The Boy from Boort

The Boy from Boort
Remembering Hank Nelson

Edited by

Bill Gammage, Brij V. Lal, Gavan Daws

PRESS

Published by ANU Press
The Australian National University
Canberra ACT 0200, Australia
Email: anupress@anu.edu.au
This title is also available online at http://press.anu.edu.au

National Library of Australia Cataloguing-in-Publication entry

Author: Gammage, Bill, 1942- author.

Title: The boy from Boort : remembering Hank Nelson / Bill Gammage, Brij V. Lal, Gavan Daws.

ISBN: 9781925021646 (paperback) 9781925021653 (ebook)

Subjects: Nelson, Hank, 1937-2012.
Historians--Australia--Biography.
Military historians--Australia--Biography.
College teachers--Australia--Biography.
Papua New Guinea--Historiography.

Other Authors/Contributors:
Lal, Brij V., author.
Daws, Gavan, author.

Dewey Number: 994.007202

All rights reserved. No part of this publication may be reproduced, stored in a retrieval system or transmitted in any form or by any means, electronic, mechanical, photocopying or otherwise, without the prior permission of the publisher.

Cover design by Nic Welbourn and layout by ANU Press

This edition © 2014 ANU Press

Contents

Preface vii
Hyland Neil ('Hank') Nelson ix

Part I: Appreciation

1. Farm Boys 3
   John Nelson

2. The Boy from Boort 5
   Bill Gammage

3. Talk and Chalk 15
   Ken Inglis

4. Boort and Beyond 19
   Gavan Daws

5. 'I Don't Think I Deserve a Pension – We Didn't Do Much Fighting': Interviewing Australian Prisoners of War of the Japanese, 1942–1945 33
   Tim Bowden

6. Doktorvater 47
   Klaus Neumann

7. Hank, My Mentor 55
   Keiko Tamura

8. Papua New Guinea Wantok 63
   Margaret Reeson

9. Coach Nelson 69
   Daniel Oakman

10. Hank of Coombs 75
    Brij V. Lal

11. Hank, My Dad 89
    Michael Nelson

Part II: Selected Writing by Hank Nelson

12. Pedalling History 95
13. A Picture: From the Past and without a Past 105
14. A Village School 113
15. Pictures at Tabara 119
16. Minimay: One of 6,000 Weatherboard Schools 135
17. From Wagga to Waddington:
    Australians in Bomber Command 149
18. Observing the Present: Writing the Past 165
19. The Joke in History 177
20. Have You Got a Title? Seminar Daze 189
21. Em Inap Nau 197

Part III

Bibliography 209

Preface

This book celebrates the life and work of Hank Nelson – scholar, teacher, communicator, mentor, writer and iconic figure of the Australian academy in the late 20th century. Besides being the premier historian of Papua New Guinea, Hank wrote memorably about the Australian experience of the Second World War and about Australian one-teacher schools. He communicated his research through books, scholarly articles, newspapers and magazines, radio and film. He was a gifted teacher of undergraduate and graduate students, whose work he supervised with care and patient understanding. While he was a distinguished member of the Australian academy, he always stood at a remove from its internal preoccupations and debates. First and foremost, Hank was a scholar who was keen to communicate with the broadest possible audience in the ordinary language of intelligent discourse.

Born in 1937 in Boort at the edge of the Mallee country of north-western Victoria, he was named Hyland Neil. In the family, he was known as Neil. He became Hank at high school. There was a boy who called everyone 'Hank', as in the American 'Hey, Joe'. Somehow the name stuck to Neil Nelson. When he started to write and publish, he decided to be Hank in print as well as in everyday life, and that was who he was for the rest of his days.

Hank attended the University of Melbourne and taught high school before joining the Royal Melbourne Institute of Technology in 1964. Two years later, he went to Port Moresby to teach at the Administrative College. In 1968, he transferred to the recently established University of Papua New Guinea, where he pioneered research and teaching in PNG's history, virtually establishing it as a discipline. In 1973, he joined the Research School of Social Sciences of The Australian National University, later moving to the Department of Pacific and Southeast Asian History in the Research School of Pacific Studies. He remained at ANU for the next 40 years, becoming a kindly and enduring presence in the lives of all he came into contact with. Hank died in Canberra in February 2012.

The book is divided into three parts. The first contains reflections on aspects of Hank's life and work by his colleagues and students, and by his older brother, John, and his son, Michael. Some of the pieces are slightly reworked versions of eulogies given at Hank's memorial service at the University House at ANU; the rest were written especially for this volume. Each contributor has written about Hank in their own voice – the way they saw him and the way he interacted with them. The tributes could be multiplied and were, at the memorial, in newspapers and online on the 'Outrigger' blog. It is interesting that the picture in the round is so consistent – with Hank there was no 'Rashomon effect'. Hank was always one and the same person: what you saw was what you got. The second part contains essays by Hank, selected to reflect the range of his work as a teacher, observer and writer of memoirs. Some pieces are slightly edited for length and clarity. More of Hank's work is widely available online and in print. A full list of his publications is in the third part, the bibliography at the end of the book.

We are grateful to many people who have helped us put this volume together. Our first thanks go to Jan Nelson, Hank's wife, who gave us advice and papers whenever asked and otherwise tolerated and encouraged us. Brett Baker prepared the manuscript and images for publication. Vicki Luker, Jan Gammage, Nic Halter and Tamai Heaton assisted us in various ways, from looking for photographs and references to typing portions of the manuscript. Nicole Haley, convenor of the State, Society and Governance in Melanesia Program, of which Hank was the chair until shortly before his death, provided generous financial assistance to defray the cost of publication. We thank the Pacific Editorial Board and especially its chair, Stewart Firth, for their encouragement, and Beth Battrick of ANU Press for shepherding the manuscript through publication. Most of all, we thank our contributors for their enthusiastic support and timely contributions. Their love for Hank showed through. They have done him proud.

Bill Gammage

Brij V. Lal

Gavan Daws

NOTE

An appreciation of Hank is in Ian Howie-Willis, 'Hyland Neil ("Hank") Nelson (21 October 1937 – 17 February 2012)', *Journal of Pacific History* 47:2 (2012), pp. 227–32. See also Gavan Daws, 'Hank', Outrigger: Blog of the [ANU] Pacific Institute, 6 March 2012.

Front and back cover photos courtesy of Jan Gammage.

Hyland Neil ('Hank') Nelson

Date and Place of Birth:	21 October 1937, Boort, Victoria, Australia
Marital Status:	Married to Jan, three children: Tanya, Lauren, Michael
Honours:	Fellow, Academy of the Social Sciences in Australia, 1994
	Professor Emeritus, The Australian National University, 2002
	AM, 2008
Education:	1958, BA, University of Melbourne
	1959, DipEd, University of Melbourne
	1962, BEd, University of Melbourne
	1966, MEd, University of Melbourne
	1976, PhD, University of Papua New Guinea
Positions Held:	1960–63, Teacher, Numurkah and Rosanna High Schools
	1964–65, Lecturer, Royal Melbourne Institute of Technology
	1966–67, Tutor, Administrative College of Papua and New Guinea
	1968–72, Lecturer, Senior Lecturer, History, University of Papua New Guinea
	1973–74, Research Fellow in History, Research School of Social Sciences, The Australian National University (ANU)
	1975–76, Research Fellow, Senior Research Fellow, Department of Pacific and Southeast Asian History, Research School of Pacific Studies, ANU
	1976–93, Fellow, Senior Fellow, Department of Pacific and Southeast Asian History, Research School of Pacific Studies, ANU
	1993–2002, Professor, Division of Pacific and Asian History, Research School of Pacific and Asian Studies, ANU
	1994–97, Professor on Secondment, History Program, Research School of Social Sciences, ANU
	2002, Visiting Fellow, Division of Pacific and Asian History, Research School of Pacific and Asian Studies, ANU; Chair, State, Society and Governance in Melanesia Program, ANU

Part I

1. Farm Boys

John Nelson

John Nelson, Hank's older brother, still resides on the family farm in Boort.

We lived halfway between Boort and Quambatook in the northern Victoria Mallee area, where Dad share-farmed on a grain-growing farm. There was no electricity in those days; kerosene lanterns were used for lighting and wood fires for warmth and cooking. There was always a shortage of water, and the temperature often hit 100°F in the summer. When we look at these conditions from the comfort of our air conditioner now, it seems that it was a very tough lifestyle, but everyone was in the same boat, so it was just a matter of getting on with life. Those were the days when horses were used to cultivate the land and pull the harvester to gather the grain.

When it was time for me to start school, we moved to another farm, now known as the Nelson home farm, which was only three kilometres from Boort. This was an irrigation farm that had been purchased by our grandparents some years earlier. There was no such thing as school buses in those days, so it was either walk or ride a pony to school.

When Neil started school, we had a Shetland pony and a jinker, which we left at an auntie's place in Boort where there was a big backyard. One of our neighbours used to ride a bike to school, and we used to throw a rope to him and tow him along. To brighten our school trips, sometimes we used to stand in the jinker chariot-style with the horse galloping and try to keep up with cars (which were not very fast in those days).

Neil was an easy-going student with no ambition to be top of the class and was content to get reasonable pass marks, which he could achieve without too much effort. This attitude changed as he moved to university.

We had a tennis court at home, and Neil and I had many great battles at tennis as well as playing tennis and football in the local competitions.

As a budding farmer, Neil had limited success. We had a small dairy, and Neil never quite mastered changing the machines from one cow to the next with a book in one hand. It was definitely a two-hand job. I remember him driving a harvesting machine on a 150-acre paddock with one tree in it, and he managed to hit the tree. It was at this stage that Dad decided Neil was not going to be a farmer and so began the concentration on education. In spite of being physically apart for 90 per cent of our lives, Neil and I maintained a very close relationship.

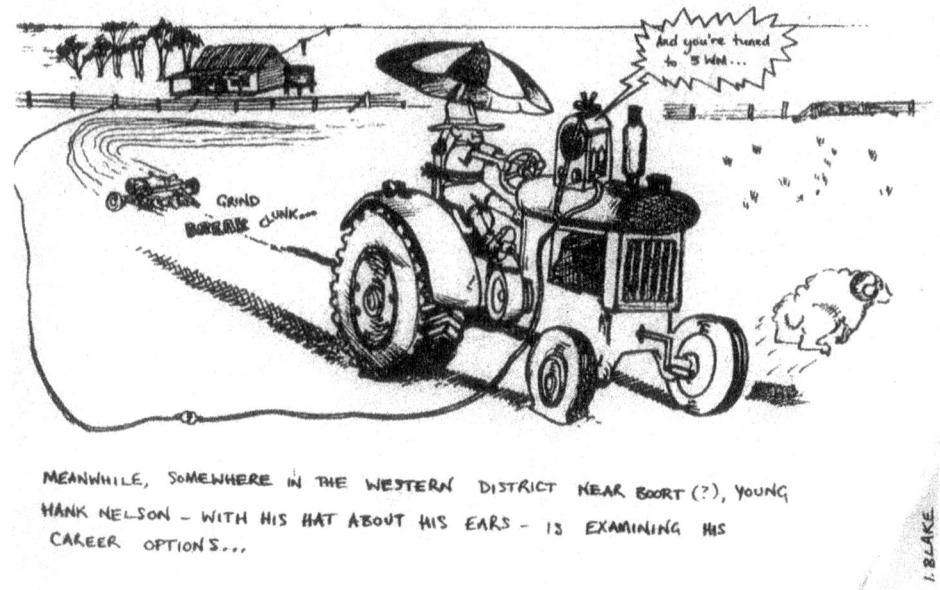

Figure 1: Young Hank Nelson on the farm.

Source: Cartoon drawn by Ian Blake.

Neil left home to complete years 11 and 12 at Kerang High School, as Boort Higher Elementary School only went to Form 4. This meant that he was home at weekends and during school holidays. Then he went to Melbourne University to complete his teacher training and so was home for university holidays. During his time at university he met up with a young lady by the name of Janet Pellas. This meant that his time of coming home during holidays was reduced, but we eventually welcomed Janet into the Nelson family. She proved to be a wonderful wife, and a great sister-in-law to myself and Margaret. Neil moved on with his teaching career, raising a family, moving to PNG and finally to Canberra, where the family now lives.

Neil and I spent many hours on the telephone, mainly on Sunday evenings, when all subjects were discussed thoroughly between us, from cricket, AFL, tennis and farming to politics. After an hour or so on the telephone, Margaret would ask me, 'What is the news from Canberra?' and my reply would be, 'There were no problems mentioned, so everything must be alright up there'.

Neil was a wonderful brother. I could not have asked for a better person as a brother.

2. The Boy from Boort

Bill Gammage

Bill Gammage is a historian of Australia and PNG who worked with Hank in Port Moresby and Canberra.

15 February 2012. Seventy years since Singapore fell and 15,000 Australians became prisoners. Hank has told their story, rescuing their memory from oblivion. Now he lay still, eyes closed, Jan and I talking by his bed. Suddenly he was looking at me. 'What are *you* doing here?' I was taken aback. Not by what he said, but I wasn't expecting him to speak. It cost him a lot. I recovered and said I was just coming to see if there were any cakes or chocolates lying around, and Hank closed his eyes.

He was born in Boort on the edge of the Victorian Mallee and grew up on a farm nearby. Farm ways and values shaped his life. He didn't drink, smoke or swear and seemed to hurry only when he played sport: cricket, Aussie rules, tennis, basketball, squash. He stood up for a fair go, worked hard, never whinged, was always helping someone. But he wasn't meant to be a farmer. He was a younger brother when farmers got bigger or got out, and he kept his head in a book. About 20 years back Boort park had a 'geep', a goat-sheep cross. Hank was a teacher-writer-farmer cross, the farmer last, so no one was surprised when he took off for Melbourne University in 1956.

In Hank's time most of the few country kids who went to uni took on what they did best in at school and trained to be teachers. Hank graduated BA 1958, DipEd 1959, BEd 1962 and MEd 1966. From 1960 he taught for three years at Numurkah High, one year at Rosanna High and two years at the Royal Melbourne Institute of Technology (RMIT). Early in 1966 he turned up for work at RMIT. 'What are you doing here?' someone asked, meaning something very different from Hank's last words to me. He was expected in Port Moresby, to tutor at the Administrative College (Adcol). No one had told him, but he and Jan packed up quickly and arrived in Moresby in March 1966.

I met him there. I'd just heard that someone was to help me teach the University of Papua New Guinea's first preliminary year history course. It turned out to be Hank. No one had told him or me until just before, but at Hank's suggestion we at once settled on a course much better than the one I'd begun. I would continue with a history of European global expansion; Hank would teach

PNG history. We crossed over for tutorials, and we double-marked everything, amazing each other at how close our marks were: if not the same, within a mark or two on a scale of 100.

His was a stupendous task. The few books available were on PNG's colonial administration, but Hank was determined to talk about Papua New Guineans, so he set about searching the only records accessible: reports, statistics, laws, regulations. He built pictures of Papuan lives under the *gavamani* – house servants, plantation and goldfield labourers, carriers, boat crews, mission helpers, police, village officials, villagers – and compared these with New Guinean lives in the *taim bilong masta*. He got students to say what their people did in those days, contrasting what should have happened with what did, comparing one district with another, steadily bringing local knowledge and perspectives into a history. He had begun that extraordinary journey which made PNG history a discipline, and ensured that it would focus forever on the experiences of its people. As a result that history shifted in emphasis from governors to governed more quickly than in any other colonial possession anywhere – in a country of over 800 languages, with few published sources, no small achievement.

The university was 'housed' in show pavilions, tin and paper mostly. No library, no study rooms, no services. Each morning a bus brought 53 men and four women and marooned them all day. One student was from Samoa, the others from PNG, mostly sons or daughters of village officials, police, clerks or mission workers. Unless the driver was drunk, the bus brought out a lunch of 'unpalatable grease', as one student put it, at the same time as the sanitary truck, and it collected the students after lectures. Hank and I formed a common front in defence of student needs. Hank had an Adcol house converted to a library and study centre, and his dark blue Volkswagen 28-826, though not ideal for ferrying a basketball team, was perennially zipping about on errands of relief and mercy.

'I went to Papua New Guinea', Hank wrote later, 'as it was one of the few (only?) places overseas where I could get my fares paid and be given a house on arrival'. That didn't last. From his first days in Moresby he was deeply interested in the country and its people. Almost daily he attended hearings into the 'wage case', on whether PNG public servants should be paid a local or Australian wage. He followed meetings of the Bully Beef Club at Adcol, where PNG public service trainees debated their country's future. He played and coached basketball for Aduni (a combined Adcol/UPNG team), supported Aduni's Aussie rules team, wrote his MEd thesis on Victoria's missions to Aborigines, and contributed more articles than anyone else on PNG affairs and future to local and Australian journals and newspapers. 'About twenty articles for *Nation*, Sydney', he tossed in at the end of his CV. Those articles are the most detailed analysis of what was happening in PNG in those volatile years.

2. The Boy from Boort

Hank transferred to the UPNG's history department in 1968. Already he was the world authority on PNG history. He wrote and taught the subject's first course anywhere at any level, and co-wrote its first two texts for secondary and lower tertiary level (1968 and 1973). His courses stood out across the university as being 'local', and he kept up a steady flow of media articles. As the best commentator on PNG, Hank was asked by Penguin Books to write a book on it. It was published in 1972 as *Papua New Guinea: Black Unity or Black Chaos*, though the subtitle was not Hank's and he did not like it.

By then he had begun a PhD on gold prospectors, miners and mine labourers in New Guinea and Papua before World War II. In November 1972 this led him, me and Elton Brash up the Lakekamu River – up the creek, as we put it. Hank wanted to see Bulldog Landing, the start of a miners' track to the Wau goldfields, and later of a wartime track. We flew to Terapo Mission on the Tauri River and met our Moveave boatmen, Tasislis (driver) and Sepi (log lookout), with a boat and a 20hp outboard. A channel took us to the Lakekamu. We camped upriver near Papa hamlet and next day pushed on for Bulldog. Unfortunately it was in Anga (Kukukuku) country, and even in 1972 coastal people weren't keen on going there. When Tasislis learnt that's where we were headed, the boat slowed, and a few hours later Tasislis said pleasantly, 'We're running out of fuel'. It took us a while to take the hint, but it began raining, so about an hour short of Bulldog we turned back and camped by the river at Halao, near an Anga house. The boatmen thought this a bad idea, especially since the house was full of bows and arrows. No Anga raiders turned up that night, but we gave the mossies a good feed and next day went on downriver. I did a bit of panning on a sandbank, got a speck, then we skimmed along with remarkable speed. For many miles the river wound through a no man's land, but near the coast houses began speckling the banks. At Urulau we yarned with two New Ireland schoolteachers, man and wife; near Papa we called to see Gabriel Ehava, MM, soldier, cooperative movement founder and former MHA, but he wasn't home; at dusk we reached Moveave Co-op sawmill and talked to two wartime carriers, and next day went back to Moresby. Terrific trip.

Straight after it Hank moved to ANU and part-time continued his UPNG PhD. As always libraries, archives, stories and numbers were his strengths, but going to sites took him beyond paper. In Moresby I kept track of his research via intermittent queries. 'Hank here. Find someone from Orokaiva and ask if so and so is alive'. 'Listen digger, were any of these blokes in the AIF?' Yes, quite a few, including Claud Castleton, prospector, who won a VC at Pozieres. 'Listen wacker, I need to see some places around Milne Bay. See what you can do'. In June 1974 five of us flew to Samarai, got a boat to Kwato, where Hank interviewed Papuan ex-alluvial miners, and flew on to Misima, where Alby Munt was washing and buying gold. Alby showed us his sluices and took us round pre-war workings all over the island, including a light rail track through an impressively deep cutting, a small version of Hellfire Pass on the Burma railway. Then we broke bush down an old mine road to Bwagoia, the jungle clutching. Hank and I talked there to Kenneth Kaiw, BEM, a pre-war administration clerk. When the Australians left in 1942 in case the Japs came, Kenneth kept census and other records up to date, insisted the school continue and paid the teachers, watched for downed pilots, and kept the administration going even during a murderous anti-government uprising. A quiet, brave man.

To Woodlark, where Kulumadau was a big goldfield before the war. Guasopa airstrip was one of Woodlark's many wartime bomber strips and was still all tar seal and Marsden matting spread by the Yanks. But within a hundred yards we were walking along the most beautiful beach I've ever seen: a long curve of white castor-sugar sand, a matching necklace of green islets edging a deep blue lagoon, a coral reef beyond, overhanging coconut palms, elegantly carved oceangoing canoes (*waga*) drawn up in the shade. We stayed in the rest house at Wabununa, where Fred and Nancy Damon were on fieldwork. Village men took us inland to some rock carvings they said were made by people before their ancestors came. That night I asked if they had stories of the first white men who came (as far as we knew) – the French missionaries in 1847–53. They laughed, and one dug the air with his hands and exclaimed, 'Travailler comme ça'. He spoke no French, showing vividly what oral history can do. Hank found pre-war mine workers still chasing colour, though not nearly as busily as the Misima men, and I bought a rough axe-head, not yet polished, from Suloga just west, the most famous quarry in eastern Papua. I gave it to Hank, and he kept it all his life.

To Goodenough, the Gosiagos' home. With them hard work is a matter of pride, so they were easily the most popular mine workers in the Eastern Division. On the north coast Hank interviewed men still proud of the work they did and the money they made. We reckoned they'd come in very handy on a wheat harvest.

As often with good historians, Hank got too much stuff, so he left the big New Guinea fields and wrote his thesis just on Papua. It was published as *Black, White and Gold* in 1977, with all Hank's hallmarks. It is a model of clear, direct writing: short sentences, active voice, few adjectives. It makes brilliant use of statistics, and of what reports did and didn't say. It is rich in Papuan names. You see the ground and hear the people, ordinary people, mostly men, in extraordinary times. It was the first detailed history of any PNG industry. In 1996 Hank used our gold circuit again when he edited the *War Diaries of Eddie Allan Stanton*, a Trobriands coastwatcher.

Hank remained the leading teacher, writer and commentator on PNG matters. From 1973 hardly a book, radio program, press comment or serious article on

PNG was done without consulting him, and many hundreds of academics, journalists, students, politicians and public servants benefited from his counsel. He established eminence in significant ways. He spoke and wrote common sense, easily attracting interested lay audiences. Academics paid by the public, he believed, should make sure the public benefits by it. He lived by this, and it led him to some significant pioneering in using film, TV, radio, sound archive and oral history to bring good stories based on high-quality research to many more people than ever hear or see academic work.

He knew film's power. He once told a seminar that whereas about 30,000 people had bought my book on Australians in the Great War, over 100 million had seen Peter Weir's *Gallipoli*. No teacher, he argued, should neglect film. He co-produced, codirected and narrated *Angels of War* (1981), about Papua's Fuzzy Wuzzy Angels on the Kokoda Track in 1942. It is still among the best of many good documentaries on PNG subjects. He then helped make *Man Without Pigs* (1989), a documentary on the return to his Mambare village of one of PNG's first doctoral graduates, John Waiko. Both films won important awards, nationally and internationally.

In radio Hank worked brilliantly with Tim Bowden. They co-wrote and Hank narrated the 24-part series *Taim Bilong Masta* (1981) on the Australian colonial experience in PNG. Hank's narration wove a story through hundreds of interviews. At a time when few Australians realised that they were colonial masters, the series told them more about their northern neighbour than anything else did. The ABC still broadcasts it.

Hank and Tim next collaborated to produce the 16-part ABC series *P.O.W.: Australians under Nippon* (1985), on the experience of Australian prisoners of the Japanese in 1942–45. They talked to dozens of survivors. One was Don Moore, from out Hank's way, a fine artist who sent Hank a stream of drawings of life, though not death, in Changi and on the Burma road. Another was Curley Heckendorf, whom each year I carted wheat and chopped thistles for. At the risk of death, Curley helped 'crutch' a wireless part into Changi. A third was Colin Brien, son of a Narrandera policeman, who survived a 'murder attempt' at Singapore in 1942, when the Japs blindfolded him, set him on the edge of a grave, chopped a sword deep into his neck and left him for dead. It was hours before he came to, and days before he got his hands free and could clean out the maggots, but he survived. His mates hid him for the rest of the war, in case the Japs tried again. Such stories are scarifying listening, shocking many who heard them, but they did valuable service to the prisoners and their country.

Both series revived a dormant public interest. Nothing like them had been attempted before, and until them neither Kokoda nor Changi was much remembered in Australia. Enriched by companion books Hank wrote, now they are among the best-known experiences of Australians in World War II. They obliged Hank to become historical consultant to numerous documentaries on PNG or the Pacific War, and from 1992 to write detailed notes at unit level to guide interviewers for the Australian War Memorial's WWII sound archive. From 1995 he assembled Australians, Japanese and Papua New Guineans to create a multi-perspective AWM website on the war in PNG, suitable for anyone over 12. Try doing that.

Still the books came. For what became *With Its Hat about Its Ears* (1989), on bush schools, in August 1986 Hank and I went chasing schools and ex-pupils on Yorke Peninsula, South Australia. We found the remains of schools like Katunga Hill and Ninnes, and at Kimba we saw former bush schools brought in as classrooms. We put up at a Kimba motel on the night the local footy team won the grand final. When we broke camp next morning, no one was about. No breakfast and no one to pay for our room. We tried a few doors, had a look round Kimba and came back. Not a sound. Hank left his address under a door, and we headed for Darke Peak. We worked out where the school there had been, but it'd been moved to Kimba, so we went on to Port Lincoln to talk to people. When Hank got back to Canberra, he had to badger the motel to get them to say how much we owed. Kimba could've been Boort.

Victoria too recycled classrooms. The one at Chinkapook went north to Manangatang. 'The Chinkie people have lost their school', Hank said. 'Can we get it back for them?' 'They'd only move it again'. Practical man, Hank, but whenever I go through Chinkie I shout out helpfully to say where their school is. At least the Chinkie classroom survived: near Lockhart in the Riverina I showed Hank Fargunyah school ruins – a few pepper trees, a post-and-rail fence, a hitching post, a patch of playground worn bare. Most even of that has gone now.

In *Chased by the Sun* (2002), on Australians in Bomber Command, Hank told the stories, among others, of two remarkable pilots, Arthur Doubleday and Bill Brill. Arthur came from west of Ganmain, Bill from Derrain North, 20 miles further west. They were farm boys. Hank and I had a look at their country – flat to undulating red loam to clay, grey box and pine, top wheat country. We knew a bit about wheat, and Arthur and Bill knew a lot about it. Before the war they worked with four-bushel bags, whereas post-war ours were only three. But with horse teams they took a lot longer to get to the silos, so had more of a breather. Arthur first, then Bill, went to bush schools, then to Yanco Agricultural High School, as I did for a year. We went through Matong, Grong Grong and Narrandera to the school, built around Sam McCaughey's mansion with its magnificent stained glass windows from Ireland. A lifetime earlier Sam sat one night with his workers around a cosy fire. A man struck a match, lit his pipe and asked, 'How did you come to make so much money, Mr McCaughey?' 'Not by sitting round a fire lighting matches', Sam said. Hank loved the story.

From Yanco, Arthur and Bill went back to the wheat, but when war came, both families had to decide who would stay to run the farm and who would go to the war. Arthur and Bill would go, and in November 1940 they met on the train to Sydney, enlisted in the Air Force together, and went back to Narrandera for elementary flying training at 8 EFTS, on Tiger Moths. They knew the country better than the map did, and on navigation tests one would get out of the Moth and say to the other getting in, 'They're cropping the middle paddock' or some such. Both passed. After training in Canada they joined Bomber Command in England, when surviving a tour of 30 ops was not common, and lucky. They learnt to hold back coming home across the Dutch coast so less experienced pilots, anxious to get clear, crossed it first and drew the German flak, letting those behind dodge it. They watched out for each other. As they neared home, one would flick open the wireless: 'You OK, cobber?' 'Yep'. 'The flying farmers of Riverina', Hank called them. By 1945 both were Wing Commanders: Arthur DSO, DFC, MID; Bill DSO, DFC and bar.

In the 2008 Queen's Birthday Honours Hank got his own gong: an AM for outstanding service as a teacher and commentator on PNG. A tribute said in part,

> *Hank established PNG history as discipline ... He shifted its focus from its administrators to its people ... He is a pivotal and inspiring innovator, an early exponent in bringing university work into the public arena via film and radio, a model in applying the highest research standards to illuminate experiences of Australians and Papua New Guineans in peace and war. Few academics parallel his range, diversity, and service, let alone to the people of two countries, Papua New Guinea and Australia.*

The gong came just in time. Late in 2009 he emailed:

Subject: Health report. Or lack of

Bill,

The Sydney visit was not disastrous but not an occasion of joy unconfined. There has been a moderate growth in the melanoma tumours in the lungs. It was pointed out to me that while these might not have any impact on me at the moment they would eventually kill me. I had grasped this possibility. The bloke at the Melanoma Unit said it was time to use chemotherapy. There was no urgency, but soon...

The Montevideo Maru film, shown last night on the Foxtel History Channel, was fairly good. I had taken a lot of errors out of the script but there were still a few statements that were slick or nearly right. But fast-moving and engaging. There was the usual lifting of film from Parer near Salamaua and dropped into the fight for Rabaul.

The Boy from Boort

And that's the way it was and is.

Hank.

Those cruel tumours grew. By 2011 Hank was pretty crook, and at two morning teas in his honour could easily have just got stuck into the cakes – he never stood back from anything sweet. Instead he gave two memorable talks. The first began, 'I trust there is no relationship between my gradual disengagement from this unit and its obvious flourishing'. He gave statistics to prove that flourishing, then listed ways in which scholars might help PNG, under the headings Corruption, Compensation to Land Owners, PNG and Democracy, Governments by Competing Groups, and Autobiographies. His talk was a typically brilliant expression of practical concern for the wellbeing of the people of PNG. At the second morning tea he spoke almost entirely on how much he and everyone owed to the school and department secretaries and office staff, a gentle reminder to listening boffins to give them the respect they deserve.

It's not easy to realise that a great mate is a great man, especially when that mate was deceptively unpretentious and egalitarian. But Hank was a great man. Few people achieve as much as he did, and fewer manage to keep their heads below the parapet so well. He was not one for public parade, but his influence was immense among the many students and staff he helped, or who heard his talks, read his books, heard him on radio or saw his films. He taught many who became PNG's leaders, offering them a view of the ways that theirs was one country. This contributed significantly to the goodwill between PNG and Australia at independence in 1975. He was a prolific and wide-ranging writer, a teacher with a touch of genius, an expert who easily reached far beyond academia. Not for him any postmodernist navel gazing. He was a superb administrator, on the side of students, careful with budgets and reports, setting no-nonsense agendas, never tempted from research and writing into more than acting in senior administrative jobs.

He remained the boy from Boort. The bush gave him perspectives few professionals have, and even rarer, he kept those perspectives. He had a rain gauge in his yard. He loved to yarn about crops, prices, fallowing, new wheat varieties coming in, water conservation. By then we could often tell what the other was thinking, leading Jan to dub us Mutt and Jeff, after two comic strip dills. That was in private. 'It pains me to say it', I once wrote under the heading *Plodder greases Queen*, 'but he probably deserves his AM'. His country voice responded, 'Haven't you anything better to do with your time?' And a favourite moment: about 1986 we were on ABC radio, live to air, Hank and our host in Canberra, me in Adelaide. We talked a bit, then were asked what we thought of some aspect. Hank spoke, then our host said, 'Bill?' I said something like, 'Well that's what you'd expect Hank to say. He's been on that line for years. You'd think he would've learnt something after all this time'. Hank came straight back: 'Bill's a careful lad, but he used to play rugby. We need to be tolerant'. To and fro we went, Mutt and Jeff. About when I regretted that Hank couldn't run a chook raffle, our host decided that we were drifting off course, got a touch panicky, and stopped us. Pity. Hank told me later that someone said to him, 'I didn't know you and Bill hated each other'. 'Yes', Hank said. 'Sad, isn't it? And I have to work with him'. Well mate, no more.

3. Talk and Chalk

Ken Inglis

Ken Inglis was professor of history and then vice-chancellor at the University of Papua New Guinea and professor of history at ANU. This remembrance was written for Hank's memorial service, 24 February 2012.

I first heard the name Hank Nelson in February 1966, just 46 years ago, at The Australian National University. I'd been appointed to the chair of history at the so far non-existent University of Papua New Guinea (UPNG), but I wasn't moving until the beginning of 1967. I was asked to find someone to teach history to a group of between 50 and 60 students who were taking a year of preliminary studies that would prepare them for work towards a degree. Bill Gammage, a recent ANU graduate, readily agreed to go. But when he got to Moresby, he found that somebody else was coming to join him. This somebody's name was Hank Nelson. Some American blow-in? It turned out that he was a Melbourne graduate in education then lecturing at RMIT, and that Hank was the name conferred on him at high school.

In mosquito-ridden tin sheds until lately occupied by a firm named Tutt Bryant, Hank and Bill teamed up to teach history to the young men and women – mostly men – aspiring to be their country's first graduates. The Tutt Bryant School of Pacific Studies, Hank and Bill called the incipient university. Hank and Jan, who had met while teaching in Victoria, were married before they went north and had children by the time they arrived. I went up from time to time during 1966 for meetings of the professorial board in one of the sheds and met some of the students at the Nelsons' house.

Hank and Bill, boys from the bush, plain speakers, good listeners, encouragers, seemed to me wonderfully well suited to be mentors for these young people. I recall conversations at the Nelsons' place with future leaders of the country, among them Tony Siaguru, Bernard Sakora, Bart Philemon and Rabbie Namaliu. (Bill reminds me that Charles Lepani was in the second-year intake of preliminary year students, in 1967.) And I remember Hank's well-informed and shrewd briefing on PNG society and culture from the driving seat of a Volkswagen on a hairy journey up into the hills behind Moresby.

Bill came back to Canberra at the end of 1966. Hank, based for a while at the Administrative College and then in the sturdy concrete buildings of UPNG, taught in two courses on PNG history, one introductory, and then one advanced. He also contributed to the Sydney-based fortnightly journal *Nation* on the rapidly changing politics of a nation poised for self-government. Penguin Books, spotting a likely author, commissioned what would become his first book, *Papua New Guinea: Black Unity or Black Chaos* (1972).

His lectures were always well prepared, clear, and unerringly pitched, neither condescending to students nor overwhelming them. He responded to a high-tech lecture theatre, installed in 1969, with some amusement. 'You feel bloody inadequate with just talk and chalk', he said, tongue-in-cheek. In the advanced class he made much use of oral history, simply getting on with it while academics in Australia and elsewhere fussed about the rewards and hazards of the approach. Our external consultant, D.W.A. Baker of ANU, judged this course the best of its kind he had come across.

Hank was a stickler for accuracy, in his own work and in the work of students and colleagues. After a lecture in which I had carelessly sketched the history of federal politics, he said with a smile, 'Hey, you just abolished the Scullin government'.

Beyond the classroom he was a quietly sociable presence at sporting events and barbecues. He was a diligent boundary umpire at Aussie rules matches. He didn't drink beer, though he was no wowser.

When I think of the special regard for Hank among students, this story comes to mind: It's 7:30 am, the time the UPNG day begins, and exams are on. Hank is supervising. As the examinees await permission to begin, one of them, Ekeroma Age, beckons to him and points to an empty desk. 'Claire must be still asleep, Hank', he says. 'You'd better go and wake her up'. So the lecturer sprints off to the women's dormitory and wakes Claire, just in time for her to get to the exam. This may be a story about the singularity of UPNG in those days, as well as about Hank.

In 1973 the Nelsons moved to Canberra, where Hank embarked on the thesis about gold mining that made him Dr Nelson and became in 1977 the book *Black, White and Gold*. As a PhD student he had been housed in the Research School of Social Sciences. Then he moved to the other side of the Coombs building to what in those days was called the Research School of Pacific Studies, and there he remained for the rest his life. At ANU he took to new fields of study – prisoners of the Japanese, bush schools, Australians in Bomber Command, all of them involving use of written and oral sources – while also pursuing subjects gestating from his PNG years.

In his advanced course in PNG history one common topic for oral history exercises was My Village during the War. The Second World War was then just far enough away for Papuans and New Guineans who had lived through it to talk candidly about their experiences, and close enough for their memories of it to be vivid. There's a direct line from the testimonies gathered in that class to the award-winning film *Angels of War*, produced and directed by Hank, Gavan Daws and Andrew Pike in 1982. Hank's other work out that year, *Taim Bilong Masta*, also draws on the collection of oral histories during Hank's years in PNG, followed up in fertile collaboration with Tim Bowden to create the splendid series of ABC radio programs on which the book is based.

Hank has become legendary both for his own work and for his wise and self-effacing contribution to the work of others, young and old, whatever their place on a spectrum from empiricism to postmodernism. In recent years he has written for general readers masterly surveys of the intricacies of contemporary affairs in PNG and elsewhere in Melanesia.

Emeritus Professor Nelson, FASSA, AM. The well-deserved honours didn't actually displease him, but he didn't find it easy to take them with a straight face. He remained the boy from Boort, evoked in a lovely memoir recalling the days when he and his brother John drove to school in a jinker pulled reluctantly by a malevolent horse named Bunny (see 'Pedalling History' in Part II of this book).

I like to imagine him in a posture well remembered by John, in a paddock on the family farm, sitting on a tractor, reading a book.

4. Boort and Beyond

Gavan Daws

Gavan Daws was professor and head of Department of Pacific and Southeast Asian History in the Research School of Pacific Studies, The Australian National University, from 1974 to 1989. This remembrance is based on words written to be spoken at Hank's memorial in 2012.

My first sighting of Hank was in the late 1960s, briefly, during a stopover in Port Moresby.

The next time was 1974, when I came to work at ANU.

My office was in the Coombs Building, and so was Hank's – though I might never have known he was there. The Coombs was designed as three interlocking three-storey hexagons, structurally joined at the hip but functionally divided into two research schools. Hank was in one, Social Sciences; I was in the other, Pacific Studies. Different turfs, different territories, different disciplines, different departments, scores of academics in scores of offices along corridors going in six different directions, on different levels, with different entries and exits.

One day, Hank and I happened to bump into each other at a landing on the stairs. We got to talking, and it turned out that we had some things in common. The two of us were pretty much of an age, we were both from Victoria, and we were both country boys – you could tell by our triphthongs. So there were natural connections.

But there were degrees of separation too. Hank was from Boort; I was from Dimboola. From one to the other it was a bit over a hundred miles, as the crow might fly. Back when we were kids, in the 1940s, that was a long way, some of it on not-too-good roads. So, no surprise that Hank had never been to Dimboola and I had never been to Boort.

Boort then was seven or eight hundred people; Dimboola, at just over a thousand, was indisputably bigger. Dimboola was in the Wimmera, definitely; Boort not exactly – it was where the Wimmera, the Mallee and the North Central District met. These were distinctions without a difference, but Hank and I did grow up differently, because I lived in town and he was a farm boy. I wore shoes, Hank wore boots, and he did a lot of clodhopping across paddocks:

> *In the 1944 drought the dry grass was blown against that fence, drift sand piled against the barrier of grass, the fence was buried and the sheep just*

> *walked over the top; over there we felled the oak trees and the grain was so straight we split fence droppers from them; that bit of rusted iron used to mend a sagging gate once fitted a bullock yoke; and over there dad yarded the draught horses and fed them before dawn so they could work all day.*

Hard yakka, the price of fair average quality wheat, dust storms, rabbit plagues: this was Hank's early education in life.

For school, he and his brother John wheeled out the jinker, harnessed Bunny, their obstreperous little black mare, and jogged into town, to Boort Primary and then Boort Higher Elementary. They each marched in with their class, the way the rules said to, and sat at the standard-issue Victorian Education Department double desk, green-topped, with attached seat and enamel inkwell, in amongst other farm boys: Doughy, Curly, Knocka, Tud, Saddles, Snakebite, and Big Barney, built like a country dunny. 'We had kids who would carry a lizard in their shirt'.

The schoolyard was dry clay. When it rained,

> *just one shower and the top ground had a skin of grey mud. It stuck to the football, and soon it had a quarter of an inch coat on the leather. Old, worn and balloon-like with use, the footy quickly had the weight and toughness of a mallee root. It burst through hands reaching for marks and wrenched and sprained thumbs. It thudded on chests. A mongrel punt hit high on the instep was the only safe kick. To try a drop or a fancy stab meant a stubbed toe and a jarring that went up the leg to the hip. Some kid might have a pocket knife, even a Rogers, and he would cradle the ball in one arm and slice away the mud like orange rind. That gave a light ball for just five or six kicks.*

Your town had its football team, the other little towns round about had theirs, and if they were close enough, you played them, home and away. At the Boort ground, young Nelson, only primary school age but rightly considered to be a good, reliable lad, was appointed chip heater fire lighter. Before he was 12, he was promoted to score board attendant. 'I thought this a more responsible and prestigious position. I have not added it to my CV'.

Come high school time, Hank and I each played football in the winter, in the dry and in the mud, on ovals not axiomatically flat and not necessarily mown. In the summer, cricket, on the same ovals, malthoid pitches or concrete and matting, with the ladies' auxiliary laying on lamingtons between innings.

Then there was the Saturday night dance. You fronted up, suited-and-tied-and-shiny-shoed-and-brylcreemed, for the Modern Waltz, Quickstep – *slow slow quickquick slow* – Valletta, Tangoette, Progressive Barn Dance, Pride of Erin, and Schottische. (A cultural history note: Hank told me something I never would have intuited – there was a sheet music 'Boort Schottische', dating from 1865.)

Here is Hank on a do after the football, an away game at Woosang:

> *The Woosang ground was a clearing, probably 'mown' by sheep. A galvanised shed for a changing room, galvanised dunnies, and a lean-to where savs could be boiled. No showers. The visiting side was invited to a dance afterwards at the Woosang hall. By the third or fourth dance, as the blokes swung into the Jolly Miller, the combination of sweat, training oil, and cigarette smoke was so dense that frail girls floated in the haze and ruckmen had to grab them and force their feet back onto the sawdusted floor.*

Boort was Aboriginal for 'smoke'; Boort Boort was 'big smoke'. The biggest Big Smoke was the city. After high school, Hank and I each headed off to Melbourne, to go to university.

The only way for either of us to have got there was on an Education Department studentship, and we lived in department hostels, Hank on St Kilda Road, me on Victoria Street in Carlton – safe places for country kids not worldly enough to be out on their own (and short of the rent for a flat).

Relocating from dusty-dry bush to big-smoke city was a significant rite of passage. Hank's rendering:

> *Those of us who left came to Melbourne still wearing the hat with corks dangling, carrying a canvas water bag and chewing a piece of straw. I did not go to a public library until I went to the one in Swanston Street.*

For 18-year-old boys in the 1950s, there was another rite of passage – National Service. I was in the second intake at Puckapunyal, in the summer of 1951, Hank a few years after that. We both had immigrant Pommies for platoon sergeants. To dinkum young Aussies like us, these alien specimens were an offence against nature, nothing on earth like real Diggers – except for being baggy-arsed, and on them even that didn't look right. The one I drew was Liverpool Irish, skinny, bucktoothed, and bone-ignorant. At reveille he used to scream, '*Get fell in threes!*' and he was scared of snakes. Hank's was called Fookin Joomp, as in, '*When I tell yers to fookin joomp, yers fookin joomp!*'

Back at university, we had an ongoing army obligation, to be infantry privates in the Citizen Military Forces. We were issued a uniform, one size fits none, with a patch, MUR, for Melbourne University Regiment, a slouch hat, and a Lee-Enfield .303, kept at home, but with the bolt taken out and held at the armoury.

Three years of repetitive parades and desultory bivouacs, and that was it for CMF. When we graduated, BA, DipEd, we were deployed to teach high school – another three-year commitment, working off our studentship bond, Hank in the country, not all that far from Boort, me in Melbourne.

Neither of us kept on being chalkies in Victoria long-term, but we did stay in teaching, lecturing in entry-level tertiary classrooms, in faraway places, islands in low latitudes with strange-sounding names, Papua New Guinea for Hank, Hawai'i for me.

And so the years went instructionally by, until we each came back to Australia, on the cusp of early middle age, to ANU, to the Institute of Advanced Studies, to the Coombs Building, Hank starting in 1973, me in 1974.

I read what Hank wrote and listened to him give seminars. He was quality, no question in my mind; and as well, it sounded to me as though the two of us had some ideas in common about doing history. By good fortune, in 1975 a window of opportunity opened up and I was able to bring him into my department.

For going on 15 years, Hank and I had offices just a couple of doors from each other, and he was the best possible person to work alongside. In fact, if I was designing a model colleague, and I had the authority to mandate the perfected version for adoption university-education-wide, I would use Hank as the template.

First thing – and it was basic – he had common sense. This is an attribute not evenly distributed among academics, and entirely absent in some. In Hank it was foundational, rock-solid.

With postgraduate students, he had a great touch. He could be personally easy-going and at the same time quietly tough-minded about quality, and he was willing to put in time and effort, way above and beyond the call, doing whatever it took to help each and every one of them to come up with their best.

Among faculty and staff, in the department and in the school at large, he was highest value. He could see what needed to be done, and figure out how to get it done, on his own, or along with others, always equable and good-humoured – zero operatics.

Just by being himself, Hank was an exemplary citizen of the republic of learning. He was not in business for the greater glory of Nelson – no big-noting, no putting on the dog. He never needed to be seen leading the big parade. He was not interested in parading for the sake of parading. He wanted things to always be heading somewhere useful, somewhere (and this was important to him) not just over the academic rainbow, way up high, but in the real world.

4. Boort and Beyond

Around the Coombs or out in the world, Hank was the best company. One time, we drove from Canberra to Melbourne for a scholarly conference, hours on the Hume Highway, that big Australian interstate country road, Hank easy at the wheel, with cruising-speed thoughts about any number of things, from Bathurst burrs and Paterson's Curse, which he knew all about from being a farm boy, to the Curse of the Seminar, which he knew all about from being a career academic.

Hank wound up being based in the Coombs for more than 30 years, and latish on he did the longitudinal arithmetic of seminars in the three hexagons in his time. In an average week, more than 50. In an average academic year, 2,000. Grand total when he did his calculating, 50,000-plus.

Statistics to conjure with. Or not. Along the Hume, we decided against, in favour of other subjects of interest that presented themselves. One of these was Aboriginal place names, on the highway or off. Gundagai. Jugiong. Wangaratta. Tumbarumba. From Hank's early days, Quambatook and Numurkah; from mine, Warracknabeal, Nhill, Gerang Gerung. We wondered about the sound of them, compared with American Indian place names, and why there should be more American songs with Indian names in them (*Oh Shenandoah, I love your daughter, Away, I'm bound to go, Across the wide Missouri* …) than Australian songs with Aboriginal names in them. Hank, never short for local knowledge, came up with 'The Boort and Quambatook Standard-Times', sung by The Cobbers.

As we were closing in on Melbourne, within day tripper range on good 1980s roads, a different question about cultural identity arose: what size did a Victorian country town need to be before it would have a restaurant with a French name? Boort never used to have one; neither did Dimboola.

The conference was at Melbourne University, more than a quarter century on from our undergraduate time. Hank gave an excellent paper, about Australian POWs of the Japanese in World War II.

When Hank spoke to audiences, including academic audiences, he practised what he preached in a piece he wrote about all his hours on the receiving end of seminars in the Coombs:

> *Those who have given the best seminars I have heard spoke without rhetorical flourishes and they used plain English with a sparkling clarity, sometimes investing simple words with grace and power, and they shifted easily between particular cases, shrewd insights and generalisations. They were also saying something significant.*

This was what Hank always aimed for in his own words, written or spoken.

Professionally as well as personally, he was plain style. He did not like writing that got in the way of reading, the way so much academic prose does, convoluted, inturned, ingrown, all pedantry, obscurity and bibliography. He liked language to show strong active vital signs, with style and substance inseparable, the two in one. And he wanted his words, live or on the page, to be understandable and interesting to other people. He never wanted to be talking to himself.

He was serious about his research, and he was as good at thinking as anyone. But he wasn't a theoretician. His way was to pick a subject that was worth the trouble, search out the facts, and make sure of them. At the same time he would be looking for meaning – and for Hank the meaning was always *human* meaning.

He was interested in history as story, and he was interested in how to tell stories. He liked the sound of voices, all kinds of voices. This led him to oral history. And he was interested in audience. This brought him to radio, to the two big series he did for the ABC with Tim Bowden, *Taim Bilong Masta: The Australian Involvement with Papua New Guinea* and *P.O.W.: Australians under Nippon*. They were great successes, in both substance and style, and they attracted big listening numbers.

Hank was up for collaborating. So was I. I had watched him road-tested with Tim in radio. I started talking to him about doing documentary films. For those in the Coombs who saw the world as an academic projection – with their own office pre-Copernicanly at the centre, and scholarly publications the only landmarks – film was off the edge of the map, risky, dangerous, even frightening: *hic sunt dracones*. But here we all were, coming to the end of the 70s, heading for the 80s. Hank could see, as I could, that people were increasingly going to be getting their entertainment – and not just their entertainment but their information, and not just their information but the way they understood the world – less and less from the printed page, more and more from TV and film. Why should academics quarantine themselves off from this? We had no doubt that good serious work could be presented responsibly, usefully, and interestingly in media beyond print, and we liked the idea of extending the reach of Pacific history by way of technology.

Hank had always been a moviegoer, beginning with the Saturday flicks at the Rex in Boort, then in Melbourne at the Odeon and the Australia, then in Port Moresby at the Papuan, the Arcadia, and the Skyline Drive-In, which were mostly for whites, and the Badili, the Bar X, and the Hohola, which put on ancient westerns and martial arts movies, mostly for Papuans.

When he was teaching at UPNG, he showed World War II documentaries at night, and anyone could come and watch, free. 'Students from all courses went, and so did gardeners, clerical staff, their families, and people living in the nearby housing areas'. For them, it was an eye-opener to be seeing their own history on the screen.

The bombing of the Macdhui as it zigzagged from the Port Moresby wharf always brought a chorus of exclamations, and there was a shout as it disappeared in blast, smoke and water-spouts. Brief glimpses of bewildered villagers caught in terrible violence provoked quiet expressions of sympathy.

For our first documentary, we decided to look at what happened to the people of Papua New Guinea in World War II. Hank knew the story, and he knew that the War Memorial in Canberra had all kinds of footage from the New Guinea campaign, shot in combat and behind the lines – rich archival source material.

Figure 2: Editing *Angels of War*. Standing, left to right: Hank Nelson, Andrew Pike, Gavan Daws and John Waiko. Sitting: Stewart Young.

Source: Photograph by Stephen Berry, published in *ANU Reporter*, 24 July 1981.

Hank and I enlisted Andrew Pike, who knew about producing. Andrew and Hank recruited Dennis O'Rourke and several other filmmakers with PNG experience, to shoot interviews with men and women who had lived through the war. Andrew brought in Stewart Young, an excellent film editor. I had some thoughts about structure and pacing. We raised money, non-academically (meaning dangerously off-the-map), and away we went.

A good collaboration is a very good thing. Making *Angels of War* with Hank and Andrew and Stewart was one of the best times I have had in my working life, certainly the best time I ever had as an academic.

The four of us came to the project from different directions, bringing our own individual aptitudes and attitudes and metabolisms and work habits; but all of us together wanted to get things done, done well, and in good time, and we wanted to see the product go out from the Coombs into the world.

Angels of War got done in good time, and it did well in the world. It won the Australian Film Institute award for best documentary in 1982; the gold medal of the major European documentary festival, Visions du Réel, at Nyon in Switzerland; and the ATOM award of Australian Teachers of Media for best film in the social sciences. It was chosen to wind up the Margaret Mead Film Festival, a showcase of international documentaries, in New York – prime time at a prestigious event in one of the biggest Big Smokes on earth, on the other side of the world from Canberra. It was acquired for television in Australia, New Zealand, Britain and Japan, and distributed in the United States. It has had a continuing life, to the end of the 20th century and into the 21st, morphing technologically, from 16 mm film to videocassette, then DVD, and now online streaming. Versions were made in several languages, including New Guinea Tok Pisin. In 2008, when a PNG government TV station went on air, on Independence Day, *Angels of War* was one of the first films picked to be broadcast; and in 2013, more than 30 years after the earliest screenings, *Sydney Morning Herald* TV featured it for Anzac Day.

All this put the case for one of Hank's basic propositions, about *scale* – the difference in the capacity of the historian to communicate the results of serious research, depending on the medium. Hank did his arithmetic, and the figures came out far different from his numbers about seminars. An article based on a seminar paper, published in a scholarly journal, might be read by a few score academics. A book published by a university press might have a print run of one or two thousand, and next to never a second printing. A radio series could be heard by a hundred thousand people, the way *Taim Bilong Masta* and *P.O.W.* were. And with film, the potential audience for well-presented serious work could increase by another order of magnitude. Worldwide, *Angels of War* has probably been seen by a million people.

For Hank, it was not just that films could attract a bigger audience but that they could reach a different kind of audience. As he said, he could have interviewed Sergeant Yauwiga, DCM, in his village on the Maprik road out of Wewak, and then written about him.

> *Yauwiga would have given his time and knowledge courteously and generously and would never have known what part of his information I had used, what I had discarded, and what shape I had given to that which I had exploited. But when the interview is filmed, and Yauwiga's comments are woven into a documentary film, then the product can go back to those who are the source and the subject. The village people are well able to comment on the context and the selection of the ideas which have been made by the film-maker. That is a much healthier cultural situation for both villagers and historians. There can be no charge of cultural theft: the taking of data from one culture and using it to enrich an academic tradition within an entirely separate culture. And when I was involved in the making of* Angels of War *I was sometimes conscious of those warm evening open-air screenings with numerous children and many audience interjections that are all part of a Papua New Guinea village film show. It was an incentive to get it right.*

You can hear Hank's voice on the soundtrack. And another voice from the Coombs as well – John Waiko, narrating and interviewing. John was a student of Hank's. He came from Tabara, a village of Binandere people on the Gira River, in the Northern Province of PNG – much, much more remote from the world of the Big Smoke than Boort or Dimboola. John was one of the first two Papua New Guineans to get a PhD, and it was his intention to carry his education back to his country. He had gone out into the big world, and now he was coming home.

Hank thought this would make a good, interesting, useful documentary. And so it did. *Man Without Pigs*, shot at Tabara, went out into the big world, winning the 1990 award for best documentary at the Hawai'i International Film Festival, the leading showcase for Asia-Pacific cinema. Again, a demonstration of reach and scale.

You can see Hank onscreen. Along with the filming of the ceremonies for Waiko's homecoming, some young Tabara men put on a performance of their village specialty, an impromptu farce. For best effect, they needed a whiteman to play a *kiap*, a government field officer. Hank looked like perfect casting, and they talked him into it, telling him his part was not hard: all he had to do was sit on a patrol box, and when he thought the time was right, call out, 'I don't understand!' and then, at another point in what appeared to him to be the plot, 'Have you got a licence?' Taking off from there, 'the Binandere actors sustained over half an hour of sight gags, lewd asides, political satire, and funny walks'.

The Tabara audience loved Hank's cameo, and if there had been acting awards at the Hawai'i International Film Festival, he would certainly have been nominated for Best Supporting *Kiap*.

He wrote a wonderful piece about the *Man Without Pigs* project. 'Pictures at Tabara' is vintage Nelson, with his trademark eye and ear for place and people, and his way of telling interesting stories that turn out to have interesting human meanings.

Hank often had several things going at the same time, yet he never seemed to be rushed. He gave the impression of being naturally slow-revving, his face undistorted by fierce acceleration; but he covered a lot of ground, in a lot of different directions, in a lot of different gears. Doing sit-down archival research for long stretches was alright with him; so was footslogging, crossing creeks that fed the Gira River on the way to Tabara, plunging into dense bush, wading through stagnant water waist-high, hauling himself up the far bank. And back at his desk he was ongoingly productive – books, articles, print journalism, conference papers, consultancies, committee reports.

As the man said, 'Good prose is like a window pane'. And as the other man said, 'Readability is credibility'. Hank was always clear, always readable, always credible. Over the years, his body of work grew and grew, and not just by annular rings; it kept accruing more and more authority. It got him elected to the Academy of the Social Sciences in Australia. And his exceptional value as an academic who was useful to his country brought him national honours, in the Order of Australia. This was a perfect fit: Hank was *Australian* through and through, substance and style – though with a curious small aggregation of cultural aberrations. He did not drink or smoke. And he did not swear. (What, never? Well, hardly ever.) These irregularities were not held to be disqualifiers for official recognition, and no mention was made of them in the citation.

I was not there to shake Hank's hand when the honour was announced. In 1989 I left the Coombs, ANU, academic life, and Australia, and went back to Hawai'i.

Honolulu is across hemispheres and time zones from Canberra. But by technological good fortune, along came email, so Hank and I were able to keep in easy touch.

For the better part of 20 years we Sent and Replied. Our back-and-forths came to number hundreds. I archived them all.

In Hank's, there was a lot about PNG, from Errol Flynn to tourism on the Kokoda Trail, to Sepik people going to England and getting on Facebook, to his wish that there was more written about individual Papua New Guineans such as the ones he taught in 1966, and how they turned out. 'Two became prime ministers, one became assistant secretary to the permanent organisation of the British Commonwealth, at least one went to jail, and one robbed and rorted outrageously and flourished'.

There were truly dreadful things too – gun violence in Port Moresby and Lae and the Highlands. I told Hank it wasn't as bad as in the United States.

When he saw the US for himself, he sent good reports, very Hank-like. Here he is at Padow's Deli, doing the arithmetic of sandwiches in America:

> *36 possibilities on his menu wall, not including mile highs, combos and subs. Then there was a choice of nine breads (not including 'biscuits' which looked like scones or small dampers) and six cheeses (including pimiento spread which technically may not have been a cheese). So Padow's had a choice of 1,944 sandwiches (not including biscuits, mile highs, combos and subs). I was so beguiled I wrote all this down.*

And while he was at it, he did some Nelsonian calculations about Starbucks: by his figuring, there was one every five acres, the same as for sheep in the Mallee in a bad year.

Other travels took him to Asia. He put together a book with Gavan McCormack about the Burma Railway. After it was published in Australia, it appeared in Thailand, in English. It was also translated into Japanese, and when Hank went to Japan, he was pleased to hear his name rendered as Hanku Neresu.

He kept writing up to his retirement, and after. In 2009, some more Nelson statistics came to my inbox:

> *In the last couple of months I have written 2500 words on the sinking of the Montevideo Maru, 3000 on Kokoda, was team leader on a 120 page report on Kokoda for the govts of Aust and PNG (I wrote 20 or so of the pages and helped pull the lot together), wrote a talk to give to 100 aircrew who fought in Europe, other short pieces, and briefed a couple of journalists on present PNG.*

He wrote as he had always written, in plain style. He never did warm to academic jargon, especially the postmodernist cultural studies kind, 'all of that interrogation of the articulate space between words, the unpacking unravelling nuancing deconstructing of the hegemonic canon'. It wasn't that he had to move his lips on the big words; it was just that he didn't see any real-world human return from it.

And, as ever, he wrote for usefulness. He often published

> *where it is close and quick. Now a lot goes out as discussion or working papers for state society and governance in melanesia (nominal chair, me). I must have written six or seven pieces for ssgm. Wise people ask me why. But to publish in a 'learned journal' will take many months – perhaps 18 – and the editor will send me the comments of the referees and in my preciousness and arrogance these will annoy me. To publish in the scholarly journals is grief and delay. And the ssgm publications are read in the region by scholars and policy formers and implementers and immediately released online.*

All this he did at low revs. 'I have not been working hard – never been writing late at night'. And he could find time for other things in life. 'I have painted much of the house, and I have read novels'.

Australian writing was one of the things we went back and forth about. Peter Carey. Peter Temple. Tim Winton. Douglas Stewart's poem 'The Mice of Chinkapook'. The poetry of Les Murray, another boy from the bush, Nabiac and Bunyah. Differences in substance and style between Ken Inglis on the Stuart case and Chloe Hooper's *Tall Man* ('creative nonfiction'). Tom Griffiths and Stephen Pyne on Australian fire history. And from there, by way of climate, back to Boort, where Hank's brother John was still running the farm: droughts and flooding rains; disputes over water rights, escalating in the driest of dry years to fist fights and talk of dynamite; and, in a wet wet year, schoolkids standing on a bridge to see a river flowing for the first time in their lives.

Hank also emailed about watching cricket and AFL football. By technological good fortune, I could watch too, courtesy of ESPN. Hank's commentaries were much better than anything in the sports pages of the online *Age* or the *Sydney Morning Herald*, sharper-eyed about the overall state of play in cricket, with more of a sense of history, from late Bradman to late Ponting. And funnier. So, Hank on Ben Hilfenhaus hooked up to a heart rate monitor delivering real-time vital signs to TV watchers. The many moods of Mitchell Johnson. And the streaker who ran out onto the Gabba wearing nothing but a stubbie cooler tied to his wrist, making for Andrew Symonds. Then, in season each year, football, past, present, future – from Bobby Rose of Nyah, and Tiger Ridley, who went to school with me at Dimboola (Bobby Watson too, uncle-to-be of Tim and grand-uncle-to-be of Jobe), on to women goal umpires, and Buddy Franklin and all the other 21st-century six-and-a-half footers, with Hank looking forward to the first Sudanese ruckman.

I have bushels of email words from Hank, many of them about his life. The full harvest would be a book's worth. I always wished he would write his memoirs. I kept encouraging him to, but he never did, and more's the pity.

What I do have, alive in my memory, are some choice bits.

The town show, and the big attraction is Jimmy Sharman's travelling boxing tent, Jimmy's abos all in a row (back then they were abos, lower case), gloves on, dressing gowns over their shoulders, Jimmy the urger whipping up the crowd, who reckons he can go three rounds, who's game? – and up jumps a big drunken lair and kinghits a skin-and-bones lightweight.

Country cricket, the visitors' opening bowler measuring off his run, he counts out his twenty paces, with an extra big hop for the twentieth, and throws down his false teeth for his marker.

And here is the one I like best. It is from a home football game in Hank's high school teaching years. Hank was a centre half-back in the great mid-20th-century tradition. His job description of the position, substance and style, went along these lines:

The big men fly, you rise out of the pack and snag the mark, you get the whistle, you take your dignified time pacing back backwards, with the ball in one hand hanging nonchalantly down to demonstrate casual self-confidence, you come to a halt and steady yourself, you lean forward, a couple of stutter steps to get into your rhythm, and you launch a stately drop kick, highly parabolic, and as you watch it in flight past midfield you pull up your socks, even if they are pulled up already, and then you pick up your man and cover him, standing with your hands on your hips – and your elbow in his ribs, nothing over-invasive or disrespectful of his human rights, you just want him to be aware that he has your continuing concern.

Hank's man this day is a nasty piece of work. All through the game he has been hacking Hank behind the play, running boot sprigs down his shins. Everybody sees it bar the umpire. First quarter, second quarter, third, Hank keeps his cool, low-revving, non-eruptive, until halfway through the last quarter a moment comes and everything lines up perfectly, and Hank goes for it – he lays the bloke out, decisively, conclusively, concussively. And legally. And from the boundary comes a cheer, a kid Hank teaches at school, his voice just breaking: *'Good on yer, Mister Nelson!'*

That sounds like the proper send-off. Good on yer, Mister Nelson. Good on yer, Hank.

5. 'I Don't Think I Deserve a Pension – We Didn't Do Much Fighting': Interviewing Australian Prisoners of War of the Japanese, 1942–1945

Tim Bowden

Tim Bowden is a journalist, author, radio and television broadcaster and producer, and oral historian. This remembrance is based on a conference talk given at the Australian War Memorial.

'Talk about your experience of working with ex-POWs when you and Hank Nelson recorded your series', Joan Beaumont said to me. 'I think our audience would be fascinated to hear your reflections on this process and your thoughts now on how POWs remember their captivity and any other insights you might want to provide'. I will do my best; how good it would have been to have Hank here. His untimely death early last year robbed us of a great historian, and for me a valued mentor and close friend.

It was Hank who rang me early in 1982, just as *Taim Bilong Masta: The Australian Involvement with Papua New Guinea* went to air. I was exhausted. This project had taken two-and-a-half years, involving the recording of more than 300 hours of original oral history testimony. I even had RSI from the manual labour of cutting and splicing the quarter-inch tapes and typing out summaries and scripts on chaffcutter typewriters well before the computer era. Hank agreed to be a historical advisor on the *Taim Bilong Masta* project and also provide on-air editorial commentary in each episode. The deal was that I would produce the radio programs, and he would write a book on the series drawing on his own research. From my point of view it was one of the great partnerships and, indeed, a professionally life-changing experience for me.

One day Hank rang me about another proposal he had in mind. He came straight to the point. 'Listen, Digger; you and I have got to do the Australian prisoners of war of the Japanese in Asia. They have never really talked about their experiences, and they are now in their mid-60s, and nearly 40 years on they probably will'.

I can't quite remember what I said, but effectively it was, 'Yes'. Thanks to a benevolent boss in the Radio Drama and Features Department of the ABC, where

I then worked, I was given the go-ahead for another two-year-plus project that would spawn another 300 hours and more of tape and unlock much unique, moving and powerful testimony. This, you see, was Hank's genius. He was not interested in working on any topic that did not produce new material. And this was certainly the case with the Australian 8th Division experience.

This time, Hank would do some interviewing on his own, but despite my best effort to teach him the tricks of the trade, his first effort with a tape recorder and microphone was not a huge success, particularly with sound quality – an important element for a radio project. I recall (as indeed he often reminded me) saying to him after listening to this first effort, 'Hank, this is truly remarkable. You are the first interviewer ever to have apparently recorded your subject under water'. But he was a forgiving soul, and his radio techniques were soon firing on all cylinders.

It is worth noting that in the early 1980s the experiences of Australian POWs of the Japanese were not widely known. Military historians tend to concentrate on campaigns and battles, and not the experiences of prisoners of war – even though for three-and-a-half years 22,000 Australians were thrown into a battle for survival that would eclipse the hardships and danger of any similar period of active service. I tried to describe our approach in a talk I gave at the Australian War Memorial in February 1984:

> *There are compelling reasons for doing an oral history project on Australian prisoners of war of the Japanese at this time. It is more than 40 years since Singapore fell to General Yamashita's 25th Army, and including our men in places like Timor, Ambon, New Guinea, Sumatra and Java, some 22,000 Australians became prisoners of war of the Japanese. Three-and-a-half years later, 14,000 would survive after varying experiences at the hands of the Asian captors – forced labour, starvation and even death marches at one end of the scale, to humane and considerate treatment complete with Red Cross parcels and prison-baked bread at the other. Those Australian servicemen – and women – who survived their prisoner of war experiences are no longer young, and most are in poor health because of the nature of their imprisonment.*
>
> *Few diaries were kept, and those that were hidden at great risk were necessarily brief. Consequently personal recollection of events in remote locations not touched on by official chroniclers of POW history remains a rich field for the oral historian. Further, official reports were compiled predominantly from the testimony of officers. The experiences of NCOs and other ranks must be given greater consideration in any realistic survey of Australians as prisoners of war of the Japanese.*

I'll return to some of those flagged aims in a moment. But what was quite staggering to us at the time was the growing realisation that most of the ex-POWs played down what had happened to them, that their experiences weren't as important as serving soldiers' because they had spent so much time as prisoners of war and therefore were not worth talking much about.

This attitude was well summed up by one of the POW doctors, Ian Duncan, recalling the situation where he was in Japan, where former slave labourers from the Thai–Burma Railway construction had been taken in tramp ships to work in coal and iron ore mines in the freezing temperatures of a Japanese winter. Duncan:

> At the end of the war I interviewed every Australian and English soldier in my camp – I was the only medical officer in the camp. And I thought it was my duty to record their disabilities. And you'd say to them, what diseases did you have as a prisoner of war? Nothing much, Doc, nothing much at all. Did you have malaria? Oh yes, I had malaria. Did you have dysentery? Oh yes, I had dysentery. Did you have beriberi? Yes, I had beriberi. Did you have pellagra? Yes, I had pellagra – but nothing very much. These are lethal diseases. But that was the norm, you see, everyone had them. Therefore they accepted them as normal.

And again, here is Ian Duncan on his experience of the longer term, when returned POWs who had wanted to shrug off their experiences and return to normal life found to their cost that they were profoundly affected by what had happened to them. We spoke in the early 1980s, more than 40 years after they had become POWs:

> I would say most of them, at least 50 per cent of them, have some form of nervous trouble. A lot of them have stomach trouble, a lot have gastric and duodenal ulcers, a lot still have chronic diarrhoea. But everyone who worked, certainly on the railway and in the mines in Japan, has some form of arthritic degeneration caused by the conditions under which they worked. I've seen X-rays of the spines of some of these men, and they are really shocking – how they get around I don't know. But they do and they make light of it. The men almost invariably come in and say, 'Well, I don't want to seem to be a bludger, but I've got this trouble', or, 'I thought I'd come along and see you. I don't think I deserve any pension; we didn't do much fighting'. And this is their attitude. They actually believe that they are not entitled to a lot of the benefits of ex-servicemen. But they are. They fought a pretty hard war. As POWs.

Hank and I found it incredible that those who had gone through so much had reservations about being prisoners of war as though they were not proper soldiers. After our 16-part series went to air, the experiences of Australian POWs in Asia became something of a growth industry, with more personal memoirs being written, documentary films made, and even a television drama series produced by John Doyle for ABC-TV, titled *Changi*. It is difficult to imagine an Australian prime minister celebrating Anzac Day at Hellfire Pass on the Thai–Burma Railway – as John Howard did in 1998 – before *P.O.W.: Australians under Nippon* went to air in 1984. But I am jumping ahead. I should say something about our planning for the series.

The word *Changi* has come to mean all that was extreme and frightful about the prisoner of war experience. But as Hank and I were to find out, for those in the slave labour work camps on the Thai–Burma Railway, in Sandakan and before the death matches, the main POW base, Changi, seemed like heaven to those sent away from it. But there were POW camps in Timor, Java, Sumatra, New Guinea, Ambon, Hainan, Borneo, Singapore, Malaysia, Thailand, Burma, Manchuria and Japan. Australian POWs also turned up briefly in unlikely places like Phnom Penh and Saigon.

Back in 1982 we drew up a list of the topics we hoped to explore in the prisoner of war series:

- Preconceptions of Asia and the Japanese.
- What did the experience teach about being an Australian? In what ways were Australians different from other prisoners?
- The mechanics of personal survival.
- Perceptions of Japanese and Korean guards, and attempts to understand their motivations and attitudes in the interest of survival.
- What did the experience teach men about themselves and about others?
- Had attitudes changed in the years since the war. What did they think now about the Japanese?
- Did prisoners' personalities and patterns of behaviour change under the stress of imprisonment?
- What did horrific experiences do to people?
- What were people's attitude to them when they got home?
- How had the prisoner of war experience affected their lives?

Broadly the interviews we were about to record aimed to cover three basic areas:

1. What happened – the varied experiences?
2. The context in which it happened – as a part of Australian history and our relationship with Asia.
3. The effects on the lives of prisoners of war since.

To prepare for the interviews, Hank and I began to read as widely as we could, beginning with books written by former prisoners of war such as Rohan Rivett's *Behind Bamboo*, Russell Braddon's *The Naked Island*, Betty Jeffery's *White Coolies* and more recent additions to the literature like Stan Arneil's excellent *One Man's War*. More personal research began in October 1981 when several thousand ex-prisoners of war gathered in Sydney for an ex-POW reunion, and Hank and I submerged ourselves in as many of the activities as possible, scribbling down names and addresses – particularly of people from areas of imprisonment where there were few survivors. Useful contacts were made with several men who had survived the awfulness of Outram Road Gaol in Singapore – the Japanese military prison specialising in solitary confinement on six ounces of rice a day. We couldn't do any interviews at the time because useful recording sessions usually take a minimum of three hours, and those at the reunion had a busy program. I did though make a point of interviewing Ross Glover, of Arkansas, a survivor of the USS *Houston*, which went down with HMAS *Perth* in Sunda Strait. He shared POW experiences with Australians in Java and Singapore and on the Burma railway, and he came to Sydney especially for the reunion.

One extremely valuable exercise happened in February 1982 when Hank and I were permitted to accompany a group of 70 ex-prisoners of war and their wives on a three-week tour to Thailand, Malaya and Singapore – culminating in a dinner to mark the 40th anniversary of the fall of Singapore on 15 February 1942. The tour included visits to the Thai–Burma Railway area at Kanchanaburi (generally called Kanburi by the survivors) and areas around some of the old Kwai River camps, formerly Tarsau and Konyu. While there were obvious advantages for me, recording the impressions of men actually standing on the River Kwai bridge or on the neglected, jungle-reclaimed bed of the railway as they hunted for bits of sleeper and steel dog spikes as souvenirs, the real benefits were to come later.

Hank and I flew with the Bamboo Tour veterans to Thailand through Singapore's Changi Airport, which several men said wryly they had helped to build. Many had not travelled overseas since their POW days and quickly cottoned on to the fact that drinks were free on the flight. They arrived in very good form, having drunk the plane dry of beer.

The most instructive thing to me about the ex-POWs was how they reacted to a tragedy before the tour had really begun. Lieutenant John Windsor, formerly of the 2/20th Battalion and a survivor of the Thai–Burma Railway, had a heart attack and died suddenly between immigration and customs in Bangkok airport. At first I thought that the Bamboo Tour might have to be called off, but that showed how little I knew. These men were accustomed to death and the loss of their comrades, and they immediately went into quick and positive action, alerting the Australian Embassy to prepare to have Windsor's body returned to

Australia. In the meantime they comforted Windsor's wife and included her in the daily bus tours to Bangkok temples and the famous canals over the next few days until she left for Australia.

One former POW said to me, quite seriously, 'You know, John always wanted to come back to Thailand'. I nodded, but thought to myself that he might have appreciated at least getting out of the airport before making his exit. I don't want to give the impression that they made light of John Windsor's death – far from it. They just took it on board and cheerfully did what had to be done and got on with the job – as they certainly did when their comrades died building the railway.

In October 1983 Hank wrote a long article for the *Journal of the Australian War Memorial*, titled 'Travelling in Memories', which I commend to you. A couple of vignettes:

> *On the tour bus a Thai guide said that it must have been the pleasure of their first visit that had persuaded so many of the men to return. A couple of the diggers laughed and said, 'Turn it up!' Most made no response – they were accustomed to greater misunderstandings. At the end of the bus trip the ex-servicemen passed around the hat and gave generously of their baht. As the contents were handed to the two guides the men and their wives burst into* For they are jolly good fellows. *They sang strongly and spontaneously. The guides could not know that they had heard the last generation of Australians who will so easily sing that community salute.*

Here's Hank again, during the last leg of the journey in Malaysia:

> *Having disposed the last of their Thai baht on the airport tax, the members of the tour party flew to Kuala Lumpur. (Pronounced 'Koala Lumpa' by one ex-infantryman, it lost all association with the Orient, or with anywhere east of the Great Dividing Range. It sounded like one of those places on the ABC Country Hour litany of names and river heights. 'Koala Lumpa' is probably out near Waterbag or Beefwood Tank, just out of Wilcannia.) On the way from the airport to the Holiday Inn the Malay Chinese guide lounged at the front of the bus and went through his well-practised patter on the constitutional and demographic facts of Malaysia. Having told us that the nine heads of the Malay state selected one of themselves to be the Yang di-Pertuan Agong, the Supreme Head of the Federation, he made his standard pause and asked, 'Are there any questions to this point?' Before he could continue, Wizza said from down the back of the bus, 'Yeah, how much is a beer?' The guide did not quite hear. Wizza spoke more clearly and loudly. 'What's the price of a beer?' Had anyone else asked the same*

question they might have been playing for a laugh – Wizza simply wanted information. The guide hesitated, gave a straight answer, and returned to his description of the bicameral legislature.

And so we began to record the POWs – trying to make sure that we selected some from every camp, from Timor to Manchuria. Even though the death toll had been high, one in three men on certain sections of the Thai–Burma Railway, there was no shortage of people still around to talk about it. Not so Sandakan, in Borneo, where in round figures, 2,000 Australians were sent on the infamous death marches early in 1945, and only six escaped to survive. Four of those six were still alive in the early 1980s, and I interviewed them all, as well as some of the officers whom the Japanese sent to Kuching after the underground network was discovered in July 1943. Only one Australian, John Murphy, was in the Japanese POW camp in Rabaul, and he was an excellent interviewee.

On the theme of how even a little homework yields great benefits, I quickly detected a change of attitude in my interviewees when I asked them, for example, which side of the railway they were on, in Burma or in Thailand, and whether they were in the most challenging work parties in the mountains, A Force on the Burmese side, and H and F Forces in Thailand. 'Oh you know about the different forces, do you', said one former POW, and he immediately began to talk to me as though I was an insider. I continued to be amazed about the frankness of people's testimonies, telling stories for the first time that had often not even been told to their own families.

Both Hank and I were keen to make sure that the surviving army nurses told their stories. They were evacuated from Singapore in the closing stages of the battle there, on a ship, *Vyner Brooke*, which was unfortunately bombed and sunk soon after leaving Singapore Harbour, leaving the surviving passengers and 65 Australian nurses struggling in the water, hanging on to any debris they could find. Separated by the currents, Sister Vivien Bullwinkel was one of 22 Australian nurses who were washed ashore on Radji Beach, Bangka Island, off the coast of Sumatra. There they were discovered by Japanese soldiers, who marched them into the water and opened fire with a machine gun. Although shot twice, Vivien Bullwinkel survived, after playing dead; concealing her wounds, she managed to join up with another group of nurses, who were put into a POW camp. The Japanese never realised that she had survived a massacre, or she certainly would have been killed.

By the end of the war only 24 of the 65 nurses who had boarded the *Vyner Brooke* were still alive. I interviewed five: Betty Jeffery (who wrote a book on her experiences after the war), Sylvia Muir, Mickey Syer, Beryl Woodbridge and Iole Harper. Only then did I approach Vivian Bullwinkel, then Vivian Statham, in Perth. I was well aware that her story had been so astonishing that it had eclipsed those of the other nurses over the years. Our interview was, in my terms, sensational. Vivian later told me she had given me the fullest account to date of her remarkable survival. I asked her why? She said, 'Well, I heard you had been interviewing the other girls, and I am always conscious that my story seems to get all the publicity. So I decided to give you a good interview'.

I remained amazed how much, and how frankly, the ex-POWs would speak of their experiences in one-, two- or three-hour sessions. However, I had a salutary experience during an interview with Sergeant Jack Sloane in Brisbane. My ABC-issue tape recorder broke down in midstream, and I had to apologise to Jack and ask him if I could come back the following morning. He agreed, but when he opened the front door, he said, 'You bastard! I didn't sleep a wink last night with all this stuff running around in my head that I hadn't thought of for years! But OK, let's get on with it and get it finished'. This worried me, and I sought advice from a clinical psychologist, who told me that it was almost surely beneficial for men to recall these traumatic events. I hope he was right. Certainly what psychological counselling there was at the time, after the war – and that was practically zilch – was to tell the ex-POWs to try to forget what had happened to them and not to talk about it, especially with their families!

An Outram Road Gaol survivor, Chris Neilson, whose bullshit detector was always well honed, reacted characteristically when a psychologist said to him, 'You've got to forget about it completely'. 'I said, "You stupid bastard, if you were there for five bloody minutes, you'd never forget it all your bloody life"'. I was certainly made aware that trawling through those traumatic experiences was an emotional overload for some. I would often have to stop and turn off the tape recorder and wait for interviewees to get control of themselves again. I'll never forget the first time this happened. I was in Perth, interviewing Arthur 'Blood' Bancroft, who was an able seaman on HMAS *Perth* when it was sunk in Sunda Strait with USS *Houston*. He began his life as a POW stark naked and covered in fuel oil on a West Java beach. He joined Weary Dunlop's Java Rabble – a label given to them by Colonel 'Black Jack' Galleghan when they passed through Changi (the major POW base camp in Southeast Asia), which they wore with pride.

After spending a year building the Thai–Burma Railway, Bancroft returned to Changi only to be put on one of the tramp ships in company with thousands of other Australians, to be sent to Japan in early 1944 to work in coal mines there. Arthur never made it. His ship was sunk by an American submarine, unaware that there were Allied POWs on board. He spent six days and six nights in the water, clinging to flotsam before being picked up by an American submarine – narrowly escaping being machine-gunned in the water when they were first thought to be Japanese.

I had reached this point in the narrative, as Arthur described being helped onto the deck of the submarine. Being a sailor himself, despite his debilitated state, he observed protocol, stood to attention as straight as he could and saluted the bridge. I said, as I looked down to check that my recorder spools were still turning, 'That must have been quite a moment'. To my utter surprise, Arthur suddenly broke into explosive sobbing. Naturally I switched off until he felt ready to go on.

This reminds me of another painful experience of my own, during the last time I spoke on these matters in this building in 1984. As part of my presentation, I played a confronting segment of tape that clearly had an impact. At morning tea I was hugely savaged by people who came up to me to say how appalling it was of me to expose the emotions of this man in that way – it was the kind of sensationalist behaviour they expected of journalists, and how dare I exploit these people in such a shocking way! I said, 'Hold on, this *hasn't* gone to air, and it won't'. But I don't think my critics believed me. In fact how I did handle this situation – because it was obvious *something* had happened – was to select a deep anguished breath just after his breakdown, to bridge the moment and rightly suggest emotional stress, and then Arthur carried on with his narrative. There is no way I was going to play it again this time, although I don't have the original tapes anymore. Happily they are now safe in the AWM collection.

One of the known facts about the Australians who worked on the Thai–Burma Railway was that they survived better than any other nationality – measured against the Dutch, the British and of course the poor unfortunate Asian labourers who had no organisation at all and died in their hundreds, some say thousands, buried in unmarked mass graves. Although the Australian officers had privileges that the ORs (other ranks) didn't have – and importantly for their own survival did not have to do the harsh, backbreaking work that killed so many men – their relations with their men were better than those of the British, whose class system insulated officers from their troops. Also many of the British soldiers had been recruited from the slums of London or provincial cities like Liverpool and Glasgow and given rudimentary training before being rushed to Malaya just before the Japanese invasion began. They were not in good physical shape when they arrived, and with the comparative lack of organisation the onset of tropical diseases and also the vitamin deficiency diseases like beriberi and pellagra– as well as the universal dysentery – put them at a disadvantage compared with the Australians who were mostly country boys, super fit when they arrived, and handy. They had bush skills and a great ability to scrounge or steal what could be had under the circumstances.

Lloyd Cahill, one of the doctors on the railway – who by the way only died a few months ago at 98 years of age – summed it up well, I thought, in this excerpt from my interview with him back in the early 1980s:

> *I always remember one fellow, 'Ringer' Edwards, who appeared in A Town Like Alice. Now 'The Ringer' was on my crowd that went up on the railway. He was one of the most amazing men I've ever met. We'd be marching up at night, and fellows would be falling over and breaking their arms in the pouring monsoon. We'd stop, and 'The Ringer' would have a little fire going within about five minutes, and how he did it in the wet jungle I don't know. But he was a tower of strength there. If you got a bunch of fellows like that around you, it doesn't matter what conditions you are living in, in the bush – you'll be okay. The poor Brits had a tough time; they did it the hard way. They had no idea how to set up a kitchen or set up latrines. Even when they were cremating people, they had no idea what to do. If you were lucky enough to be with a good bunch of Australians, you could see most of it through.*

Kevin Fagan, another legendary doctor on the line, put it this way:

> *I felt that the Australian other ranks had a greater sense of group loyalty than the British. There was this terrible class thing in the British mind. It's horrible. I've seen British officers at the end of a long day's march, as soon as they arrived at the camp, just flop down on the ground. Someone would say, 'What about the men?' 'Oh so-and-so the men. I can't do any more'. Whereas a fellow like Reggie Newton would be scrounging around trying to buy a few eggs for the sick, trying to organise the men to be together, finding out where everyone was and whether anyone needed a doctor – and all this before he even thought of eating or sitting down.*

Still on this point of the survival skills of Australians, I'd also like to quote from the interview that Hank did with ex-POW Hughie Clark:

> *If one of our blokes was crook, someone always took him food. I was taking an egg down to a mate in hospital when this raspy-voiced Englishman said, 'There's no doubt about it. You always stick together'.*
>
> *Australians didn't die alone. I saw plenty of Englishmen and Dutchmen dying on their own – but not Australians.*
>
> *I can explain it by comparing the way people behave in a city with those in a country town. In a country town the people might not like each other, but they know one another, and when something goes wrong, they rally around. In a suburb people don't know other people and don't feel responsible. Our army was like a country town – other soldiers might well have been in the city.*

For as yet unexplained reasons, the white Dutch were not popular with the Australians on the railway. I asked Ray Parkin, a survivor from HMAS *Perth*, why this was so. Even this talented wordsmith found it difficult to explain. 'I don't know', he said. 'It's just that they *knew* everything', and wanted to talk about it whether the listener wanted to hear or not. Lloyd Cahill told me that when they all got back to Changi after the railway was finished at the end of 1943, he saw a large hand-printed sign in the Dutch camp: 'We are your loyal allies, and not those fucking Dutch'. I never did track down what all that was about. Certainly Australian relations with the British and the few Americans on the line were much more cordial. Whether the almost universal Australian distaste for the Dutch helped survival, I can't say.

I mentioned that the relations between Australian officers and their troops were better than in the British army, and this was generally so. But in the Asian prisoner of war situation, the Australian officers found themselves – as did the British officers – in a privileged position. They were accorded status by the Japanese and paid a little more, but importantly they did not have to do the hard, back-breaking work that killed so many Australian and British troops on the railway.

In battle, officers die in numbers out of proportion to their men. But in the Asian POW situation, being an officer was like being issued with a ticket to go home. Hank, with his usual thoroughness, researched this assertion:

> *The statistics confirm the claim by the other ranks that as prisoners they did the dying. The 2/29th Battalion lost 12 officers and 58 other ranks killed in action. Even when it is taken into account that many other ranks were classified as missing believed killed, the officers died in battle out of proportion to their numbers. But as prisoners, two officers and 381 other ranks died. In H Force, the death rate for British and Australian officers was 6 per cent – for the men, it was over thirty per cent. Among the Australians in F Force, three officers died in comparison with 1065 other ranks. On the* Perth *18 officers were killed in action or were drowned, but none died as prisoners of war – 331 ratings were killed or drowned and 104 died while prisoners. The battle conditions which made junior officers vulnerable were reversed when the Allies surrendered.*

Not all the Australian officers behaved well, although most did. The doctors are remembered as heroes by the ex-POWs. Major 'Roaring Reggie' Newton of the 2/19th Battalion was outstanding in his unceasing abilities to stand up to the Japanese to get a better deal for his men and was often beaten and humiliated for his efforts but just kept going – continuing his pastoral care of the men of his beloved 2/19th even after the war was over until the day he died.

Some officers began their imprisonment by interceding on behalf of their men but could not take the bashings and stress and decided that they wanted to get home; these tended to take a back seat to avoid the unceasing confrontation.

A few were legendary for the wrong reasons and could never attend any unit reunion after the war because of their shameful conduct. Lieutenant Colonel Gus Kappe came back to Changi from the Thai–Burma railway fat, in marked contrast to his skeletal men. As well as feathering his own nest with extra food from his officer's allowance – some officers pooled their extra pay and did share with their men – Kappe even turned over his own men to the Japanese for punishment.

George Aspinall, who did not name Kappe to me at the time, told me of his experience with him on F Force:

> *There was one particular officer who was renowned for laying back all day doing nothing, issuing orders and making life very hard for the rest of the men that were working. To some extent he was cooperating with the Japanese to their detriment. The men detested this particular person. Even today they don't talk about such things publicly; they prefer to let bygones be bygones. But when a group is talking privately, some of these names come, and there's a real hate session. It did anger people. But we were supposed to be soldiers; we were supposed to take orders from our superior officers. We perhaps tried to live up to a code, something set by our forefathers in World War I.*

Don Moore speaks of another case:

> *There was one officer known as the White Jap. He was entirely dedicated to his own self-preservation. He was affluent by POW standards. He had money that he could lend where he would be paid back three times the price in English currency when he came back.*
>
> *This money had come from the proceeds of a canteen which he ran at a camp of which he was the commander. In this case it was private enterprise purely and simply for himself. This fellow I speak of has never been back to any reunion that I know of.*

To add insult to injury as far as his hard-done-by soldiers in F Force were concerned, Colonel Kappe was awarded an Order of the British Empire (OBE) for his war service.

It was all very well, Hank and I recording all these extraordinary stories, but were they all true? This is a question that all historians must constantly ask, and those collecting oral testimonies must be similarly on guard. I once facetiously named that formidable raconteur and author Samuel Langhorne Clemens, better known as Mark Twain, as the patron saint of oral history. Twain once said words to this effect: 'The further I go back, the better I remember things – whether they happened or not'.

Most practitioners of the noble art of oral history are aware of the cautionary tale of a wonderful little old lady in Melbourne who gave fascinating anecdotes and detail of life in the suburb of Collingwood in the 1930s — when someone realised she was running about one episode behind the ABC's period drama *Power without Glory*. This is where Hank Nelson performed a sterling role in keeping me, the journalist, as honest as could be with the *Australians under Nippon* radio series.

Sometimes when more than one person was interviewed about the same incident, an event could be verified by more than one source with crosscutting between the speakers. Coverage of the ship nicknamed the *Byoki Maru* (sick ship) from Singapore to Japan is an example. A description of the AIF (Australian Imperial Force) men enlarging a leak below the ship's waterline so they could take a shower is counterpointed with wonderment by former sailors from the HMAS *Perth*, who also recalled the same incident.

Here's a more tricky problem, resolved by paperwork at the AWM. Hank Nelson:

> We often found that our informants made factual errors in dates and numbers — but we came to have increasing confidence in their personal narratives and judgements. At one stage Tim Bowden interviewed Chris Neilson, a survivor of Outram Road Gaol, the place of secondary punishment and also the prison in Singapore for those who had offended against the Japanese. Neilson said that he had attempted to escape from a work camp on Singapore island. But when one of the party of five became intensely ill they brought him back to camp, and intended to try again the next night. As they rested during the day they were suddenly awakened with a boot in the ribs — the Japanese arrested them for attempting to escape. Neilson said that the senior Australian officer in the camp, Lieutenant-Colonel RF Oakes, had informed the Japanese, presumably because he thought that the escape would bring reprisals on him and the remaining prisoners. This was in spite of the fact that it was the duty of all captured soldiers to attempt to escape. At this stage I told Tim that we could not publish the Neilson story without confirmation.
>
> Now one of the great advantages of working with the memories of prisoners of war is that prisoners were rarely involved in significant events when alone. There were nearly always witnesses, and through the ex-unit associations those witnesses can be found. Neilson named a junior officer who was present and who kept a brief diary. He had notes about Neilson's arrest, but could not confirm that the senior Australian officer had informed the Japanese. I then started going through the statements made by the prisoners at the end of the war. Without great difficulty I found the sworn statement of another escapee, Driver Reg Morris.

He had details of the escape attempt, gave all the names of those involved and the dates, and said that on the escapees' return with their sick mate, Oakes 'saw fit to hand us over to the Japanese'. We let Neilson's words go to air.

Sometimes the discrepancies between the oral and written record could be checked back with the interviewee. This happened in the case of Lieutenant Rod Wells, who had been arrested in connection with the secret underground movement at the Sandakan camp in Borneo in 1943. Wells, among other things, had helped in the construction of a clandestine radio. One detail concerned a permanent injury to Wells's left ear during a *Kempeitai* (Military Police Corps) torture session. In my interview, Wells said he was made permanently deaf when his torturer hammered a wooden skewer into his left ear and perforated his eardrum. In his 1945 deposition, read by Hank Nelson, he attributed his deafness to being hit over the ear with a billet of wood. When queried on this on Hank's behalf, Wells said that when he made the original deposition, he believed that the blow with the billet of wood had caused his deafness. But some years later his doctor told him it was definitely the skewer that had done the permanent damage. There was in fact no inconsistency. Wells had what he thought was better information by the time I interviewed him. But enough of keeping journalists honest.

Radio cassettes had just started to be produced and sold by the ABC, and several thousand sets of tapes were snapped up by our listeners, extending and continuing the reach of *P.O.W.:Australians under Nippon*. In order to highlight some of the individual stories not able to be pursued in the 16-part series, I produced a further ten half-hour programs titled *Survival*, featuring the experiences of eight prisoners of war, including Chris Neilson and the remarkable Vivian Bullwinkel. Hank published a book on the series with the same title, a chapter for each program. I also wrote a book (my first), *Changi Photographer – George Aspinall's Record of Captivity*, based on extended interviews with George, and which published many of his photographs for the first time.

So Hank Nelson's phone call in 1982 triggered an immersion exercise in prisoner of war experiences that has been a considerable part of my professional life. Working with Hank for all those years was simply wonderful, and I cannot believe that he is no longer here. The urge to ring him about something still occurs daily. But he neglected to leave his telephone number – how very inconsiderate of him.

6. Doktorvater

Klaus Neumann

Klaus Neumann is a historian who writes about historical justice, social memory and refugee policy. He is a research professor at the Swinburne Institute for Social Research in Melbourne.

'I am certain that the doctorates here at The Australian National University have a very high international standing but I know almost nothing about the university systems of Germany and am therefore not in a position to make any comparisons between the two', read the first response I received in early 1984 when exploring the possibility of applying for admission to The Australian National University's PhD program. The respondent was Hank Nelson – the fact that he did not mention his position or title struck me at the time as being as noteworthy as the information his letter contained.

From others I learnt that in Australia, postgraduate students have *supervisors*. A supervisor, I was told, is not the same as a *Doktorvater* (literally 'the father of the doctorate'), the senior academic looking after a doctoral student in Germany, Austria or Switzerland. I thought that was good news. In my experience, a *Doktorvater* (or *Doktormutter* – although some 30 years ago she would have still been very much an exception) was a rather elusive figure. German professors were notorious for not recalling the names of their doctoral students and could often be contacted only during a once-a-week, one-hour *Sprechstunde*, when students could be seen queuing outside their office for a precious five-minute audience. In my attempts to find a German professor to take on a student wanting to study the impact of colonial rule in Papua New Guinea, I had sent off several letters that had not met with a reply. In the end a historian specialising in late 19th and early 20th-century southern Africa agreed to be my *Doktorvater*. His main role would have been to examine my dissertation rather than to advise me on how to research and write it. He was however reputedly more conscientious than some of his colleagues, who met their doctoral students only twice: once to approve of their project and the second time to take receipt of the completed thesis.

I left my *Doktorvater* once ANU had offered me a PhD scholarship. As I was preparing to move to the other side of the world, Hank Nelson kept writing to me, patiently answering my many questions, trying to accommodate my ever-changing travel plans and putting up with my poorly-worded anxieties: 'I am sorry to cause some hustle for you again', I told him six weeks before my scheduled departure for Australia. 'Please let me know in your next letter at which time and by which phone calling number you can be got'.

By then I was officially enrolled because I was expected to complete any necessary archival research in Europe before moving to Australia. The ANU student administrators, who would have been justifiably nervous about paying a stipend to a student they had never sighted, instructed me to furnish detailed fortnightly reports about my progress. I did exactly as I was told (or so I thought), only to be advised by Hank: 'I require only very brief reports – 1 page'. Although he had become my main point of contact with ANU, I hadn't yet understood that he was already my supervisor – but then I still did not know what exactly a supervisor's role was.

How Hank himself understood his role became clearer late one Saturday evening in June 1985 when I arrived at Canberra Railway Station carrying a backpack and a typewriter. Hank was there to pick me up and to deposit me at a college where he had booked a room for me. I can't recall what was said in our first encounter – or rather, I don't know because I do recall being horrified to discover that I could not comprehend Hank with his broad Australian accent. I did understand, however, that I was meant to explore Canberra's city centre the next morning and that Hank would pick me up in the afternoon to take me for a drive.

That Sunday, Hank tried hard to make me see the positives of Canberra. But by the end of the day, I was despondent. Having lived in Europe all my life, Civic (on a wintry Sunday morning in 1985!) wasn't exactly my idea of a city centre. And the fact that Hank took me to see an ugly bunker-like building in Mitchell, a very long way from anywhere, and told me that I would spend some considerable time there added to my despair.

I was amazed by the fact that Hank would spend his Sunday afternoon with a mere PhD student, including introducing him to his family. At the same time I was dismayed because I grasped so little of what he was trying to tell me. The next day, I met him again at ANU and told him that rather than schlep my typewriter to the National Archives in Mitchell, I needed to do an intensive English language course because I didn't understand him and was daunted by the prospect of having to write in English. That was the only time when Hank flatly refused a request of mine.

I was very tempted to run, to return home while it was still summer in Europe. But somehow Hank convinced me that it would only be a matter of time before my English comprehension and writing skills would be up to scratch. He did not comment on my intense dislike of Canberra but had no objections to my decamping to Sydney for a while. In fact, throughout my time at ANU he was very relaxed about my physical whereabouts. He must have been surprised when I later extended my fieldwork in Papua New Guinea from a few months to a couple of years, but he remained confident in my ability to eventually come up with the goods. In October 1987, while I was in my second year of living in Raluana Village near Rabaul and had not yet produced a single draft chapter of my thesis, he wrote:

> *I wonder whether you ought to try a different location for some writing? I have no objection to you staying in Raluana, and I do not care much how long you take – although there are practical matters about visas and things like that. If you want to try a spell in Sydney or anywhere then do so. Do not ask for formal permission from ANU because it would only worry people. I raise this merely in case you are inhibited from going elsewhere for fear the bureaucratic wrath of ANU would fall upon you. My unofficial advice is to go wherever the typewriter taps most smoothly.*

Hank took it upon himself to shield me from the university's rules and regulations – and more importantly, from those who took delight in enforcing them. I suspect he must have been asked to explain why his student was away in Papua New Guinea for a total of two years, but he never mentioned having to stand up for his wayward charge. I encountered the bureaucratic wrath of ANU only once, when I applied – initially unsuccessfully – for a substantial extension of my scholarship on account of having suffered from malaria. The student rep on the committee later told me that Hank had been blamed for my tardiness and rebuked by his colleagues for supervising me 'too loosely'.

Whether I was in Canberra, Sydney or Raluana, Hank kept talking to me. He sent me long letters; some of them were typed on letterhead paper, but most were handwritten on a notepad ('I hope you can read all this: It is the handwriting equivalent of age, a mouthful of buai and no teeth', he once noted apologetically). When I was at ANU, he tried to engage me in conversations in the Coombs tea room – over cups of coffee that tasted like anything but coffee.

Without my realising it, he tried to educate me: not only about PNG but also about Australian politics, history, literature, film and sport. While I foolishly treated his stories about Australian prime ministers, poets and cricket captains as attempts at making conversation, I truly appreciated his other efforts to make me less stand out as an ignorant foreigner: he had taken it upon himself to teach me how to write. I had always been interested in writing in German, but most of the English I knew I had learned when working as a volunteer with young offenders in the English Midlands. I thought that in order to write a dissertation in English I simply needed to learn the basics of English grammar, increase my vocabulary and then substitute my German words for English ones. 'The prose is satisfactory', Hank wrote to me after reading one of my first attempts at composing an essay, a few months after my arrival. 'But remember that English is better if it's simple, direct (active voice) and in short sentences'. That was news to me. Why would anybody trying to be sophisticated prefer a ten-word sentence to one meandering over a couple of pages?

Over the following three years, Hank taught me to think and express myself in English, to reinvent myself and unlearn much of what I knew about writing. He showed me how to be exact and parsimonious with words. He taught me to love creating texts in my second language. It was a thrilling learning experience.

Hank was a patient teacher, but he was unwilling to make allowances for the fact that I was not writing in my native language. As far as he was concerned, I just needed to improve. Two years into my candidature, he was still chiding me: 'Your prose is satisfactory, and some paragraphs are good, but keep working on achieving a continuous clarity. Use more short sentences. Use short, active-voice verbs. In English, the Anglo-Saxon terms are nearly always preferable to (better than!!!!) the latin'. At the same time, he was concerned that I would despair about the extent to which he corrected my texts:

Do not think that because I make suggested alterations on your prose that you do not write well. I am addicted to altering prose. In fact if this letter were on the screen rather than being fixed instantly on the paper, it would be much changed before it got to you. (And I notice that some of it would greatly benefit.)

I tell my PhD students that the better their prose, the more I may feel compelled to make comments and alternative suggestions. Sometimes I make more corrections on the second draft than I have done on the first – after the student has already incorporated all my previous suggestions. Hank taught me to cherish sentences that are laconic yet laden with meaning, unadorned yet beautiful, with a message that is precise and complex. I can sense him looking over my shoulder when I read the work of a student who is skilful and ambitious as a writer: 'You need to keep pushing her', I hear Hank say; 'there is nearly always room for further improvement'.

Hank did not teach me to mimic his own style of writing. Rather, he encouraged me to identify a way of writing that suited *me* – provided, of course, I respected what he considered to be basic rules regarding precision and economy. I now believe – and keep reminding my own students – that the chance to develop an *individual* style suited to writing a 100,000 word thesis is perhaps the best thing about doing a three-year PhD.

Very soon after my arrival in Australia, Hank began telling me exactly what kind of text he eventually wanted me to write: 'Keep thinking about that balance between tight, engaging narrative, sharp arresting observations tied to the narrative, and broad speculative conclusions. That's what makes good theses and good books'. Hank always encouraged me to write for audiences other than two or three likeminded scholars and to experiment with non-academic formats. He wanted me to do as he had done as a PhD student: write a good book, which by default would also be a good thesis.

While Hank had definite ideas about the difference between talented and poor researchers and skilful and hapless writers, he did not expect me to emulate his own practice as a historian. A German *Doktorvater* is often trying to reproduce himself through his students. In Australia, too, supervisors sometimes seem to think that the ideal student is a disciple following in their footsteps. Hank would have been far too modest to expect anybody to become his disciple. Yet he felt also sufficiently comfortable about his own work to be able to be tolerant and generous when it came to that of others. While he had no penchant for theorising, he never discouraged me from trying to make sense of my research by reading the work of philosophers and social theorists. Many of his colleagues in Pacific History were virulently anti-theoretical, to the extent that the mere mention of Adorno or Derrida would trigger laments about the demise of the humanities in general and the corruption of the historical discipline in particular. Hank would heap scorn on scholars who resorted to academic jargon because they were poor writers, but he always respected those with original ideas, however complex or theoretically informed.

Unlike Hank, I tended not to trust my stories to be analytical in their own right. I felt the need to add theoretical reflections when he was content to let a descriptive narrative speak for itself. We never argued about this point, as it seemed to be a matter of personal inclination rather than of principle, but I knew that in this respect my writing had little in common with his. In those days, history departments were often split along two fault lines: between empiricists and theorists and between those embracing the first-person singular and those shunning it. With regards to the latter, Hank and I found ourselves on the same side. He wrote:

> *Do not be reluctant to put yourself and specific occasions in the thesis. I trust I won't get you into trouble with conservative examiners. It is not only that I distrust the pretentiousness of the omniscient style of history in situations like this, but you are obviously a particular observer-fieldworker historian and this has ramifications. You have a specific perspective, specific experiences, and specific interaction with informants denied the reader of archival documents and newspapers.*

Referring to an article he had written for the literary magazine *Overland* (and which I had admired when he sent me a draft), he acknowledged that such an approach wouldn't necessarily win me many friends:

> *You need not go as far as I did in the Tabara article in which my colleagues thought I was either just being funny or I was incompetent. I may have been both a comedian and incompetent, but I was also trying to say something about Tabara and comprehension across cultures.*

While Hank did not expect me to have read any of his pre-1985 books or articles, he shared everything he wrote once I had become his student. For him, supervision was no one-way traffic between a teacher and a student. While I was in Papua New Guinea, Hank worked on his book about Australian one-teacher schools. He sent me drafts and seminar papers but also discussed at great lengths the problems he was encountering. 'I am having great trouble getting the Bush Schools book completed', he confided in late 1987.

> *I have over a hundred pages, but they are not sequential and they are not consistent. Some is anecdote, some is about the generation of Aust literature, some is about teaching Aborigines in desert camps about the glories of the British Empire, and some is detailed history of education among farmers. All the problems have been made by me.*
>
> *At least I had no money in the stock exchange.*

Hank was a private person. But his letters were not only about the issues that had brought us together in the first place: Papua New Guinea and doctoral thesis. He also wrote about his everyday life in Canberra. One of his favourite topics was the change of seasons. 'We had a taste of summer. Again I made a premature switch to shorts', he told me at the end of one November. In another letter, he wrote: 'In March we have more summer – well a few days over thirty degrees. All this strange behaviour of the weather must be the result of French bomb tests, daylight saving which interferes with God's time, or covert socialists in Canberra'.

His lighthearted remarks about the weather or Australia were to help me stay connected. But they also prompted me to reciprocate and explain to somebody in Canberra what it was like living in Raluana. They encouraged me to practise translating my experience long before I started drafting the first chapters of my thesis. I learned about Tolai culture and histories not least by trying to write about them. Hank knew I would. A few weeks after I arrived in Papua New Guinea for my first stint of fieldwork, he gave me this piece of advice:

> *Write a lot, not to me but self-indulgently. Perhaps self-scarifyingly, because writing is never a sensuous pleasure and rarely an intellectual delight. You must keep writing because when you leave the field much that is now available to you will no longer be accessible. What seems to be insignificant now may become important.*

He was well aware of the poverty of the grand ideas I then had about Papua New Guinea, but rather than ridiculing them before I had seen the place for myself, he held out a promise:

> *Keep writing so that by the time you reach Canberra you will have a store of words and sentences, and not just wandering, wondering speculations. And the exercise of writing will sharpen your eyes and your questions. Keep writing because you may want a record of your first or second or third impressions. It is strange how quickly your responses change so that the exotic becomes ordinary and the inexplicable becomes rational – and other puzzles arise.*

Puzzles aplenty arose during my two years in Papua New Guinea, and I tried to make sense of them by writing to Hank about them. I tried to sharpen my eyes and my questions. In his letters, Hank kept reminding me that I needed also to sharpen my prose.

By the time I submitted my thesis in late 1988, I was familiar with the role of the PhD supervisor in the Australian academy. I also knew that Hank was an exception. In fact he was a *Doktorvater* in the literal sense of the term: somebody who was partly responsible for the creation of my dissertation, and somebody with whom I would form a bond that in some respects was reminiscent of that between father and son.

7. Hank, My Mentor

Keiko Tamura

Keiko Tamura completed her PhD under Hank Nelson's supervision in 1999 and has held research positions at ANU, Kobe University and Kyoto University. She is a visiting fellow in the School of Culture, History and Language at ANU.

A message from Bill Gammage on Hank's passing reached me in Kobe on 18 February 2012. It was a bright and sunny day, but cold and clear. Occasionally white snowflakes danced down from the blue sky, glittering in the sunshine. From my hotel room on the 8th floor, I could see the Rokko Range clearly in the north of Kobe. Downward gaze spotted locals and tourists milling in the narrow streets of the Chinatown. They were shopping, eating tasty delicacies and chatting among themselves. I could almost hear the noise and smell the food down there. But I did not want to mingle with the crowd. I stayed in my room, as I felt immense sadness that Hank was no more. Even though we all knew that was imminent because of his declining health, I was still shocked when it finally happened. I have been reflecting on my engagement with Hank, which spanned over two decades. Although the sadness and sense of loss are still with me, I feel I was so lucky and privileged to get to know him, first as a respected academic, then as my supervisor and as a colleague over that period. I always ask myself, 'What Hank would say?' when I wonder what I should do.

My first encounter with Hank was totally uninspiring, solely due to my blunder. Then his presence gradually grew bigger in my academic career. Before I realised it, he was my mentor, to whom I always turned when I needed some crucial advice. Sometimes he gave a decisive and definite response and advised me to tackle the issues. Sometimes he just listened and waited until I decided for myself. What stays with me is his smile whenever I told him about some exciting news, discoveries or plans. He was happy to share good news with me but not overly emotionally involved when not-so-good news was shared. Over two decades, Hank became my confidant.

I saw Hank for the first time in the early 1990s when I went along to his lecture on Rabaul at the Australian War Memorial. I do not remember why I decided to attend the talk because my interest in the Pacific War had not developed at all then. Rather, I was actively avoiding anything to do with the war. On the day I saw Hank for the first time, he entered the lecture venue with a shy smile, walking with crutches (after injuring his leg playing tennis, I later found out from him). His trademark moustache reminded me not of Henry Lawson, as my Australian colleagues would say, but of Nigel Mansell, a champion British

The Boy from Boort

Formula One driver whom I was a big fan of around that time. During the talk, alas, I started to nod off, only to be woken by a sudden shudder as someone behind me knocked the chair leg with his foot. I woke up with a shock and felt awfully embarrassed but at the same time annoyed with this presumably militaristic method of handling the sleepy audience. I told myself never to attend any talks at the Memorial in the future, and I never imagined that I would form a long association with the Memorial several years later through working for the Australia–Japan Research Project. As for Hank's lecture, I cannot remember what he talked about.

The next encounter with Hank was in August 1991 when I first learned about the issues on the Australian prisoners of war. I attended a seminar on the Thai–Burma Railway that was co-hosted by Hank and Gavan McCormack.[1] The seminar brought together not only Australian and Japanese historians but also a group of Australian ex-POWs and a former camp guard of Korean descent. The Australian POWs included Edward (Weary) Dunlop, Tom Uren and Hugh Clark. The Korean ex-guard, Yi Hak-Nae, travelled to Canberra because he wanted to apologise directly to the Australians for his conduct.

My lack of knowledge on the topic was mainly because I belong to the post-war generation of Japanese who grew up during the 'economic miracle' period. At school we received the so-called 'peace education', where the importance and virtue of peace were drummed into us. It was a fairly simple binary ideology: peace was good, and war was evil. Let us talk about peace, but don't talk about war. Throughout my schooling, it was almost a taboo to learn about the Pacific War. For us, the war started with the Japanese attack on Pearl Harbor in December 1941 and ended in August 1945 after two atomic bombs in Hiroshima and Nagasaki, but what happened in between was not clear. We did not learn how the China–Japan war had started in 1937 or how and why the Japanese troops fought miserable battles in New Guinea and surrounding islands. As for the prisoners of war, I had heard of the film *The Bridge on the River Kwai*. For me the film was simply one of many Western war movies with a catchy theme tune, 'Colonel Bogey March'. I was not interested in those war films as the Japanese depicted in them were never favourable – rather ugly and fanatic. My knowledge gap was actually much wider. I am embarrassed to confess that I did not even know that Australia fought against Japan in the Pacific War until I came to Australia. For Japanese, the Pacific War was the war between Japan and the United States. I learned about Australia's involvement only when I started to work as a Canberra tour guide for Japanese tourists when I was a student. During visits to the Australian War Memorial with young Japanese honeymooners, I happily recited the Japanese submariners' bravery in the

---

1   See Gavan McCormack and Hank Nelson (eds), *The Burma–Thailand Railway: Memory and History*, St Leonards, NSW: Allen & Unwin, 1993.

Sydney attack and pointed out some Japanese good luck flags in order to stir up their emotions, but I made sure to avoid any objects that showed the cruelty carried out by the Japanese. I simply was not sure how I could tell those dark stories to the Japanese visitors.

The 1991 seminar on the Thai–Burma Railway revealed to me many stories that were horrific. I felt ashamed to learn about the inhumane treatment of the prisoners by the Japanese military. At the same time, I was moved by the gracious acceptance by Edward Dunlop of Yi Hak-Nae's apology. In contrast, Tom Uren and some other POWs told Yi that they understood his intention but could not accept the apology, which made me realise how deeply they were scarred by the experience. Hank's contribution was felt, but for me it was overwhelmed by other emotive impacts. At the end, I regarded the seminar as an interesting and stimulating intellectual experience, but I was not ready to be involved in further painful issues of war. It took me another several years before engaging with these issues under the guidance of Hank.

I started my PhD research on Japanese war brides in 1993 with a scholarship, after a few previous false starts. Nic Peterson (Department of Archaeology and Anthropology) and Gavan McCormack were appointed as my supervisors. I approached Hank to be on my panel as an advisor, and he agreed readily. My research method was rather unusual for PhD research in anthropology, where research students usually spend up to 18 months carrying out fieldwork away from the university. Instead, I was going to collect the research data through a series of life story interviews with the war brides in conjunction with archival research. I framed this research plan so that I did not need to move away from Canberra since my two sons were still young then. What I was hoping for from Hank was his expertise in oral history research. Our association started finally, and how lucky I was to learn so much from him.

Throughout my PhD years, Hank was the one from whom I drew intellectual and moral support most. I received much advice and wisdom from him during these years. One of the first things he said to me was, 'You will start receiving Christmas cards from your informants'. Another was, 'Don't write a thesis; write a book', as other ex-students of his have testified. He also wanted his students to have a prospective reader in mind. As Margaret Reeson has written, his suggestion was a matron in Broome Hospital. It took me some time to figure out what he meant by these pieces of advice, but later they all made sense. The significance of receiving Christmas greetings from the informants meant building personal trust and respect with them. The generation of women I interviewed expressed these sentiments by putting me on their Christmas greeting lists as the Australian ex-POWs must have done for Hank. I found an equivalent of the Broome Hospital matron in Jude Shanahan, one of the long-term administrators of the Division of Pacific and Asian History. She was intelligent and curious but not an expert in particular subjects. She was always ready to hear the progress and appreciate my research findings. As Hank said, I did receive Christmas cards from Japanese war brides for many years, and part of my thesis was published as a book in 2001.[2]

For my PhD research, Hank's understanding of Australian servicemen and their culture was indispensable. The men who were too young during the Pacific War went to Japan as members of the British Commonwealth Occupation Force (BCOF), met Japanese women, fell in love and brought them back to Australia. Hank remembered the arrival of Cherry Parker, the first Japanese war bride in Australia, in 1952. These were the insights that I could not learn from books and archival material. Yet the most significant insight Hank gave me was in understanding why the women decided to tell their stories and how they talked about their experiences, as Hank's work on the Australian POWs shared common factors with my research.

Hank and Tim Bowden worked on the major oral history project on Australian POWs for the Australian Broadcasting Corporation in 1984. The 16-part radio series and subsequent book by Hank significantly influenced how Australia remembers and commemorates the POWs and their experiences. My PhD project, although much smaller in scale, had some similarities. The ex-POWs and Japanese war brides started to tell their stories in the public sphere in their old age after many years of silence. At the beginning of their research, Hank and Tim attended the 40th anniversary national reunion of ex-POWs in 1981 in order to establish contacts. Then the next year they travelled to Thailand with the veterans. The start of my research also coincided with the 40th anniversary gathering in Melbourne to celebrate the Japanese war brides' arrival in Australia. I subsequently travelled to Hawai'i with the women when they joined a larger group of Japanese war brides who had married US servicemen. These interactions allowed researchers to meet and recruit the informants, while the informants themselves could measure the researchers for their worth. Another important common factor was the content and timing of their narratives. While the nature of Japanese war brides' experiences was significantly different from the POWs', both groups shared the feeling that other people who had not lived through the same experience would not understand. The women's stories were filled with the personal anguish of dislocation and the sense of isolation in the new country. They were also conscious of the social stigma towards them in Japan, where people questioned their marital motivation. The women were reluctant to talk publicly for fear of being misunderstood, just as the POWs had been. Like the ex-POWs, the women did not tell their stories to their children, partly due to their lack of English fluency but mainly due to their concern about

---

2   Keiko Tamura, *Michi's Memories: The Story of a Japanese War Bride*, Canberra: Pandanus Books, 2001. (Reprinted in 2011 by ANU E Press.)

whether the children would understand and appreciate them. In order to avoid the disappointment of being misunderstood, both groups were very hesitant to open up to outsiders. Yet as they reached their old age and had time to reflect on their lives, they started to make sense of what happened and its consequences. Hank was generous to share his expertise and gently guided me to explore why the women started to tell their stories to a researcher when they had not even told them to their own families.

When I started to write the women's life stories in my thesis chapters, Hank became a keen and responsive reader. His comments were generally encouraging yet at the same time included always some difficult tasks that I needed to work on. I kept his note from 24 April 1998 for one of the war brides' stories. Here he wrote,

> *Keiko, You are going to write a good book. The life stories are excellent – engaging, amusing, disturbing. The more detail you can fit in the better. You are aiming for frank, conversational prose – prose (as you are aware) that reflects personality and social status.*

I remembered I was so happy to read his encouraging words but at the same time wondered how I should produce convincing English prose when the original interviews were carried out in Japanese. Some details I wanted to include were appreciated by Hank greatly. For example, I wrote how a Japanese grandfather handled his 'mixed-blood' grandson. His teenage daughter had fallen in love with an Australian man in Tokyo, eloped to marry him without parental consent and gave a birth to a son. When she was hospitalised for TB treatment, the young son was sent to her parents. The grandfather was initially reluctant to accept the boy because the mixed-blood baby would be a source of embarrassment in the neighbourhood, but he gradually became attached to his grandson. He carried him on his back for walks at night although he made sure the boy wore a hat to hide his light-coloured hair. Hank told me that he found the grandfather's reaction so interesting that he read that section out to his wife, Jan. For me, that was one of the best compliments I received from Hank.

In 1997, the Australia–Japan Research Project was established at the Australian War Memorial with substantial funding from the Japanese government. The project was to promote research and understanding of the war history between Japan and Australia through research database construction and bilingual publications on the internet. With Hank's recommendation, I applied for a research position and got it. In hindsight, that was the turning point of my research career. Over the next 13 years, the project evolved and covered a wide range of topics such as Australian and Japanese soldiers' experiences in New Guinea, the Cowra Breakout and the aftermath of the Japanese midget submarine attack in Sydney. Through my work on the project, I gradually accumulated knowledge and understanding on the war. My initial avoidance in dealing with war started to change to realisation that these were the important issues to study.

In December 2001, a symposium on the Pacific War in Papua New Guinea was held at Rikkyo University in Tokyo. Hiromitsu Iwamoto, Hank's ex-student and one of the symposium organisers, invited me and Hank to Tokyo. Hank was accompanied by Jan, and other members included Bryant Allen from ANU and Peter Stanley and Peter Londey from the Australian War Memorial. I was asked to act as a tour conductor to deliver the Australian delegation from Canberra to the university in Ikebukuro. For Hank, it was his second visit to Japan. We flew from Sydney to Narita and caught an airport bus to Ikebukuro; then we realised that nobody was there to meet us at the coach terminal. Instead of waiting around, Hank and Jan decided to set off for the hotel with some others. Bryant, a human geographer, was given the task of reading the local map. When I eventually arrived at the hotel some time later, the first group was nowhere to be seen, and hastily a search party was sent out. It turned out that the hotel was located on a discreet back street of Ikebukuro's red-light district and was rather difficult to find.

The symposium went smoothly in spite of this adventure at the beginning. I presented a paper on the Japanese military nurses in Rabaul and invited one of the ex-nurses, Mitsu Sakata, to the symposium. Hank and Mrs Sakata felt mutual affinity instantly during the reception. Although neither of them spoke the other's language, somehow the Rabaul connection seemed to draw them together. Mrs Sakata treasured for many years a silk scarf that Hank presented to her. Hank and Jan extended their stay to explore Tokyo. By the time they returned to Canberra, he was so proud that they could manage to find their way around in the complex Tokyo transport system, particularly the Yamate Loop Line.

Hank maintained neutral attitudes on Japan even though his research on the POWs had a lot to do with the country and its people. He must have heard horrific stories of mistreatment of the ex-POWs under Japanese control, but those stories did not seem to affect negatively his attitudes to the country and its people. Hank and Tim Bowden initially expected the ex-POWs to talk a lot about their sentiments towards and interactions with the Japanese soldiers, but the Australians were more interested in talking about their relationships with other POWs. Hank never asked me to explain why the Japanese soldiers and their colonial camp guards had behaved in such brutal ways to the POWs. Neither did he try to explain their behaviour from cultural relativism. He was open to and friendly with the Japanese researchers. Over the years, I introduced many of my Japanese colleagues to Hank. Since his POW book had been translated into Japanese and was widely read, they usually expected to meet an authoritative figure who might make some moral judgements on Japan and its military. On the contrary, they were surprised when they met a humble academic with a shy but friendly smile. He treated them with openness and engaged in discussion without making any judgement on Japan.

I had a chance to work closely with Hank when we organised an international symposium on the POW experience at ANU in August 2006. The symposium, 'Towards Better Understanding: Reflections on the Experiences of Australian Prisoners of War of the Japanese', was jointly hosted by the Division of Pacific and Asian History, ANU, and the POW Research Network Japan (the Network). The Network is a Japanese group whose members come from variety of backgrounds in academia, journalism and education. The members are involved in research on POWs and a reconciliation movement. Aiko Utsumi, who took part in the 1991 ANU POW seminar, was one of the representatives of this energetic organisation. I was contacted by the Network for the possibility of organising a symposium in Australia so that not only Australian and Japanese researchers could present their papers, but also some Australian ex-POWs would attend and discuss their experiences for the international audience. I went to see Hank for his opinion when I received the enquiry. His response was short and definite. He pointed out that the average age of surviving ex-POWs was already 86 years old, and we should not wait too long before organising such a symposium. Although I knew it was going to be a daunting task to host a symposium, his conviction motivated me. The two-person local committee started its work. Hank provided me with moral and intellectual support throughout the preparation period.

The symposium was a success. Twelve members of the Network travelled from Japan to Canberra, and several of them presented their research papers. Australian and New Zealand researchers presented their research. With Hank's advice, we invited Rowley Richards, a prominent medical doctor and ex-POW who had had the 'full tour' as a POW since he was captured in Singapore, sent to the Thai–Burma Railway and then transported to Japan, including the sinking of the transport ship on the way. He spoke about his experiences and his stern views on Japan. Several ex-POWs attended the symposium with their family members. For some families, it was the first time to hear their fathers talk of their war experiences. I believe one of the main reasons for its success was Hank's involvement. His paper, 'Australian Perceptions of the POWs of Japan', opened the symposium and set the scene. The participants felt confident that a symposium in which Hank Nelson took part would be worthwhile.

I returned to Australia from Japan on the day of Hank's public memorial at University House. A long queue at passport control in Sydney Airport caused a long delay, and I missed the connection to my scheduled domestic flight. When I finally arrived at the Common Room, proceedings had already started. The room was filled with people, and many speeches were delivered, but for me the most memorable event was Ted Egan's singing of 'Sayonara Nakamura' at the end. The song is about a young Okinawan pearl diver named Nakamura, who died of bends off Broome, and it was chosen by Hank to be played in the private funeral that had already taken place. Ted Egan, who happened to be in Canberra when Hank died, wanted to attend the memorial gathering. When he learned that his song was played at the funeral, he offered to sing the song at the memorial. Ted sang solo beautifully without any musical accompaniment. While I was listening to the song, I could picture the sea, the pearling lugger and the diving gear divers wore, from my visit to Broome. The song laments the loss of young life so far away from home. The chorus section was haunting:

But it's goodbye now, farewell;

Say goodbye to Okinawa

For today they'll bury you

In West Australia.

You will never be as one

With the Land of the Rising Sun

Sayonara. Sayonara, Nakamura.

We will never know why Hank chose that song other than the fact that he liked it. Yet for me I felt like Hank was bidding farewell to us all. Sayonara, Hank. I felt so lucky to get to know you. Thank you and *arigato*.

8. Papua New Guinea Wantok

Margaret Reeson

Margaret Reeson is an independent scholar with an interest in Papua New Guinea and Pacific church history as a result of living in PNG 1961–1978. She took a course in Pacific history with Hank.

In Papua New Guinea, a *wantok* is one who shares your language and your tribal connections – a 'one talk'. In a country of over 700 distinct languages and many dialects, it is a powerful sign of relationship to be able to communicate with another person in a language you both understand. It suggests that you will discover mutual friends and allies and find that some landscapes and places are familiar to you both. In that sense, Hank Nelson and I were *wantoks*. We both understood the language and the landscapes of that tribe of outsiders who, over many decades, travelled to Papua New Guinea from somewhere else and came to value the people and stories of that beloved, frightening, beautiful, confusing, frustrating and unforgettable land.

Hank and I did not meet in Papua New Guinea although we were both there during some of the same period. He was in Port Moresby, and I was in the Southern Highlands in the 1960s and 1970s. The mission community on the outskirts of the small mountain township of Mendi in the Southern Highlands and the isolated mission at Nipa several mountain ranges further west were remote in every way from the world of the new University of Papua New Guinea where Hank worked. The first time I heard Hank's name was when a book he had written arrived in the little book shop my husband had established in Mendi. Later books of his were also read with interest.

Long before I had the benefit of any guidance from Hank Nelson, I had been developing a keen interest in writing and in history. The early seeds for this were sown at high school in Parramatta, New South Wales. One of my first friends there was a descendant of a family who traced their roots to the very beginnings of the colony; her tales of her family home with furniture linked to fables of convicts, officers and dramatic encounters with local Aboriginal tribes were enthralling. Living in the Parramatta area as a young person, I was aware of the evidence of the early colonial period.

Later, as a young single teacher, I arrived in Papua New Guinea in 1961, appointed to a small mission school in Mendi, in the Southern Highlands. The people of that area had seen their first white face, their first wheel and their first piece of paper only ten years earlier, and the children in that school were the first generation to become literate. 'History' was unfolding before my eyes. It seemed important to try to record what I was seeing. That first writing effort broke the basic rule of 'write what you know' as I attempted to tell the story of culture contact through the eyes of two Highlands men. Even so, it was my first experience of the delights of exploring archives and gathering oral history from my friends Wasun and Sond. An added challenge was that we were working between languages – in English with Wasun, in which he was not fluent, and in Sond's Mendi language, in which I was not fluent. Despite everything, this book was published in 1972, and I knew that I would love to write again.

An invitation to write a series of brief chapters on 30 'great Christian lives' for an educational project in Papua New Guinea proved a new challenge. The 30 names on the list ranged from 2nd-century martyrs to 20th-century Papua New Guinean characters. As a publishing exercise it was a failure. As a private education and as an introduction to church history it was a success. Even though for most of the period of writing I was out of reach of any library (the internet was unheard of) and had to rely on the bookshelves of friends or generous acquaintances for resources, it was a time of discovering the richness of story, memory and myth over the centuries of Christianity in its various manifestations. The world of those 30 Christians was my world. Future writing would be in the context of church history.

In the years following independence in Papua New Guinea, by now with a family of school-age children, we returned to Australia in late 1978 to settle in Canberra. In time it was possible to write again. Still working outside the guidance of the academic or professional world, I wrote several more books, and they were published. Each of these enterprises taught me more about the process of writing history. Again more unwritten rules were broken. The story of a young woman who lived in the young colony of New South Wales and as a missionary wife in Tonga during the early years of the 19th century was based very closely on primary sources – original letters and diaries found in the Mitchell Library – but because I wrote it in the first person as if she were telling her own story, without providing footnotes, readers assumed that it was fiction. Another effort, an attempt to rescue someone else's manuscript about the Highlands of Papua New Guinea, demonstrated the need to be thorough in one's research before committing to one's document. In yet another of my manuscripts, following an Australian family over a century, I learned the importance of comparing the various versions of oral history against other evidence; memory can be very slippery. Maps, images, contemporary newspapers, visits to sites, old letters and other family archives were all used to build the story. A manuscript about a working woman among the homeless in Sydney taught me to observe and listen very carefully, to read between the lines, to check and check again and, as with other documents, to spend time in places that were significant to the story rather than relying on the descriptions of others.

Enter Hank Nelson. By now I was someone without a university education who had had five books published. For most of them there had been excellent advice from an editor in preparation for publication but no direction about historical method. Through an introduction by a mutual friend, late in 1991, Hank met with me to pass on a document that had been recommended for my latest writing project. It was soon clear that Hank was someone who knew more about the theme that was now capturing my attention than perhaps anyone else. We found, as *wantoks* do, a number of areas of shared interest. We both had a strong and continuing interest in issues relating to Papua New Guinea. When Hank learned that I was beginning to explore the experience of the Methodist missionary nurses, teachers and missionary wives who had been impacted by the coming of war to the islands of New Guinea in 1942, he was immediately generous with advice. Although I was outside the academic world of ANU and had no formal call on his time and expertise, Hank took me seriously, assured me that my project was worth doing and was warmly enthusiastic about suggesting sources of vital archival documents. We met a few times during the course of writing, talking about the loss of the *Montevideo Maru* on 1 July 1942 and the effect of the long mystery of its loss on the surviving families; when the book was published in 1993, I asked Hank to launch it.

A new possibility emerged in 1992. I had always assumed that a university education was beyond my reach. With an unimpressive leaving certificate result from 1954 and my only formal qualifications a teacher's certificate after two years of training, it had seemed impossible. But now it was suggested that I should attempt a master's qualifying program at ANU with a view to doing more work about all the families from the islands of New Guinea who had been impacted by the loss of the *Montevideo Maru*, not only the mission families. This was a program that I had not known existed, and so I visited Hank to ask for advice about it. Again he was helpful and encouraging, which was very important for one who felt unsure about her capacity to work at the level required. Although he knew that I was unfamiliar with the 'correct' language in which to describe it, he assured me that I did have a grasp of the process of writing history and pointed me in the direction of the path that could lead to a master of arts. Hank always seemed such an ordinary good bloke, so human and unassuming, yet a fount of vast knowledge and wisdom. What had seemed impossible became possible under his direction. I was able to complete the master's qualifying work and began work on the master's program in 1994. To my great satisfaction my supervisors were John Knott and Hank Nelson.

So began a period of regular meetings with Hank. Having found my way to his room through the maze of the Coombs building, I would find Hank engrossed in whatever project was occupying his mind that day, slightly rushed but always welcoming. Although I was one of the few students with whom he could not have a decent talk about cricket, there was always something of mutual interest. Often we were tempted to stray briefly from the work in progress to themes of PNG politics, memories of *kiap* (patrol officers) and *didiman* (agricultural extension officers), Big Man and explorer, missionary and *raskol*. We also discovered that each of us had begun our formal education in a little one-teacher school somewhere in rural Australia around the same year. Hank's writing on prisoners of war intersected with my own, and his knowledge of the period of war in the islands of what is now known as Papua New Guinea was able to direct me to less obvious sources and steer me away from major error. Occasionally I would uncover a hidden gem in the depths of the mine of the archives and would take it to Hank with much excitement; almost always he already knew about it but would share my enthusiasm. In time the work was completed, deemed acceptable and later published by Melbourne University Press in 2000. Although I feel a sense of unease at the way I bypassed the discipline of an undergraduate experience, I am grateful for Hank's contribution to my education.

Hank had a capacity for introducing people in his circle to others who he thought would appreciate the opportunity to meet them. In this way I met some of the people working with the Australia–Japan Research Project and was invited to contribute a paper at a symposium at ANU in 2000: 'Remembering the War in New Guinea'. Through Hank, Keiko Tamura and I discovered a deep human connection as each of us had been exploring the grief and uncertainty of the families, both Australian and Japanese, whose men had been lost in that miserable time of war. It was the same story, we realised, viewed from different hemispheres but with the same profoundly wounded humanity weeping for their lost men.

The connection with Keiko Tamura was to continue. Keiko introduced me to two Japanese women who were researching the experience of foreign prisoners of war and internees held in Japan during the war years. Through a series of email exchanges about our mutual interests, it became possible to arrange to meet Yoshiko Tamura and Mayumi Komiya in Japan in 2007. After my return from this adventure, I met with Keiko Tamura and Hank to show photos and tell them the story. Together we looked at images of my exploration with Yoshiko and Mayumi of the Commonwealth War Graves cemetery in Yokohama and the harbour-side streets of that city searching for the site of the Yokohama Yacht Club, where the Australian nurses from New Guinea had been interned in 1942. Most moving was the photograph of the group seated around a table with an array of Japanese delicacies in a private home. (I was told later that it is unusual for foreign visitors to be invited into a private home.) We were on the site of the house in Totsuka where the Australian nurses from Rabaul had been interned in the later years of war. Around the table were the daughter-in-law of the woman who had been their cook, a 93-year-old lady who remembered them well; her son, who had been given a garment knitted by an Australian nurse when he was an infant; the two researchers; some neighbours and us. Through interpreters we told stories of those years of war, sensed something of the memories of distress of our one-time enemies, shared a meal and exchanged gifts. It was a strange and wonderful encounter. To be able to recount to Hank this story of a small reconciliation was a gift. He had been the one who began the sequence of connections that led us to that moment.

At intervals in the years since I was Hank's student we have met in various settings, usually at events associated with ANU. When I began a new writing project, a joint biography of a 19th-century missionary couple who had been pioneers in New Guinea in the 1870s, unsurprisingly Hank already knew about them. There was not much about Papua New Guinea that had escaped his notice. As always, he was encouraging in what proved to be a very extended and labour-intensive piece of work and was willing to offer advice on possible sources. In 2011, when he was already facing the challenges of his illness, he agreed to meet me for a conversation about my work. Although there had been only a brief period of two years when he was under any obligation to give me his time and wisdom – and that time was now 15 years in the past – he was still generous with his time to someone outside the academic system. On that occasion he offered some practical suggestions about possibilities for finding a publisher. That conversation led directly to the eventual publication of my manuscript by ANU E Press.

A piece of advice about writing that Hank gave to many of his students was to picture our audience and write for that person. He suggested to me that I imagine that I was writing for the intelligent, busy matron of the hospital at Broome, who would be interested in my ideas but would be impatient with fancy, convoluted, tangled language. As I had never been a speaker of the impenetrable dialect of academe, that suited me. So it was that for my most recent writing project I kept three people in my mind: Helen, a widely read woman with an interest in the human story, particularly the experience of the women; Bruce, a chap working for the contemporary incarnation of the organisation about which I was writing; and Hank Nelson. Hank did not see the finished work but knew that it was to be published. I hope he would have given it a grin of approval.

9. Coach Nelson

Daniel Oakman

Daniel Oakman is a senior curator with the People and the Environment team at the National Museum of Australia. He is currently developing an exhibition about cycling in Australia and working on a biography of the cyclist and politician, Sir Hubert Opperman. He maintains a strong interest in the history of Australian relations with the Asia-Pacific region.

No one has ever called me Danny. No one, that is, except Hank – and Americans. Thinking back to the first time he called me that, I'm sure that (like so many others) I reasoned that Hank probably had some familial connection to the United States. Anyway, we had just met, and I let it pass. Soon it took on a life of its own, and I quickly became 'Young Danny'. It then seemed too late to bring it up; too late, too embarrassing and, somehow, a bit rude. In truth, I liked it. In part because he always delivered my name with the same kind of irrepressible enthusiasm that he projected onto all manner of things: history, good writing, a tightly fought test match. In time, when I heard a call down the corridor for 'Young Danny', I felt it reflected the good-natured paternalism that characterised our relationship.

I'd completed two theses before embarking on my doctorate in 1998, and I knew very well that a student always owes debts to his or her supervisor. And by the end of almost four years under Hank's supervision, I had racked up quite a few – the first before we had even met. When I applied for a scholarship to The Australian National University, my 'foreign' degrees (they were from Monash University in Melbourne) were deemed less worthy than their home-grown Canberra equivalents, and I slipped down the merit list. Months after I started at ANU, I discovered that I had only been offered a position in the Division of Pacific and Asian History because someone had lobbied strongly for my admission to the program, presumably on the strength of my proposed topic and not my ranking by the university. This stroke of good fortune saved me from a career at the Australian Bureau of Statistics, where I was working at the time.

That someone, of course, was Hank Nelson, who had noticed my proposal to write a history of Australia's role in the formation and operation of the international aid program known as the Colombo Plan, once a conspicuous symbol of Australia's post-war regional engagement. By the late 1990s, although the Colombo Plan had, among many other things, sponsored thousands of Asian students to Australia, it had faded from popular memory. But not from Hank's. In an early meeting he told me that just after World War II, non-European students in Australian universities numbered in the mere hundreds, but by the end of the 1970s, tens of thousands of Asians had studied in Australia under the scheme. This, he thought, was a phenomenon worthy of a book, and I would be best to start thinking of my work as a draft manuscript. At this same meeting, he gave me three cassette tapes from his bookshelf. They turned out to be a wonderful six-part oral history-based documentary, written and produced by Tim Bowden, on the Colombo Plan and the Australian Volunteers Abroad program. *Crossing the Barriers* was first broadcast in 1993, and Hank provided historical commentary throughout the series. Not for the last time, Hank had delivered a quiet surprise that he genuinely hoped would help improve my work.

Hank utterly confounded my ideas about the role and influence of a supervisor – and what an academic historian might be. Early in my research my mother asked about my supervisor. The best I could come up with was that Hank looked a lot like Henry Lawson, and his style was not unlike that of Australian Rules footballer and coach, Ron Barassi. 'Good work, Danny!' 'Rip into it!' This is what being supervised by Hank sounded like. Once while I was doing my grocery shopping in a north Canberra supermarket, I heard a shout down the aisle: 'Nice chapter, Danny; looking forward to the next one!'

Like any eager young player, I was drawn to the coach's candour and encouraged by his confidence. I fell under his spell. The yarning, the long anecdotes, the always clean and appropriate jokes and the serious conversations about good scholarship were all part of Hank's charm. For me, it was all about his voice. That casual, knockabout tone was at once deeply familiar and absolutely alien. I grew up in what I joked to Hank was the Far East: the outer eastern suburbs of Melbourne: Bayswater, Fern Tree Gully, Boronia and Wantirna. Today the inhabitants are called aspirational. When I lived there, we were called bogans – and no one was cashed-up. A crushing anti-intellectual climate that took years to overcome pervaded my high school years. Hank sounded like the people I grew up around. But I'd never really heard people who spoke like this talk so passionately about the things I had grown to care about. Surely people who sounded like this didn't have an enthusiasm for learning, a passion for historical investigation and, most importantly, a desire to share this history with the world outside the academy. Hank's lack of pretence and his love of clear, engaging scholarship was the perfect antidote to any misgivings I might have had about the academic world.

Just as Hank offered respite from the worst examples of academic self-regard, he also had little time for the self-absorption and self-indulgence common to many doctoral students, especially those lingering a little too long in the comfort of the Coombs building. He always told me that it was a privilege to have the freedom to research and write on a topic of my choosing for nearly four years

9. Coach Nelson

– a privilege that I was unlikely to experience again in my working life. How true. He also told me that it was just as unwise to spend too long on the one subject. Towards the end of my time with the Research School of Pacific and Asian Studies, I told him over coffee that I reckoned I would finish writing and submit my thesis in three months. 'Three weeks sounds a bit better, Danny'.

Hank had me writing almost from the beginning. We avoided theory, embraced the richness of the archival material I was uncovering and began building the story of the Colombo Plan. The chapters were falling into place. Well, mostly. When I faltered, I received firm advice at exactly the right time. A misguided attempt to grapple with theory yielded 5,000 words of nonsensical jargon. Hank gave me the benefit of his views on the parlous state of academic writing, especially the erroneous and confusing use of the word 'narrative'. 'Is this really the kind of book you want to be writing?' Well, no, it wasn't. That was another hallmark of Hank's supervision. In many ways, he knew what you could do (and what you really should be doing) better than you knew yourself. At the very least, he knew it before you did, and he was confident that you would catch up – eventually.

Good supervision is often about what is left unsaid. As my writing progressed, it became clear that I had been testing Hank's patience. I went to school in the 1970s and 1980s and was among the first generation of students unburdened by having been taught the formal rules of grammar, punctuation or spelling. My early chapters were filled with the almost illegible scrawl of Hank's pencil. It was just what I needed. In the space of six months, I learnt more about the basic grammatical rules than I had in all of high school. Evidently I still had some way to go. The more I wrote, the less my drafts bore the marks of Hank's pencil. Fantastic, I'm really improving here, I thought. I was somewhat deflated to discover two editions of the government style guide in my pigeonhole some months later. 'Thought these might be useful, Danny'.

Writing a full-time doctoral thesis tends to result in a kind of institutionalisation. For me, the essence of Hank's supervision was the way he prepared his students for life on the outside. He encouraged us to look beyond the hexagonal walls of the Coombs building. Mostly he kept us mindful of our audience and the need to write with clarity and precision. But there were other things to learn. One of the things I admired most in Hank was his ability to deflate professional pomposity, to starve it of oxygen and render it impotent. After a year or so reading files at the National Archives, I wrote to the former Secretary of the Department of External Affairs, Sir Arthur Tange, requesting an interview to discuss the origins of the Colombo Plan and how the policy was administered during his tenure in the 1950s and early 1960s. Tange wrote and then telephoned to tell me in no uncertain terms why he would not grant me an interview. It was clear, he said, that I had not consulted the archives with sufficient rigour and that his policy was only to speak to those who had. Then he hung up. No goodbye. That was it. I told Hank. He paused, read Tange's similarly curt letter and said, 'Sod the old bastard'. Another time, I mentioned to Hank that I would like to show a chapter on the Colombo Plan's role in the demise of the White Australia Policy to another Coombs-dwelling academic. 'You could, Danny', he said, 'but, you know, you'll probably find that you've got it all completely wrong'. I took his wise advice and never contacted the staff member in question.

I knew little of Hank's early work as a historian of Papua New Guinea and the Pacific. His biggest impact on my work was his 2002 book, *Chased by the Sun*. Hank's account of Australians who served in Bomber Command during World War II came out as I began to transform my thesis into a popular, publishable book. While I had taken Hank's advice to not write a dissertation for a handful of examiners and instead write a book, it still needed work; a lot of work. There was much to admire in *Chased by the Sun*. It had all the hallmarks of Hank's style as a historian: breadth, economy, balance, humour and a sensitivity to the essential humanity of those engaged in profoundly stressful and inhumane acts. With the scholarly apparatus removed, Hank could marshal a carefully selected anecdote or quote to great effect. Take this short vignette about the effect that bombing German cities could have on bomber crews. Hank described a captain calling his navigator, busy over his maps and charts, to see the firestorm engulfing Dresden. The navigator stood behind the pilot with tears running down his face. 'Christ, you poor bastards, you poor bastards. I never want to see that again, skipper, don't ever show me again, what poor bastards'.[1] Where so many military historians, overly concerned with operational details, had failed before, Hank moved seamlessly between a compelling narrative about military operations, civilian life and the complex emotional and moral universe of those involved in the bombing of Germany. On many occasions, I turned to this book seeking inspiration and always received a master class in building narrative tension without compromising historical rigour.

While Hank was naturally modest about his successes, he could be disarmingly candid about his failures. He told me how ABC Books had rolled him on the subtitle of *Chased by the Sun*, insisting that it should be '*Courageous Australians in World War Two*'. 'Well, they weren't all bloody courageous', he told them; 'mostly they were fucking terrified'. I note that in the second edition (with a different publisher) the offending adjective dropped. For me it was reassuring, if greatly disappointing, that someone as accomplished and compelling as Hank could be overruled by the marketing department. His experience was instructive. It helped ease my own frustration with the publishers of my first book, when they dismissed my suggestions over the subtitle.

---

1   Hank Nelson, *Chased by the Sun: Courageous Australians in Bomber Command in World War II*, Sydney: ABC Books, 2002, p. 272.

I want to end by letting Hank have a say. When I started writing this piece I replayed my tapes of *Crossing the Barriers* and was struck by his explanation of how the Colombo Plan came into existence. I can transcribe the words, but try to imagine hearing it on radio. It is classic Nelson, spoken in his unmistakable flat tone, but animated by an insistent, short and punchy delivery.

> *1950. That was two years before Australia allowed Cherry Parker, the first Japanese war bride, to enter Australia. 1950. Australia had a population of 8 million, and in that 8 million less than half of one per cent were born in South, Southeast or East Asia. That was about the same percentage as it had been at the census of 1933. And it wasn't going to be much different in 1961. But in January 1950, Percy Spender, the newly appointed Australian Minister for Foreign Affairs in the Menzies Government, flew to a conference of Commonwealth foreign ministers in Colombo in Ceylon … What became the Colombo Plan came into operation in January 1950 … The Australians were both compassionate and self-interested. Australians wanted protection from what they thought were threats from Asia. They wanted to help Asians. And they wanted goodwill in Asia.*[2]

His voice is still with me. It tells me to forget the blockers, the snobs or the uninterested. It tells me to get on with it. Just after I learned of Hank's death, I went home and picked up my copy of *Chased by the Sun*. I turned to the title page. He didn't have to write anything here, but I suspect that he knew that his small act of generosity, of inclusion, might help boost my confidence. It might be typical Nelson egalitarianism, but it felt like more of a graduation than sitting through an hour of names in Llewellyn Hall to receive a mass-printed certificate. It reads: 'Danny. Fellow historian. Hank'. It meant a lot to me then. Ten years later, it still does.

---

2   *Crossing the Barriers,* ABC Radio National, 1993.

10. Hank of Coombs

Brij V. Lal

Brij V. Lal is professor of Pacific and Asian History in the School of Culture, History and Language, College of Asia and the Pacific at The Australian National University. He was Hank's colleague in the Coombs Building for 20 years.

Hank was a name before I met him in the flesh. I was in the Coombs tea room when I looked up to see a man slowly making his way down the stairs. 'Dr Nelson', I said. 'G'day', he boomed, this tall, modest, unglamorous, even laconic man with a drooping 'Henry Lawson' moustache; 'the name is Hank'. And so he remained for me for the next 20 years, and for countless others: an iconic figure, an authentic, down-to-earth Australian, not an American with a broad Australian accent, as his name seemed to suggest. Boort, Hank's birthplace, is in north-western Victoria on the edge of the flat, red-brown Mallee country of dead sheep, frequent droughts and interminable distances, and he casually presented himself to visitors as nothing more than an ordinary 'boy from Boort' in perpetual wonderment in the august halls of the academy. But no one was fooled. Behind that unselfconscious country-lad façade was a sharp, shrewd intellect with practical understanding of the ways of the real world and a deep appreciation of the vagaries of the human condition. As a guide in fair weather and foul, there were few to equal his skills. As teacher, writer, scholar, administrator, supervisor, colleague and encourager, Hank was one of a kind.

Hank had been in the Coombs Building for 17 years when I joined in 1990, his reputation solid as the world's leading historian of Papua New Guinea. He died with that reputation intact. But Hank was more than just a great scholar, of whom there was no shortage in the Coombs. He was to many younger colleagues a generous mentor and a kindly presence, a guide and a tutor as well. He was my closest colleague for much of our time together in Coombs, and he opened many a window for me on the land he loved so passionately.

At the most personal level, he introduced me to the intricacies of Australian sporting culture gradually over the years. This he did for others as well, including foreign academic visitors perplexed by the arcane rules of cricket or the incredible athleticism of Aussie Rules players in tight-fitting jerseys and short shorts. I have never been able to follow the rules of the latter despite Hank's best efforts to teach me. The Coombs tea room served as the tutorial venue. One Monday morning, following long-established ritual, Barry Smith, another distinguished denizen of Coombs, and Hank were talking Aussie Rules at morning tea when, very new to Australia, I inadvertently blurted out, 'Ah, is that the game they play in the southern states?' Barry looked at me straight in the eye and said with mock menace: 'You Third World fool, you. Aussie Rules is not a *Victorian* game. It is *the Australian* game, and don't you ever forget it'.

On the way back to our offices, feeling suitably chastised and slightly embarrassed at such elementary ignorance, I asked Hank the reason for Barry's belligerence, or pretended belligerence. 'Cast an eye of pity on Barry', Hank said, gently smiling. 'He is a Victorian'. And a Hawthorn man, as I later discovered, like the great Monash historian Geoffrey Serle, who once famously declared: 'I am an Australian and a Hawthorn man. Stuff Victoria and Melbourne'.[1] This from a bloke who wrote a two-volume history of Victoria in the 19th century![2]

Hank did not have a favourite football team, Jan tells me, unless it was Boort playing in the North Central Football League. Then he barracked for it full-throated. Otherwise, he would decide which team he wanted to win after watching the game for the first five minutes. No wonder he got on well with all and sundry in the university's football community. Hank was a proud Victorian but not one to impress his attachments and interests on others, unlike so many from that part of the world who were (and are) defiantly different, and casually indifferent to outside opinion about themselves.

Hank tutored me and many other newcomers to Australia in the country's literature and scholarship. I had read at school and at university in Fiji novels by Patrick White (*Voss*) and Randolph Stow (*To the Islands*, *Tourmalin*), which rather surprised and impressed Hank: these books, at that time, in that remote, colonial backwater. 'The Poms did do some things right, and you are a living proof of it, mate', Hank used to say to me. He introduced me to many newer Australian authors I did not know, such as Robert Drewe (*Shark Net*, *The Body of Contented Men*).

Australian novels or novels about Australia were Hank's passion. Sitting in a doctor's waiting room killing time in Sydney during one of his frequent forays there in the last years of his life, Hank read most of Peter Carey's *Parrot and Oliver*, and he emailed me: 'He writes sharp, smart prose. It was good to be immersed in his art'. Hank was like that: he read widely and shared his passion with those he knew cared for books and good writing. I still have with me a second-hand copy of Margaret Kiddle's *Men of Yesterday* that Hank gave me. It has this magical opening sentence: 'Once, in the land men now call the Western

---

1   John Thompson, *The Patrician and the Bloke: Geoffrey Serle and the Making of Australian History*, Canberra: Pandanus Books, 2006, p. xvii.
2   Geoffrey Serle, *The Golden Age: A History of the Colony of Victoria, 1851–1861*, Parksville: Melbourne University Press, 1963; *The Rush to be Rich: A History of the Colony of Victoria, 1883–1889*, Carlton: Melbourne University of Press, 1971. Later, Serle turned to writing biographies, including one of General John Monash, as well as a cultural history of Australia.

District of Victoria, the mountains touched the clouds and from their summits fire sprang forth'.[3] Hank knew that world well. His master's thesis was on missions and Aborigines in western Victoria.

I suppose the gift of history books was also Hank's way of telling me what he thought good history writing was, or should be: literate and literary, composed with flair and imagination. The last big book he read before he died was Bill Gammage's *The Biggest Estate on Earth*.[4] 'It is brilliant', he said to me as he lay stricken in bed at Claire Holland Hospice by Lake Burley Griffin in Canberra. He would not have been surprised at all, but rather much pleased, to see it win a clutch of big prizes in Australia. And one of the last books we discussed over morning tea before Hank left Coombs for good was Jim Davidson's life of the historian Sir Keith Hancock, *A Three-Cornered Life*.[5] A day later, Hank wrote to me:

> *I meant to make a further point about the Davidson biography of Keith Hancock. He deals well with a couple of incidents when Hancock as director or head of department was confronted with intractable and perhaps either mentally obsessive or disturbed colleagues: Lindsay and Ellis. I know little of the Ellis story and nothing of Lindsay. These are salutary stories. I concluded that I had been relatively lucky in my undistinguished administrative career. I trust that you never encounter a Lord Lindsay.*

I did not, and now nearing retirement, do not expect to.

In his farewell speech organised by the Division of Pacific and Asian History on 24 August 2011, Hank remarked with characteristic generosity: 'With Brij, I enjoyed many conversations in this tea room about two important topics: cricket and good prose'. Cricket was certainly our mutual passion, and it featured in many of our conversations. It featured in the farewell party we hosted to mark Hank's retirement. He drew up the invitation list himself for a party 'in the Pavilion of the China Tea Club at the close of play on Thursday November 28, 2002'. The batting order would be as follows: Amirah Inglis (left-handed), Keith Willey (right-handed), Ken Inglis (selector), John Waiko, Bill Gammage (captain), August Kituai, Ian Willis, Tim Bowden, Jude Shanahan (keeper), Gavan Daws (selector), Keiko Tamura, Daniel Oakman (night watchman). Commentary: Professor Donald Denoon; Presentation of Awards: Professor Brij Lal; Man of the Match: Professor Hank Nelson; Best and Fairest: Professor Hank Nelson; Modest Acknowledgment: Professor Hank Nelson. 'Stumps'. Sad word that, when you think about it, signalling the end of play and metaphorically of

---

3   Margaret Kiddle, *Men of Yesterday: A Social History of the Western Districts of Victoria, 1834–1890*, Carlton: Melbourne University Press, 1961, p. 3.
4   Bill Gammage, *The Biggest Estate on Earth: How Aborigines Made Australia*, Sydney: Allen & Unwin, 2011.
5   Jim Davidson, *A Three-Cornered Life: The Historian WK Hancock*, Sydney: UNSW Press, 2010.

life itself until, if you are lucky, a new beginning the next day. All this says as much about Hank's passion for the game as it does about some of the people in Canberra who mattered to him – and to whom he mattered. Such playfulness, such innocent fun, speaks to life in the academy of another era – when time was found for serious matches between academic departments, when perfectly sensible people took time off to watch an engrossing day of play, when 'What's the score?' needed no further explanation.

Hank's advice about good prose: certainly. He himself wrote 'crisp, clear sentences in the unaffected language and accents of common Australians', as one anonymous observer put it. He wrote with the patience of readers in mind, and it is no surprise that his books were very well received by the wider reading public and are still in print, to the quiet envy of some of his colleagues whose eyes and energies were more focused on the verdict of their fellow professionals in the cloistered halls of the academy. Many people in the department sought the service of Hank's editorial pen, or rather, pencil.

I was no exception. Hank read most things, certainly nearly all the smaller pieces, that I wrote over the last decade or more. He would return the text with pencil marks in the margin: ticks for the phrases and paragraphs he liked and suggestions for revision where there was opaqueness and ambiguity. Stewart Firth remarks that with Hank, 'no request for comment on a manuscript was turned down', and he never stinted his time. 'He always encouraged others in the field, seeing them as co-workers rather than as competitors, and, best of all, returned manuscripts promptly'. 'Prompt and helpful' are the words Doug Munro uses to describe Hank's responses to his queries as review editor of the *Journal of Pacific History*. Perhaps promptness was a habit Hank had picked up from his days of high school teaching, for few academics I know are ever prompt.

Hank gave me two pieces of writing advice that have served me well. 'Shorter sentences, mate, shorter sentences', he would say whenever he came across a meandering three- or four-line clunker in my prose. And 'avoid "however": a lazy writer's word'. I have avoided *however* ever since. 'I am in despair in our misuse of the language when I read an opening such as this', he once wrote to me about a submission to a scholarly journal that he had been asked to read: 'Imbricated histories are evident in the work of Australian filmmakers in Papua New Guinea, through contestations and shifts in the documentary practices that mediate the visual archive constituted by such work over the last century'. He continued: 'I started rewriting it, changing "Imbricated" to "Overlapping", "contestations" to "contest", and "constituted by such work" to "made", but then decided I did not know what the sentence was trying to say anyway'. All this was so unnecessary: 'Mystifying vocabulary and sentence structure are all the more regrettable where the writer has clearly done a lot of research and could tell us something new and interesting'. Hank is right. If an author is asking his or her reader to work that hard, it had better be well worth it.

Hank always had a bee or three in his bonnet about bad prose. Once, upon reading an impenetrable, obfuscatory passage by a person being considered as a panel member of a research review committee for our school, Hank wrote to Robin Jeffrey, Dean of the College of Asia and the Pacific: how could a scholar with this kind of prose be allowed to have anything to do with the research school, to come anywhere near it, Hank implied in his message. The passage Hank quoted had some choice gobbledygook such as 'the fixation of speech through inscription', 'the indexicality of the performance and moves away from the dialogical situation', 'metadiscursive notions', 'the intertextual world which are not the culture as texts', 'the flow of substances between different generations or domains of the universe'. 'I am keeping an open mind', Hank informed Robin, tongue-in-cheek. Robin wrote back acknowledging Hank's fine-tuned radar for detecting academic weasel-words: 'Keep on keeping the mind open'.

Supervision is an integral part of the life of a research professor, and Hank had his share of graduate students during his time at ANU. Good supervisors know that students come from varying backgrounds and levels of training in their disciplines, and they have their own needs and requirements. One size does not fit all. Hank understood this better than most, open, democratic and tolerant of a wide range of views, encouraging his students to reach their own conclusions based on thorough assessment of evidence with all its contradictions. Klaus Neumann says his relationship with Hank was 'based on mutual respect'.

> *At no time did he attempt to make me follow his lead, make me adopt his assessment, or steer me towards his own way of approaching the Papua New Guinean past. He pointed out flaws in my arguments and never held back any criticisms, but he let me find my own way. He would closely read what I had written and listen attentively to what I said, and respond by asking questions and not passing judgments.*

Still, Klaus says that 'from him I learnt more about writing Pacific Islands' history than from anybody else'.

August Kituai, from Papua New Guinea, agrees. 'He provoked me into discovering my strengths and predilections, and into persevering with unorthodox ideas'. He found Hank caring, supportive and encouraging. August's two years of fieldwork in Papua New Guinea were successful, he says, 'because it was accompanied by an extensive correspondence' with Hank. August also picked up from Hank something of the art and technique of writing cross-cultural history. He was 'most struck by his ability to listen sensitively to Melanesians and Europeans talking to him, which translates into a "gentle" rendering of people's memories into writing'. Hank's writings lack 'explicit theoretical reflections', yet, August continues, 'through his poetics of history he ponders about issues that would be absent from any theoretical historical narrative'. August thought both Hank's 'respectful treatment of the subjects of his writings, and his reflectivity, are aided by, if not an outcome of, his admirable use of the English language'. Respectful treatment in Hank's case meant, among other things, concern for the place of common people in history, using seemingly small and insignificant incidents to see wider trends about the operation of power in small-scale societies, for instance, or to consider why certain imported institutions worked in developing countries and others did not. 'In many ways, you are an unsung hero', August said, 'but knowing a little about you, that is how you prefer to be'. *Lookim yulong sampela taim, wantok.*

Hank was a conscientious examiner of theses and dissertations. A good thesis needed little commentary, he used to say to me; it was the weak ones that did. In these instances, he would produce several single-spaced pages of corrections and advice on revision. I know that sometimes he took a week to examine a thesis. I don't know if the examinees knew how lucky they were to have Hank's detailed comments. He was sufficiently concerned about the ethics and practice of dissertation examining in history in Australia to write an informed survey piece on the subject:

> The PhD examiners are gatekeepers. The candidates come up to the gate, two men for every woman. One man takes his thesis from under his arm, and presents it to the three gatekeepers. The candidate waits, shifting from foot to foot. He is called forward, and told to go through the gate; or make changes on the spot; or go away, alter his thesis and try again; or go away and never come back. The gatekeepers are keepers of standards: standards of a discipline, a profession, an institution, and the national and international standing of a PhD.[6]

Throughout the 1990s until his retirement, Hank carried more than his share of administrative responsibilities at several levels. He served as the associate director of the Research School of Social Sciences in the mid-1990s when he was on secondment there for a couple of years. He served as the associate director of the Research School of Pacific and Asian Studies in the early 1990s and subsequently as convenor of the Division of Pacific and Asian History. After retirement, he served as chair of the State, Society and Governance in Melanesia Program. Hank did not actively seek administrative work for its own sake. He was

---

6   Hank Nelson, 'The Gatekeepers: Examining the Examiners', *Australian Historical Association Bulletin* 68 (1991), p. 12.

first and foremost a scholar and a writer, who performed administrative duties out of a sense of obligation and perhaps also as a collective insurance policy. On those committees on which I served with Hank, representing our division or our school to the outside, Hank's modus operandi was clear. The brief had to be properly mastered and effectively defended in crisp, clear sentences. If the issue at stake was critical, prior networking helped. The mood of the meeting had to be properly judged. If the prospect of success was negligible, a strategic retreat had to be struck rather than expending capital on a foregone conclusion. There was no residual bitterness towards opponents but a strong determination to live to fight another day. Putting it another way, you can carry only so much powder and shot, so it is best to keep it for attainable ends.

Research and writing and teaching were the main game in academia, Hank always believed. Whenever he saw my name on yet another committee, he always said, 'No one will remember the committees you sat on, mate. They will remember the words you have written'. Hank's advice recalls the wisdom of Winston Churchill: words are the only things that last forever. Some administrative duties had to be done, Hank agreed, but he was particularly saddened by the strategy of some early career academics to advance their promotion prospects through committee work. Like Hank, I belonged to the older school about the proper vocation of scholars, though I also understand the enormous demands the academy makes on the time and energy of people now, demands not necessarily related directly to academic work, especially on women who are dragged to sit on endless committees in the interest of 'gender balance'.

Hank was not a micromanager. He had the big picture laid out and let his staff manage the day-to-day affairs of the department or division.

> *I soon learnt that the less I did the more smoothly the department ran. My laziness triumphed over my humility. I chaired meetings, sat on committees, and graciously stood aside from the detail of running the department. I less graciously accepted praise for the running of the department.*

There was no sense of hierarchy in relationships, scant regard for protocol, and everyone addressed each other by their first names. Throughout the 1990s, the Division of Pacific and Asian History had a wonderful group of administrators, the best, bar none, with whom I have worked: Dorothy McIntosh, Marion Weeks, Jude Shanahan, Julie Gordon, Oanh Collins and Jenny Terrell, all now retired. With their complementary skills, they nurtured a real sense of community in the division that made working in it a distinct pleasure.

Hank's comments on each of them would ring true to all those who were in the division in those years. Marion Weeks gave 'excellent pastoral care' to doctoral students and beyond that 'gave aid and advice on formatting, printing and editing theses. In retrospect, she earned an honorary PhD'. Julie Gordon was the department's 'cheerful hospitality staff member', keeping a tab on 'who was having or fathering babies, having a significant birthday, publishing a book, being promoted, leaving or arriving, gaining a PhD, going to hospital'. Before anyone knew it, Julie had bought a card or arranged to send flowers. Jude was the resident artist, designing 'several of the best books to come out of the department'. Oanh was the early bird of the department and known and admired for her legendary efficiency. 'I would sometimes bring in some typing for her to do', Hank remembered. 'I would say to her: "There was no hurry. Just attach it to an email when it's finished". Then I would race down the corridor to see if I could beat it to my desk. Often I failed'. Jenny held the *Journal of Pacific History* together for 40 years with tact and skill, succeeded admirably by Vicki Luker.

And then there was Dorothy. 'She was our boss', Hank said, borrowing my earlier description, a fortress of rectitude never breached. 'She never raised her voice, never looked under stress, never demanded deference'. Hank recalled something that would be familiar to most of us who at one time or another acted as head of department.

> *Sometimes I would be at home and Dorothy would ring to explain that there was a visitor claiming to have an appointment or that there was a meeting about to begin. There was no reprimand in her voice. My reply was always the same: 'Right, I will be there in ten or twelve minutes'. This had happened so often we both knew the time. When I arrived the visitor would be calmly sitting in the Records Room or Dorothy would have gathered the papers she thought I needed for the meeting.*

Those days of easy camaraderie in the corridors of Coombs, the sense of being in it together, are a distant and vanishing memory.

Hank came to ANU with his reputation as the pioneering scholar of Papua New Guinea history cemented, though he remarked with typical bemused humility that since there was a rarity of Australians in the ranks of historians in the Coombs, his appointment had to do with affirmative action. He was the 'father of Papua New Guinea historiography', Donald Denoon wrote, a person who almost singlehandedly, and always with great modesty, created a new field of study. This was a rare achievement, recalled Bill Gammage, 'for few men have the opportunity to "create" the history of a country, and fewer still do it well'. His publications attest to the range and productivity of Hank's scholarship. His early work was solidly focussed on Papua New Guinea itself, with the behaviour, beliefs and policies of Australians there, with the experience of those who fought in World War II or were caught up in it, with the spread and efforts to control the disease kuru.

Hank was partial to Papua New Guinea and Papua New Guineans, some people said, not always approvingly — meaning that he cared rather less about other parts of the Pacific. Hank was undoubtedly partial towards PNG. His love for the country and its people was deep and genuine and his disappointment with its many missed opportunities real. His affection clearly showed in his fluent Tok Pisin conversations with visiting Papua New Guinean politicians, civil servants and students, many of whom he knew very well. His young family had lived in Port Moresby from 1966 to 1972, he began his academic career there, and he wrote prolifically about its past and present. Hank's knowledge of other parts of the Pacific was less direct, less personal, more derived from secondary reading and detached, vicarious observation, but that would broadly be true of most people I know working on the region. It is certainly true of me. The Pacific world is simply too vast and too complex for one person ever to know its many subparts intimately. We acquaint ourselves with some small part of it and learn about the rest by osmosis.

So, yes, Hank was partial, but not parochial. He was well up on broader Pacific regional history, current on political developments in the region, Fiji in particular. He read and commented on submissions to the *Journal of Pacific History* on a range of topics. He supervised dissertations on non-PNG topics: on the Colombo Plan by Daniel Oakman, for example, or on Pacific regionalism by Sujatmiko, while serving on numerous other supervisory committees. He was up on Francis Fukuyama[7] and on the burgeoning literature on 'failing states', which some observers thought Melanesian nations were on the verge of becoming. Hank frequently cautioned against large perilous comparisons over time and space. Theory had to emerge from concrete experience closely observed.

Hank also wrote fine books on rural Australian one-teacher schools and life generally (*With Its Hat about Its Ears*) and on Australians in the Bomber Command (*Chased by the Sun*). Then there was a book, co-authored with Gavan McCormack, on the Thailand–Burma Railway, launched by Prime Minister Paul Keating and translated into Japanese, which greatly pleased Hanku-san. Towards the end of his career, Hank reflected obliquely on how he might wish to be remembered as a scholar of history, what he had tried to do, the approaches he had used.

> *I like to take a perspective from somewhere in the Coral Sea, looking north and south, explaining Papua New Guineans to Australians, Australians*

---

[7] An American political scientist and author of *The End of History and the Last Man* (1992), who argued that the triumph of Western liberal democracy may turn out to be the final form of government. Later Fukuyama turned his attention to the problems of small states, including those in Melanesia, in which context he visited Australia, where Hank met him.

to Papua New Guineans, Australians to Australians, but not completing the reflections by trying to tell Papua New Guineans about Papua New Guineans.

Hank moved between two seemingly disparate fields of research with consummate ease. Ken Inglis remarked on the uniqueness of Hank's strength. 'Scholars of Australian history', Ken said, 'tend not to be well acquainted with work on the Pacific, and vice versa; only observers familiar with both fields are well placed to recognise the scope of Nelson's work'.[8] For Ken, Hank 'displayed most impressively the quality which the late great W.K. Hancock characterised as *span*, both by moving between Melanesian and Australian history and by working in other media as well as print'. Greg Dening, himself a cultural mediator and boundary crosser of great distinction, concurred. Hank, he said,

has been for some years the most prominent Australian academic in mediating the complex and sensitive intercultural part of Pacific history. He has done this with innovative methodologies and by exploiting the widest possible range of media for such a history.

Further, Hank had 'taken the more difficult task of engaging himself in modern and current Pacific history, where the sensitivities are alive and strong'. And Greg made the point that Hank realised the audience of such histories had to be much wider than a handful of academics.

With equal ease, Hank moved between the past and the present. Much of his work on Papua New Guinea during his last years was on the contemporary affairs of that country. Alan Gilbert, who taught with Hank at the University of Papua New Guinea in 1967 and went on to become the vice-chancellor of Melbourne and Manchester universities, wrote perceptively that Hank showed an 'awareness of the "great themes" underlying the particularities of time and place with which individual historians are concerned, and a profound sense of the importance of the past as a means of understanding the present'. This distilled understanding was communicated to the larger public in a variety of ways. As Hank said, 'While working in universities I have written for newspapers and magazines, done radio interviews and talked to journalists who have rung me on various matters'. In one year alone, just as an example, he gave interviews on violence in the Highlands of PNG, secession on Bougainville, the bombing of Darwin, the experience of prisoners of war, the fall of Singapore and themes in Australian nationalism.

Many of his articles in his last years came out as working papers for the State, Society and Governance in Melanesia Program. They were read by scholars and practitioners of policy alike and quickly made available online, whereas

---

8   In recent years, Peter Hempenstall and Clive Moore have moved assuredly between Australian and Pacific history.

publishing in 'learned journals' — a quaint phrase, if ever there was one — could well take a long time and then reach only a miniscule audience. Hank published where he wanted to, to be read rather than just to get ahead. He had nothing left to prove, no further academic brownie points to earn, no more promotion ladders to climb. One of the last papers he published was on the numerous crises in the latest Somare government. It appeared in *Inside Story*, a non-refereed online publication. It was titled 'Cranks Emerging', after a quote from an article in the *Post-Courier*. 'The writer may have meant 'cracks', mused Hank, 'but let the reader allow both wit and insight'.

Donald Denoon remarked that Hank was *always* concerned with 'outreach' — to other researchers, of course, but also to ex-prisoners of war, ex-students, former residents of Papua New Guinea, examiners and writers and supervisors of doctoral theses, Papua New Guinea villagers and many others. He had never met a scholar with such a wide and respectful audience as Hank, whose correspondents included the late Bruce Ruxton, the irascible former president of the RSL, and Rabbie Namaliu, a prime minister of PNG. Bill Gammage ranked Hank among the best-known historians in Australia dealing with cross-cultural issues, alongside Henry Reynolds and Geoffrey Blainey. But Hank was unassuming, like Bill, and always stood a pace or two apart from the cult of the academy. He was a highly creative scholar, attuned to the demotic, serious in his commitment and loyalty to his craft but not a solemn person, ponderous; indeed, a certain light touch was one of Hank's endearing attributes in talk and in prose.

Humour was always just below the surface, tactfully deployed to lighten a conversation or defuse a contentious point. 'Struth' was a word I picked up from him. From him, too, I learnt many an Australian colloquial expression that lubricated casual conversation, to show that I was in the know. 'Short of a sheep in the top paddock' was a favourite, along with 'a sandwich short of a picnic' and 'high as a nerd's trousers'. 'An opinion is like an arse: everyone has one', he used to say to me whenever I was down about being unjustly attacked in the media. A politer version of this was, 'Everyone is entitled to have their own opinions, but they are not entitled to have their own facts'.

From the very beginning, Hank combined rigorous scholarship published through conventional scholarly outlets (university presses and academic journals) with shorter articles in newspapers and periodicals. Hank was determined to communicate to a lay audience beyond the academy, and he did that with precision and clarity borne of experience and intimate knowledge of the subject. Whenever he heard me on the radio, he would write encouragingly:

> *You spoke well on the Fiji coups on ABC radio. The ANU got a good run. I am sure that there were many things unsaid on air, and you were conscious of that, but we listeners were not, and what we got was considered comment obviously drawn from knowledge and a long perspective.*

He did the same with others. Hank 'deserves to be mentioned in all despatches', wrote Norman Davies, the British historian Hank had brought to the division as a visiting fellow.[9] Ken Inglis is spot-on that Hank was 'an unusually good encourager and critic of work by colleagues, and a sensitive co-operator'.

Alan Gilbert saw Hank as a 'pioneer of multi-media approaches to historical scholarship'. There were two in particular: radio documentary and films. His foray into the former began in collaboration with Tim Bowden of the ABC in the late 1970s when Hank was enlisted as a consultant to the series *Taim Bilong Masta: The Australian Involvement with Papua New Guinea*. From some 350 hours of original interviews over two years came two dozen 45-minute radio documentaries produced by Bowden and a book by the same title produced by Hank. Collaboration between the two also produced the book *P.O.W.: Australians under Nippon*, written by Hank. Later Hank worked with the ABC on a radio documentary on one-teacher bush schools because he thought it important to acknowledge the part played in Australian history by those young people sent to the back of beyond to educate bush children, because these had all but disappeared from the scene. The book that came from the series was the deeply evocative *With Its Hat about Its Ears: Recollections of the Bush School*. 'Even well-disposed listeners and viewers are often unaware of how much original research has gone into what they are listening to and seeing, so artfully has it been blended in', said Ken Inglis. He noted that Hank's 1984 radio feature on Douglas MacArthur and John Curtin 'taught me things I could not find in any printed account of the relationship'. That, from Ken, among Australia's most esteemed historians, is significant praise.

What impressed Bowden most about the book that came from the series was Hank's ability to produce a work of scholarship 'while not alienating the general reader'. For Hank, the oral project led him to ponder 'how people, as individuals and groups, edit and articulate their memories'. All this, Hank said, 'raises many significant theoretical and empirical topics to pursue', including the 'influence of different media on what is said and unsaid, and what audience is reached and what readers and audiences learn'. It pleased Hank that his work on the prisoners of war was used by at least two playwrights and two novelists. David Malouf acknowledged his debt in his prizewinning novel, *The Great World*. And it led to other radio projects, including one on Australian Volunteers Abroad,

---

9   Davies is the author of the monumental books *The Isles: A History* (1999) and *Europe: A History* (1997), both over 1,000 pages each.

who went overseas from the early 1950s. Australian War Memorial staff warmly remember Hank for all the interviews he did for them on World War II. He drafted their questionnaires, different for each unit.

Hank was a great believer in making films and using them to disseminate scholarship. Films also had the potential to resolve an ethical dilemma. 'Pacific Islands historians who make films have a chance to return the product of their research to the people they have studied, and in a more accessible form', Hank said. 'It is a moment of pride for people of small language groups to hear their own language coming from the speakers, and to know that those familiar combinations of sounds will be heard in distant places by unknown people'. He even harboured the heretical thought that someday graduate students might be able to submit the results of their research on film! 'The examiners will have to be told about the help of others with editing, photography and sound, but in many of the sciences doctoral research is a group activity, and the publications stemming from the research have joint authors'. Historians, Hank said,

should always be writing, trying to write better, and getting great enjoyment from fine writing by others. I just want historians to use other media, reach more people, communicate better with students, and perhaps in the process produce better history – on pages, sound tapes or film.

I suspect he would add online now as well.

Hank wrote in the ordinary language of intelligent discourse, 'complex thoughts underpinning simple expression, and deep wells of knowledge informing common sense', in Bill Gammage's words. Hank was a real worker, not one of the drones who were sometimes thought by people elsewhere to disproportionately populate the halls of ANU. Donald Denoon captured a common consensus: 'An exemplary citizen of the scholarly world: avid and perceptive in research, excellent in pioneering new forms of scholarly communication, omnivorous in the range of his interests'. This appreciation is tinged with the regret that 'he was so competent in management that he was increasingly diverted into organisational matters', which he executed 'with humanity and dispatch', regrettably at much cost to his own work.

With Hank, the professional and the personal were always one and the same, Gavan Daws recalled, 'and this made him an exemplary colleague – none better – and a genuinely good citizen of the republic of learning'. More than most, Hank's work expressed in simple readable prose and his many documentaries and innumerable radio interviews were celebrated in countless communities across the nation and region, from Boort to Boroko and beyond, of researchers and students, old diggers, rural folk, politicians, bureaucrats, film makers, villagers and ordinary people. That is a fine legacy for the 'boy from Boort'. *Em inap, man blong Boort.*

NOTE

Much of the material for this essay comes from Hank Nelson's files in the ANU archives, and for that reason I have seen no need to provide detailed documentation of specific files for the quotes used here, but I am grateful to the people whose words I have used. Jan Nelson provided additional material, and I am enormously grateful to her for her gracious support and friendship over the years. For their comments on a draft, I thank Doug Munro, Vicki Luker, Peter Hempenstall, Stuart Macintyre, Klaus Neumann and fellow contributors Gavan Daws and Bill Gammage.

11. Hank, My Dad

Michael Nelson

Michael Nelson works as a management consultant in Canberra.

Hank Nelson was my dad. I miss him greatly. My family and I are fortunate to have him in his books, documentaries and radio programs, and in our memories. And now in this book we can share the memories of others too.

Dad's public and professional face was expressed through his work. Although I love these fruits of his labour, and will probably enjoy them even more now as a way to connect with Dad, they do not represent what Dad meant to me.

Dad was my teacher. He was a teacher by trade, first high school, then university, but to me he was a teacher of everything. Swimming. High jump. Triple jump. Kicking an Aussie Rules ball. Catching yabbies, and exactly how rotten the meat for bait needed to be. Driving a car and the intricacies of what distance you should leave between your car and the car in front of you when driving on two-way highways. Fixing a bike. Paving. Writing essays. Oiling a cricket bat. The history of just about every town in Victoria and New South Wales. That afternoon tea is the most important meal of the day, closely followed by morning tea. Even a trip to a movie like *Beverly Hills Cop* starring Eddie Murphy could be educational. 'Mick, the director wants the audience to quickly get into the movie by using upbeat music near the beginning, and then use happy music during the closing credits as we walk out', Dad said, referring to 'Neutron Dance' by the Pointer Sisters and 'Stir it Up' by Patti Labelle.

Dad taught me to play cricket too. He was a good, although careful, batsman. He wasn't much of a bowler. I suspect that combination leads to the opposite blend in the next generation. I was a fast bowler. No matter how busy he was, Dad always found the time to go to 'the nets' with me. Unfortunately for him, when I was playing representative cricket and most wanted to practice in the nets, he was approaching 50 and his reflexes were slowing. Not something a young fast bowler has much sympathy for.

How to get away from sporting events before the rest of the crowd exits was another thing my dad taught me. This skill was most utilised on cold, wintry Friday nights in the 1980s when watching the successful Canberra Cannons basketball team play at 'The Palace'. Leaving with the rest of the crowd meant being stuck in a very cold Mazda 626 waiting for the traffic to disperse. To avoid this, Dad and I would head to the top of the stadium and watch the final few seconds from the top balcony, walking around to the exit that would provide the most direct path to the car. As soon as the final buzzer rang, we would sprint to the car, beating the traffic and getting home to a house kept warm by Mum. Dad always seemed so pleased that we were able to avoid the traffic while still seeing the end of the game.

Dad's obsession with getting away quickly from sporting events backfired when we went to see Australia play England in a 1986–87 one-day international cricket match at the SCG. With a couple of overs to go, Australia was well in front. We left our seats on the eastern side of the SCG in the O'Reilly stand and started to make our way around the southern end of the ground, past The Hill. By the time we were halfway around, England needed 17 runs off the final over, with Bruce Reid about to bowl to Allan Lamb. While it was easy to watch the Canberra Cannons from the top of The Palace, it wasn't so easy to watch the cricket from behind screaming fans at the SCG, and we were also competing with about 40,000 spectators rather than 4,000. As we were exiting the SCG we could hear the roar of the crowd as Lamb hit 18 runs off five deliveries. I was there, kind of.

Dad taught me that in all likelihood one or both of my Achilles tendons would break at some point in my life. Dad played a lot of squash when I was young, and eventually he broke an Achilles tendon. This is a fairly common squash injury. Upon recovering, Dad decided to focus on tennis. The incidence of Achilles tendon injuries is lower in tennis than in squash, although with hindsight we can say probably not low enough. He proceeded to break the same Achilles again. This time I got to fully experience his injury. I had to hold my dad's foot in place at the old Canberra Hospital so that a cast could be set with his toes pointing down. They must have been short-staffed that day. From then on every Achilles twinge and pain has filled me with dread. So far, I have avoided breaking my Achilles through a variety of preventative methods – shoes with orthotics, no shoes at all, stretching, strengthening, worrying – and yet the pain and twinges continue. Playing basketball in my middle age may not be the wisest activity.

Dad's teachings were endless. How to cook eggs on toast when I was a teenager, but only because he had malaria; Mum was with him in the hospital, and I was hungry at home. Never to go to a museum with him: he once took 45 minutes to get through the first ten steps of the National Museum of the US Air Force at Wright-Patterson Air Force Base in Dayton, Ohio. In that time I had walked through three hangars of aircraft. Why did they have to put the Pacific Campaign display right at the beginning?

However, of all the things Dad taught me, two stand out. First, he taught me how to appreciate people and see the best in them. Second, he taught me to teach.

11. Hank, My Dad

My experience following the death of my father is probably similar to others. I often think I see him, usually in shopping centres. For a split second I think it's him, and then remember it can't be. It's a bit strange, mainly since I don't think he spent that much time in shopping centres. Similarly, I regularly notice things that I think, 'I should talk to Dad about that', and realise I can't. So many things have already happened since his death that he would have been amazed by.

Many of the things I enjoy I now find difficult to do without thinking of Dad and missing him. I can't watch the AFL, cricket or basketball without having conversations with Dad in my head. 'How good is Gary Ablett Jr?' 'Imagine how badly the Australian cricket team would have performed if they hadn't replaced Mickey Arthur with Darren Lehmann?' 'Can Canberra disown James Hird?' 'Tim Duncan deserved to win the NBA title'. These conversations now get lost in the ether.

Fortunately there were other conversations with Dad that haven't been lost. I was lucky to move back to Canberra from Sydney in 2007, which allowed me to spend increased time with him. I was even able to be Dad's chauffeur several times when he had to go to Sydney's Westmead Hospital for his chemotherapy treatments. The goal was to get to Sydney, have the treatment and then get to Berrima in time for lunch, often at the 1834 Surveyor General Inn. We would talk all the way to Sydney and all the way back, about anything and everything. Even the conversations about how the new plants were growing on the M5 median strip, or the fastest route to take to the hospital, were precious.

More recently I've been reminded of emails and letters I received from Dad over my life. More conversations that weren't lost. Dad's emails were like literature, like poetry, and I was rewarded with this prose whenever I emailed him.

How do I want to remember Dad? Trudging around the garden in his gumboots? Looking up from his work papers over his glasses? The way he would curve his tennis serve? Brutally correcting my high school essays? Eating his Weet-Bix with banana for breakfast while listening to ABC Radio and reading the newspaper and taking up the whole kitchen bench? Playing a delicate late cut? Kicking the footy with him on a small patch of grass outside a country woollen mill while Mum shopped? Watching *Mr Bean*, *The Young Ones*, *Fawlty Towers*, *Porridge* or *Open All Hours*? Telling me the background of every player in an AFL match? Most of all I'll remember the way he called me, or rather yelled, 'Mick!'

Part II: Selected Writing by Hank Nelson

12. Pedalling History

Conversations *(June 2000)*, pp. 70–84.

Today as I left the Gwydir Square shops on my Speedwell Ladies Sports Bicycle (3-speed Sun Tour hub) I passed an elderly man in his battery powered wheelchair. Perhaps it is unnecessary to record such a small triumph; but I pass so few other wheeled travellers. We exchanged no greeting. He kept carefully to the left, and as I glanced back I noticed that he was still going steadily east along the bike track around the oval. I had thought he was on his way back to the old people's flats, but he was now well beyond those havens of the elderly. I hope I did not distract him and lead him into a wilderness of unrecognised streets and houses. At least his battery would have faded before he jolted on gravel tracks where capital becomes bush.

An elderly suburban bike rider, I think of other domestic journeys taken over fifty years and five hundred miles away. They seem so close.

My brother and I drove a horse and jinker to school. The jinker rolled along on car tyres, and over the tyres were high, wide mudguards, and we could sprawl across them and gaze at the neighbours' familiar fence posts, droppers and strainers rhythmically marking our passing. But the tyres punctured, or the tubes perished, or the valves failed. Dad fixed punctures by roughening the tube around the hole, clamping an oval patch in place, lifting some of the patch surface with a pocket knife, lighting it with a match, and watching the burning surface generate the heat that miraculously welded patch to tube. Dad got sick of fixing tubes and pumping up tyres, and changed the wheels to standard, thin, iron tyres. Our carriage then became a gig.

Each morning and afternoon we harnessed the reluctant Bunny to the gig. A sturdy black shaggy mare, Bunny should have been a placid pony pet. In fact she was wilful, cantankerous and sly. If you were half asleep as you reached up to unbuckle the collar, adjust a trace or shaft, she would suddenly snap her teeth on a shoulder or bum. Sometimes the jangle of the bridle or the clunk of the bit against her teeth would give warning, and you would have time to leap aside. The thickness of winter jumpers were some protection, but if there was only a flimsy summer shirt between Bunny's grass-stained teeth and your skin, then you wore a horse-bite tattoo for three or four days. Having left her mark, Bunny just turned away and resumed her apparent docile acceptance of being a gig pony. We were not fooled: the broody bitch was savouring her moment of triumph.

Bunny was almost impossible to ride. She did not waste energy on extravagant displays of bucking or bolting, but she would suddenly shy-slip sideways jolting the rider. Or she would stop suddenly and refuse to cross a bridge or go through a gate, snorting in simulated alarm. If tied to a fence while you checked the irrigation water, she would pull back and snap the reins or rub the bridle against a post and slip it over her head. After you had walked home she would be standing at the horse trough, waiting calmly to be unsaddled.

Even when burdened by the gig, Bunny liked to race. The school kids coming in from Barraport shared a crowded car. On days when they went in the car of those parents who had a modern sedan – like Jack Piccoli's Studebaker – the Barraport mob swept past with a scatter of quick waves, but when Neville Hawthorn took his turn in his old pre-war box-shaped tourer, John would stand up and like a Roman chariot driver, flick Bunny with the reins, and with a lot of yahooing urge Bunny into a canter. With exuberance flowing from boy to horse and the Barraport mob leaning on and shouting from Hawthorn's open-sided car, Bunny could sometimes extend her stumpy legs into a gallop. For a hundred yards we could keep pace with Neville's old car and cautious driving. But Bunny was no stayer. Soon her stride was so short that the shafts were rocking up and down, and that was about all the movement we had. Hawthorn's car puttered steadily around the salt lake and out of sight. Bunny settled to her steady trot, sides heaving at the unaccustomed effort.

The formed red gravel road was hard on horses' feet, and most of the time Bunny plodded along the side-track, following the three parallel tracks cut by the horses' hooves and thin gig tyres. She knew the way so well that where we crossed from the left of the road to the right at the top of the rise, she needed no guidance. On a drowsy day when we were both reading, John just gave a glance to see if there were any stray cars, and left the reins slack. Bunny crossed the road and trotted on.

Going to school we passed no farmhouses. There was just Maloney and Warren's slaughterhouse on the top of the rise. Sometimes we saw the windlass turn, and knew that the carcass of a bullock was being hauled up for skinning, cleaning and quartering. At their Godfrey Street shop with its flywire door, sawdust-strewn floor and heavy chopping block, Maloney and Warren proclaimed 'Fresh Supplies of Meat Daily'. In summer they killed after dark or before dawn, but in the winter we saw evidence of truth in advertising.

The first house, screened by struggling gums and threatened by drifting sand, was isolated from the rest of the town. It belonged to the Wardhaughs. Bob, who met the train and did the town deliveries, had an easy downhill run as he left his house. His doorless 1920s truck with its box cab needed that rolling start. Bunny might have matched Wardhaugh's truck for speed, but we turned off the Barraport Road, crossed the Wycheproof Road and followed the dirt track that led into Wright Street, bouncing on limestone corrugates without startling good residents – who would have told Dad.

The *Champion* arrived regularly at Elliot's newsagency, and John picked up his order. I read many feet of its austere columns that came all the way by slow boat and empire ports from Fleetway House, Farringdon Street, London. Rockfist Rogan, Captain Rogan of the RAF, climbed into his Spitfire, and watched for the Hun in the sun as Bunny jogged along. Rockfist's pal, Curly Hooper, gave a quick thumbs up, shoved the stick forward, and 'whoosh! There was a searing flash of light …' Out of the habit Bunny slowed as she approached the crossing at the Wycheproof Road. Danny of the Dazzlers, centre-forward, 'hit the ball on the run, and sent it tearing towards the far corner of the goal …' The 'footer fans' at Sunrays Park roared themselves hoarse. Jock McCall, skipper of the Dazzlers, said 'Nice work, Danny'. A cloud of dust from Pud Diamond's new gravel truck drifted across the double-columned pages: I did not bother to look up. Colwyn Dane, ace detective, and his young assistant, Slick Chester, searched the convict's clothes for clues. Dane was about to turn away when his eye caught something. He 'whipped out a magnifying glass from his pocket and peered at some hairs on the drab jacket'. The boy 'tec looked on anxiously. 'What is it, guv'nor?' Rabbits scrambled to their warren under the giant cactus as Bunny turned through the first railway gate. But I saw rabbits every day, and was not distracted. Ginger Nut, the boy who takes the biscuit at St Juke's, said 'Crumbs, just hark at old Greggy!' And Jumbo Merlin, Ginger's tubby pal, chimed in 'Corks, there goes Greggy again'. Ginger winked to his chums in the fourth form: 'We'd better hand in our lines in later'. And Bunny was slowing as she passed under the pepper trees, walked a couple of steps and stopped outside the gig shed.

I had never seen a soccer game, a detective, even the outside of a private school, did not know what a centre-forward was, never used or heard such words as 'footer', 'guv'nor, 'corks', 'crumpets', and 'hark at'. 'Hark at!' If Doughy Dwyer or Tud Storey had used 'Hark at' everyone playing kick-to-kick at Boort School would have stopped and jaws fallen open. Such an astonishing use of prissy, archaic language would have been an unprecedented lapse of taste or simply beyond comprehension. Yet I read the *Champion* avidly, entered completely its most English of English worlds, and I did that without ever confusing Ginger Nut and his wizard wheezes and jolly japes at St Juke's with the ruck and tumble on the top ground at school, and without ever wanting Boort School number 1796 to be like St Juke's. I did not doubt that Boort was a better school.

I identified most with Danny Roberts of North London United, forever young, forever on the edge of international selection, forever playing against the odds, and forever – with the final blistering kick – defeating cads, rotters and bad sports. John and I tried playing a couple of soccer games using the oval Australian football and the mouth of an old galvanised iron tank lying on its side as the goal. But it was not a success, and we soon returned to using hands as well as feet and all the skills of Australian football. Hitting a ball with your head seemed abnormal, even stupid. It still does. Deep down I knew that if Danny tried a quick back heel into space, trapped the ball again, and in a blistering turn of speed tried to weave his way around Boort's fullback line, then Peter Chalmers would not have been taken in by the feint, Laurie Crump would not have let the ball pass through his outstretched fingers, and Morrie Boyle would have already been breaking into space knowing the Crumpie would be feeding the ball to him. Danny, still recovering from Pete's shoulder in the chest, would have watched this from ground level. Afterwards in the shed the Boort men would have talked about that Pommy mug. He was just a fancy dancer. A two-bob lair. They never learn.

There were other horses and gigs on the road. Hills drove one to school, and they came in on the Wycheproof road, so we travelled the last quarter of a mile on the same track. But the three older Hills soon left school and the two youngest switched to bikes. The Byrnes boys came in on the Charlton Road, so we did not see them. It must have taken them nearly half an hour in the gig. When the older Byrnes boys left and Mrs Byrnes got a job as a teacher at the primary school, John, the youngest of her sons, drove himself and his mother to school in an old side-curtained Oakland car. John was only about fourteen, and he parked discreetly under a broad pepper tree below Dunstan's garage. John and Mrs Byrne then walked the rest of the way, around the post office corner and past the police station, where the local constable was as discreet as they were. Jack Gould and Mr Hawkins still drove gigs around the town, and the elderly Misses Beattie, looking (as I later learnt) like Daisy Bates, wore boots and bonnet. And we might see Charlie Robertson driving a long-shafted break with a spirited young horse tied alongside; but he was training pacers and was in a different category. By 1951 when my brother left school we were the last of the children driving a horse to school, and the grocers, bakers and milkmen were abandoning their horses, carts and deliveries.

Sonny arrived from up north somewhere in about 1945. A beautiful black pony, he had none of the shaggy characteristics of the Shetland or the short legs and boof-head of many ponies. He was a well-proportioned half-horse. As a stallion, he was kept in his own yard with his own high-railed fence and galvanised iron stall. Dad had ideas of breeding ponies, but Bunny was as cooperative in motherhood as she was in most other parts of her cantankerous life. Whenever Sonny escaped his yard and ran free of human constraint, his stallion instincts drove him to herd and control mares and drive off any colt or gelding he thought was a competitor. But away from other horses, Sonny was always alert and gently affectionate. He responded quickly to rein or heel, almost anticipating the rider's request. Often asked to carry heavy riders through the day, he was tireless, never expressing his fatigue in petulant stamping, head-shaking or mulish refusals. If a mad-eyed steer, tail in the air, broke away from a mob, he was off in pursuit, racing close and swerving left and right with the frantic beast.

As he was yarded, Sonny had to be fed and watered every day, a job that often fell to me. I scooped loose chaff from the barn into a five-gallon can that had once held oil and carried it across to Sonny's yard, knowing that there would be well-mannered enthusiasm for both the chaff and the carrier.

But once Sonny nearly killed me. One hot day I was riding him through an irrigation channel, and the water was just below his belly and lapping on the stirrups. Suddenly he stopped, pawed the water a couple of times, and gently settled and rolled. Something in his horse brain had told him that it was time for a dip. I just had time to fling my feet out of the stirrups and throw myself to one side into the water. I emerged spluttering to see Sonny holding his head up and rolling from side to side. When he had finished he simply stood up, scrambled up the bank and shook himself like a giant dog. I gathered the reins, looked at the oozing, mud-encrusted saddle, and we walked home together. Had Bunny done that I would have known that she had every intention of grinding the rider into the mud, and once free would have bolted for home. But Sonny was unconscious of the alarm he had caused.

Sonny stayed long after all the draught horses had gone, long after the swingle trees were eaten away by white ants, long after the heavy dray and wagon had rested for years in the one place and long after the team's harness had hardened and its buckles rusted.

When Sonny finally got so old his fine legs would no longer support his still willing heart and balls, Dad got his cousin Ian to take him down the paddock and shoot him. I do not remember Dad declining to shoot any other old injured (or just useless) animal.

As I ride down the bike track from Kaleen to Giralang, cross Maribyrnong Street, and roll down the easy slope through the tunnel of poplars, I wonder about mud. Canberra has no mud. There is mown grass, tall grass, asphalt and concrete, but no mud.

Boort was in dry country, but I remember mud. Mud that caked on boots and we walked an inch, even two inches, taller. All houses had mud scrapers; ornate at the front and discs or mould boards off ploughs at the back. At school just one shower of rain and the top ground had a skin of grey mud. It stuck to the football, and soon it had quarter of an inch coat on the leather. Old, worn and balloon-like with use, the footy quickly had the weight and toughness of a mallee root. It burst through hands reaching for marks and wrenched and sprained thumbs. It thudded on chests. A mongrel punt hit high on the instep was the only safe kick. To try a drop or a fancy stab meant a stubbed toe and a jarring that went up the leg to the hip. Some kid might have a pocket knife, even a Rogers, and he would cradle the ball in one arm and slice away the mud like orange rind. That gave a light ball for just five or six kicks.

When we did our right turn and began the march into school that turned into a saunter, some would break away and scrape their boots. But the bare boards of the passage and aisle between the desks were soon covered in half an inch of mud. Great clods fell from heels and lay under desks. The mud dried quickly, and passing soles crushed it and turned the top layer to dust. After school Ma Burgess shovelled, swept and hosed it out the door.

The mud stuck to bike tyres and riders stood on the pedals as though on a hill climb. The space between the tyres and the mudguards packed with mud, and the strongest riders could not force the pedals to turn. They pulled the mudguards off, but soon the mud jammed in the forks, and men walked along the side of the road carrying mud-encrusted bikes. Kids with chilblained hands and bikes jammed with mud cried as they pushed their bikes slowly towards school. Mud defeated bikes.

Drought made mud. The average rainfall was 14 inches a year. But, as one cocky said, 'It was a bloody unusual year when we got the average'. When we traced a low with tight black concentric circles making its way west across the continent, the Victorian forecast was always 'Rain on and south of the ranges'. Just where the ranges began was uncertain. Big Hill south of Bendigo was one possibility and that was close to 100 miles south of us. Wherever the rain fell it was a long way from us. In 1943 we had just eight and a half inches, just a shower more than they had in 1902, and 1902 was a great drought, the year when they sent train loads of water up the Robinvale line, and when all the wheat varieties – Queen's Jubilee, Straight Vote and the Prolifics – withered. But this was a record drought on a drought. No grass protected the topsoil and by 1944 even the roots had withered in the earth. When the west and north winds swept across the ground they whipped the soil away and left clean red clay pans that expanded with each wind. The tops of rises, most exposed to the wind and drained of all moisture, were vulnerable. So were gateways where cattle and sheep tracks came together, and hooves trampled the dry grass and cut and loosened the dirt. The fans of bare ground spreading out from gates looked like careless townies had ignored the notice 'Please shut the gate and use Federal Fertiliser'. It seemed that winds seeking escape had seized the opportunity, rushed the open gates, and carried the topsoil with them. Only Godfrey Street in town was a strip of tar, all other roads were gravel or just banked dirt. In the long dry they corrugated and fine dust collected in potholes. Showers turned roads into mud. Twenty or thirty points were not enough rain for seeds to germinate and keep growing, and it did not fill dams; but it was enough to make acres of mud. It was falling on clay pans, on earth skinned of all vegetation. Cars fitted with chains churned along roads. Drivers picked eccentric routes and left rutted wheel tracks as evidence. And when they struck hard gravel the chains clattered and banged and clods and sparks flew.

Mud has gone from most Australian lives. Men going to work and kids going to school or rabbiting do not wrestle bikes through mud. Kids do not walk on mud stilts. They do not collect the clod heels and with a relaxed flick send them in a skimming arc at some unsuspecting lounger. Barefoot kids do not walk with sausages of mud squeezing between their toes. Men do not divert left or right to the scraper before they go in the back door.

The tall grass beyond the mown edge of the Kaleen bike track dies brown, is bleached white and then turns grey with rot and age. It is perfect cover for rabbits. And once I saw a young one on the slope near the underpass. The genes in that half-rabbit were remarkable for their luck and their resistance to 1080 poison, myxomatosis and calicivirus.

Some mornings before school we slipped rabbit skins from the wires on which they had been stretched and dried, tied them in a bundle with binder-twine, and threw them in the back in the gig. On the way to school we diverged north into Victoria Street to the corrugated iron shed where Wally Evans, wool and skin buyer, carefully checked the weight and quality of our skins. When Wally's searching hand or eye found the skin of a nursing doe, or one that was ripped, he dropped the price, and with slow deliberation fossicked for the seven or eight shillings that he had decided was a fair price, handed them over, and we escaped from the heavy smell of skins, tallow and daggy wool.

Some kids said that they put stones inside skins to increase their weight, and old Wally never knew. We never tried anything like that and as Wally thought that the handing over of two bob was a serious transaction we doubted that he paid for many stones.

We killed thousands of rabbits, and had no effect on the total that burrowed in dam banks, were caught in car headlights, and were so thick in the distance that the ground rippled with their movement. In the morning we could lean a rifle on a post in the house-yard fence and take shots at the rabbits along Mercer's fence line. On winter evenings we set traps, carefully covering the jaws with paper and dirt, and hammering in the anchoring peg. We set them at burrow entrances and on dung hills, drawing mordant pleasure from the thought of catching some buck just as he squeezed out the first pellet. In the morning we had to 'go round the traps'.

We usually had three or four dogs, a couple of sheepdogs (prick-eared, intelligent and always looking for human companionship), a heeler (tough, single-minded in pursuit of cattle-hocks), and a greyhound (bred to chase). When the dogs put up a rabbit they worked as a pack. The greyhound, head low and fine legs flashing, led, but when the rabbit turned it careered past and the slower dogs, cutting across, took up the chase until the greyhound again came up through the pack and made another dive at the desperate rabbit. It might take four or five sprints and turns before the greyhound seized the rabbit. As Aussie, one of the greyhounds, grew old, he sometimes made a looping run straight for the nearest burrow. He flattened his brindle body into the earth, and we cheered on those times when Aussie chose the right burrow, and the rabbit, so close to safety, ran down his throat.

Whopper replaced old Aussie. Where Aussie had been fine of limb and skin and suffered when he slid on turns or staked himself on roots, Whopper was a tough crossbreed. Big and stupid, he never recognised insult or rejection, coming back for more when he was pushed, cuffed and kicked out of the way. He lacked Aussie's speed, but he would rabbit all day.

Once Aussie or Whopper had picked up a rabbit, the heeler, the boss of the pack, would claim it. If the heeler's jaws crunched the limp body of the rabbit there was no chance of selling the carcass and the skin might be ripped. When we were on foot, John and I would be left far behind and have to run nearly half a mile across the paddock to retrieve the mangled rabbit.

We poisoned, ripped warrens apart with deep ploughing, and hosed carbon monoxide from engine exhausts down burrows. Whenever irrigation or floodwater rose close to a burrow we dug trenches and sent a stream of water into the warren. Having thrown a few shovelfuls of mud into most of the entrances, we stationed ourselves above the other with an axe-handle and clouted the rabbits as they came out. Those that escaped our brutality were picked up by the dogs.

I must have killed thousands of rabbits. Once before a science lesson in which we were to watch a rabbit dissected, the teacher, Mr Fincher, handed me a rabbit and asked me to kill it. I thought nothing of it at and went to kill it right at my desk – grabbing it just above the ears with one hand, around the back legs with the other, and with a quick stretch and turn breaking its neck. Mr Fincher told me to go outside and do it. I thought this strange behaviour, but complied. I went one step out the door, came back without stopping walking, and gave him the warm limp carcass.

Myxomatosis was released at Gunbower in 1950, and soon the myxo had destroyed the rabbits and changed the lives of boys, farmers and skin and meat buyers. It seems hard to believe that I did all that rabbiting before I was thirteen. Fifty years later my mother in-law was given a rabbit to cook, and she asked me to skin it. I wondered if I knew how. I got a sharp knife —how we had valued our skinning knives and how we had worked a fine edge in spit on the whetstone! I opened up the inside of one back leg, and never hesitated.

Snakebite Bartlett lived further out the Barraport Road, and rode a bike to school. Sometimes we would chuck him a piece of rope, he would hitch it to his handlebars, and we towed him along behind the gig. Snakebite knew a lot of yarns, and was the first person I ever heard recite 'The Good Ship Venus', verse after verse after verse. But Snakebite learnt no poetry in the classrooms of Boort School. The rope kept him within easy earshot, and he was a good travelling companion. We tried to coordinate our travels so that we met at our railway gate. If we got there first and decided not to wait we left a large white quartz stone on the gate post. But often it was uncertain whether Snakebite had been and gone or we were looking at the stone left from the previous day. In summer, as we looked up the road to see if he was coming, the first sign of Snakebite was the flash of sun on bike spokes. Then a black elongated rider and bike, distorted by heat haze, crossed a distant bridge over an irrigation channel and slowly a recognisable Snakebite came into view. I have not forgotten why he was called Snakebite: I never knew.

At various times there were three of us in the gig. Auntie Wilma was driver when I started school in 1943. Mum's young sister Wilma was born in 1927. Only just turning sixteen when she came to live with us during the week, she was somewhere between John and me as kids and Mum and Dad as adults. Pretty and vivacious, she knew and could sing the latest songs – 'My knees are a knockin, There is hole in my stockin' – knew what was on the flicks, could dance the Hokey Pokey, and pushed the limits of the strict Methodism of her elderly parents. Because the men of the district had volunteered or been called up by the army, Wilma got a job previously taken by men; she became a teller at the National Bank. If you jumped up to look through the bars on the bank window you could sometimes catch a glimpse of Auntie Wilma in her blue uniform. If she could not get her balance out, she had to stay behind until all figures added up. If the balance was a penny out, and she had searched the columns for an hour, she might just get a penny from her purse and give it to the National. While we waited for Wilma and her lost pennies, we started harnessing Bunny, and John was adept with the winkers, even the heavy collar, but could not drag the jinker forward and get the shafts into the harness. We mucked around until Wilma appeared through the pepper trees, and quickly got us on the road.

Later, after Wilma had left, we sometimes had a cousin staying with us: Randal, Russell or Maurice. All of them lived at least ten miles out of town, and no school bus went close to their farms, so one of them stayed four nights a week and travelled with us. So three boys chattered their way along. Sometimes we equipped ourselves with stones to throw at the white posts on the side of the road or any other suitable target. Our main protection against the weather was a stiff canvas-backed rug which we could curve around our backs and over our heads when rain was slanting the way we were driving, or when travelling into the weather we could pull it up to our noses and just have three half-heads peering on to a frosty or rain-soaked morning. With a few tugs on the rein John guided Bunny so that the iron tyres snapped through the thin ice on puddles and we left shattered shards of ice glistening behind us.

When John left school, after finishing his fourth year of high school and sitting for his Intermediate, I sometimes rode a horse to school. Not the cantankerous Bunny but one of the stock horses that Dad kept. If I was on my own, it was easier and faster to saddle and ride than to harness a horse in the gig and drive. But the horse had to be left in the long backyard of Auntie Lizzie's place in Victoria Street, and it had to have water during the day. Dad had never learnt to ride a bike, and there had never been a bike at our house. It was therefore a moment of revolution and liberation when Dad bought me a standard gent's freewheel Hartley bike. With a bike I could ride straight into the school yard, dump it without a thought in the bike rack, and when we played sport on a Wednesday afternoon I could take my bike down to the football or cricket ground or swimming pool, and leave from there. I could also ride it to the pictures on some Saturday nights. On the way home its battery powered light showed flickering, abnormal images on a familiar road. In the ten years I went to school in Boort I do not remember a bike, owned by adult or child, ever being stolen. No bikes had locks – no one had heard of a bike with a lock.

After I left home, Dad gave my Hartley to a nephew. He rode it to school, but one day decided to escape his known world. With a howling wind behind him he went for miles. He was well beyond the perimeter of the search, and it was a long time before he was found. He kept the bike. The fading silver Speedwell that has carried me around the capital's northern suburbs is my second bike.

13. A Picture: From the Past and without a Past

Conversations *4:1 (2003), pp. 18–29*.

At Boort Primary School Number 1796 in northern Victoria, we lined up four times a day: morning, midday and after the two playtimes. Except on Monday mornings, when boys saluted the flag and we all mumbled a pledge to cheerfully obey parents, teachers and the law, there was no ceremony. Called to attention, we turned right, and marched in pairs into school. Through the double doors, we stepped (no tramping) along the wooden-floored corridor, past the racks hung with hats, dangling leather school bags, a couple of hessian bags with scrap material shoulder straps, and one forgotten cardigan. We entered by grade. The little kids, infants to grade two, turned into the first room on the left, grades three and four into the next room, and grades five and six turned right into the room opposite. With just seventy or so in the primary school when I started in 1943, we had twenty to thirty children in each of the three classrooms.

Through my six years all three teachers were women. It was Miss Chalmers who finally seized me and, holding me tightly by the right wrist, forced me to bowl with an extended, straight arm. She saved me embarrassment, but I never learnt to bowl with the speed or spin to threaten any but the most incompetent of batsmen.

All rooms were austerely furnished with green-topped double desks with seats attached. The desks increased in size from row to row and room to room, and the desks' two enamel ink wells were inserted and filled when we made the momentous change from pencils to pens. Each room had a fire place, the wood fire lit on winter mornings; the teacher had a small table and chair, centrally placed for surveillance; and on one wall of each room were blackboards, and another window. We all sat so that the light of the windows came from the left as we faced the blackboard. Left-handers would have been writing in the shadow of their own hands and arms, but left–handers were compelled to labour with an awkward right hand, and to direct all vertical strokes, thick on the way down, fine on the way up, to slope to the right. Girl monitors were responsible for dusting and flowers. Even in drought when grit-filled west winds seared every surviving plant, there were, we were told, no excuses for leaving all the vases empty. There were always tips from the sugar gums and other trees and bushes that could be used. Boys, excluded from flower arranging, were told they shared responsibility for bringing them to school. My brother and I never brought one flower or gum tip.

The Boy from Boort

The pictures on the walls were landscape prints behind glass. A teacher working at the blackboard could glance up and see the reflection of her class. Without turning, Mrs Foley would say, 'Neil Nelson, stop poking Norman Baldwin with your ruler'. It seemed a demonstration of the mysterious powers of teachers to know when a rule was broken, or even under threat.

One picture was different from all the pleasant prints. It was what appeared to be a photograph in a wooden frame, but may have been a copy of a detailed drawing. It had hung next to a classroom doorway, and was then shifted to the corridor near the entrance to the headmaster's office. It was of a young Aboriginal woman standing with a skin cloak pulled around her shoulders. She was, the label said, Jerrybung, Queen of the Boort and Loddon Tribes. She remained in the primary school after I shifted into the extension that housed Boort Higher Elementary School. I remember no other picture of an individual, not even of King George VI. Not of General Charles Gordon of Khartoum, hero of Empire, killed in 1884. The local government district, the Gordon Shire, with its meeting place in Boort, was created the next year, and Boort had a Gordon Street, and one of the school 'houses' was Gordon. But in my eleven years at that weatherboard school sited just under the crest of Boort Hill, I do not recall one teacher referring to that unique picture, or Queen Jerrybung, or her tribe, the Djadjawurung.

The Aborigines were not absent from our classes. In many years we drew and labelled '*mia mias*', spears and boomerangs. Children were asked to bring along spear points and grindstones found in paddocks when ploughs turned the distinctive black soil of what were always known as 'blackfella's ovens'. And we all knew that '*boort*' was the Aboriginal word for 'smoke', or that '*boort boort*' meant 'big smoke', because Aborigines, it was said, sent smoke signals from the highest point of the Hill, up where the concrete water tower gave the town supply its pressure. Living in an area littered with Aboriginal words – from Barraport to Wychitella and Borung – I knew the meaning of no other Djadjawurung word.

The *Victorian Readers* that went from the First to the Eighth Book contained many stories of Aborigines. In the Fourth Book we read what were said to be legends 'told by the blacks to their piccaninnies': 'Why the Crow is Black', 'How the Sun was Made', 'The Magpie and the Children' and 'How Mussels Were Brought to the Creek'. The notes included in the Readers confirmed the attitudes of those times. We were asked to notice the repetition of words and told that 'Children and savages are fond of this'. We were asked why 'our native blacks are dying out'; but we were also told about the different seeds that 'blacks used for grinding', asked if we knew what yams were, and instructed that many 'savage tribes' had an animal 'totem' and it was 'held sacred'.

The *Readers'* stories of Aborigines in meetings with whites included extracts from Aeneas Gunn, and we were assured that Bett-Bett, the central character in *The Little Black Princess*, had now grown up and become Mrs Bronson. In the story *A New Years' Day Adventure in Australia*, a lost drover's son was saved by two Aborigines who 'were very kind', and the drovers 'treated the two blackfellows well' giving them 'damper, tobacco and meat, and a whole bullock besides'. In the questions we were asked to think of other 'instances of kindness on the part of the blacks'. One incident described in the Fifth Book stayed with me. It was set on the Loddon River which made its slow wandering way to the Murray east of Boort, and the author mentioned the Four Post which I wrongly assumed was the Four Post that we passed on the way to Bendigo. In fact Samuel Carter's boyhood reminiscence was about events between the upper Loddon and Wimmera Rivers, 150 kilometres from Boort. Carter wrote of being attacked by Aborigines and, while no one was killed in that incident, it was apparent that violence and intimidation between blacks and whites on the squatter frontier were common. But I knew no stories of any Aborigines in the Boort area doing anything, and certainly nothing of any being killed. The map that retained so many Aboriginal names was not interspersed with Ambush Creeks, Skull Lagoons or Murdering Swamps.

We had one chance when we might have looked seriously at Aboriginal history. In our final year at Boort Higher Elementary School, in fourth form, we sat for the Intermediate examination in the local hall under the watch of the local Methodist minister. One subject was Australian history. Our main text was R.M. Crawford's *Ourselves and the Pacific*, first published in 1941, an imaginative and pioneering text that located Australia in the Pacific. But Crawford gave but one index entry and one short paragraph in the text to the Aborigines. The sections on the inland exploration and the advance of the squatters had almost no mention of the Aborigines. Unlike nearly all the other fifteen and sixteen-year-old students in my Intermediate year, I was a student of two books: I had inherited my brother's copy of Ernest Scott's *A Short History of Australia*, revised in 1947. While Scott was brief, he concluded: 'The worst features of the fading out of the native race arose from sheer brutality and treacherous murder by white settlers and their convict servants'. The process, he said, was 'grim and hateful'. No books then available to students in country schools said more, and none was as blunt.

So although we had no texts with any details about Aborigines in the present or the past, in all but our last years at school we had learnt something of them, and we had read extracts from many of those who had written about them: Gunn, Henry Kendall, Charles Bean, Mary Gilmore, Katie Langloh Parker. We had learnt the standard prejudices of the time about savages, child races, and people destined to fade away; but we had also looked at illustrations of nardoo plants and grindstones, read stories of Aborigines behaving admirably, and a few of us had had access to Scott's judgement that some settlers were guilty of 'the lowest depth of mean homicide'. Our education in Aboriginal history was not – as is often said – absent, but deficient. The gaps were largely because by the 1940s and 1950s so few scholars had done the research to establish the depth in time, cultural complexity and diversity of experience within Aboriginal Australia. For me, sitting at my desk in school 1796, the Aborigines always seemed to exist in distant times or places. There was no connection with any events that had happened in the landscape that we looked at, played and worked in, and travelled across. There was no connection with the lonely Jerrybung in her skin cloak.

The picture of Jerrybung dated from either 1856 when John Kerr, the magistrate at Fernihurst, drew her, or from 1863 when a photographer preserved images of the Aborigines camped on Lake Boort. I saw Jerrybung as she had been about eighty years earlier. I was one lifetime from the woman in the picture. My father and grandmother had both gone to the Boort Primary School. Even if Jerrybung had died immediately after her image had been preserved, she was in Boort within twenty-five years of my grandmother. Both my father and grandmother must have known people who had known Jerrybung. My great-grandmother, Granny McRae, was alive and well when I started school; my brother and I left our horse under the pepper trees in her backyard. Granny McRae might even have known Jerrybung, or some of the other Aborigines photographed in 1863. That closeness, to what I thought of as my place, of another people and culture, of particular people such as Jerrybung, never occurred to me in the 1940s, and can still surprise me.

Through my years at school in Boort I thought that I knew no Aborigines. It was not, I believed, until I was about sixteen and travelled outside the Boort area and saw the people who lived in the river camps near Swan Hill and Echuca that I encountered people who were obviously Aboriginal. It is only in recent years that I realised that one family living close to the school was almost certainly part-Aboriginal. The husband, George, was always called 'Darkie'. Even that gave me no clue. George was well known as he had been a talented sportsman, having played for the Boort football team as a teenager in the 1930s. But he injured his knee when there was no corrective operation, just the hope offered by bandages and quacks. Local men drove him all over the state hoping that one of the blokes said to be good with knees would get him back on the field. They failed, of course, and as George had played in a team with three other men who went on to play in Melbourne, there were stories that George would have worn the 'Big V' (represented Victoria).

I had my own reason to admire George. In about 1948 Boort was playing football against its bitter rivals, Wedderburn. Fights had broken out on the ground, the two captains were slugging it out at centre half-back, and among the sparse spectators on the far side of the oval close to where I was operating the score board, Charlie, a Boort man well known to me, was fighting a thug from the 'burn. Both landed thudding blows, and the thug was being urged on by three or four of his drunken mates. Moving quickly up behind Charlie, George waited. Suddenly the thug saw George, dropped his hands, and said, 'I'm not fighting with you, Darkie. I'm not fighting with you'. He turned quickly, and he and his mates hurried off. To a ten-year-old it was amazing; the humiliation of enemies by reputation. I could not wait to tell everyone.

George's son 'Saddles' was an older boy at school with me. I do not remember anyone suggesting that 'Sads' had any Aboriginal inheritance. If we had been conscious of it, we certainly would have commented in our casual, unthinking racism. No one did. While I was in primary school George and his family left the district, and passed out of local knowledge. But there is, then, just the chance that I was in primary school with someone who was part-Djadjawurung, even a relative of Jerrybung. Those people apparently so distant may have been known to Granny McRae, may have continued to live as a result of the mixing races on the frontier, and their descendants, just three or four generations on, may have been with me at school.

At Melbourne University I did not study Australian history until 1958 when I was in my third year. I was well taught. Jack La Nauze, Bob Gollan, Geoff Serle, Barry Smith and Don Baker were then in the Melbourne History Department and strangely all later went to The Australian National University. The main text books were Gordon Greenwood's edited essays by six historians, *Australia: A Social and Political History*, 1955, and Manning Clark's two volumes of *Select Documents in Australian History*, 1955. Neither lectures nor books said much about Aborigines. Greenwood and Clark have more on Chinese than Aborigines. But some historians were then aware of the absence. In 1959 La Nauze wrote: 'The Australian aboriginal is noticed in our history only as melancholy anthropological footnote'.

I had completed my last class as a student of Australian history just as John Mulvaney was starting a new scholarly interest in Aboriginal history. He surveyed the literature and the little archaeological work that had been done and, in 1962, as a result of his own work at the Kenniff Cave site in Queensland, he said that Aborigines had been in Australia for more than 13,000 years. He had begun the collection of evidence to establish that the Aborigines had a history of 30,000, 40,000, 60,000 … years, so important to their own self-perception and claims to possession of Australia. But it was not until the 1970s that much new work began to be published on black and white relations on frontier settlement.

In 1963 I had to choose a topic for Master of Education thesis. I decided to write on the early attempts to 'civilise' the Aborigines of Victoria – then the Port

Phillip District. I cannot now be sure why I chose to write on what was still an unfashionable topic, and when I did not know just what evidence was available to allow me to describe and comment on what had happened between 100 and 130 years earlier. But it was certainly true that I still wondered about the people who lived and died on the paddocks, swamps, creeks and wind-blown hills of those northern rivers and the Mallee fringe that I knew so well. And I retained the image of the lonely Jerrybung who had no history.

In 1964, in the basement of the State Library of Victoria, I read my way through seventeen boxes of reports and letters in which Port Phillip District colonial administrators had set out their dealings with Aborigines. In breaks between teaching at the Royal Melbourne Institute of Technology, I went down the curved iron stairs into the library basement, and there a man wearing a grey dust jacket showed me to an old table and chair where I worked. When I first took the papers from their boxes I was delighted to find that they were still tied in red tape. 'Government red tape' was not so much a metaphor but an extension of a reality. In those files I read the reports of the earnest Edward Parker, born in London in 1802, apprentice printer, candidate for the Methodist ministry and school teacher. From 1839 he was Assistant Protector of the Aborigines in the Loddon district. After travelling widely, Parker set up his station near Mt Franklin. It was named 'Jim Crow', but probably before 'Jim Crow' became the disparaging term for a Black American song and dance man and before it was extended to imply segregation.

In his travels in the Loddon Valley, Parker encountered cases of Aborigines being killed by settlers. In one incident an Aborigine known to Parker realised that he was about to be shot and grabbed his attacker around his legs. He was shot in the shoulder while pleading for mercy. As Aboriginal evidence was not accepted by the courts and whites would not incriminate each other, Parker soon knew there was 'no chance of justice being obtained for these unfortunate people'.

Parker learnt the Djadjawurung language (he called it Jajorurong), and made notes about beliefs and practices. But his attempts to civilise the Djadjawurung came to little and as a result of sickness, dislocation, despair and violence, the Djadjawurung were rapidly disappearing. By the early 1850s there were only about 150 of them. After Parker resigned in 1850, the station lingered on for a few years. Parker said that his failure to educate the Djadjawurung children was 'one of the most painful of the many painful remembrances of my official career'.

The bundles of red-taped papers had taught me something of Djadjawurung, but Parker had been in the south of their lands, about 150 kilometres from Boort, and close to where Carter had set his reminiscences. Parker recorded no names and no stories of the people who were photographed in their camp on Lake Boort in 1863. As Parker was the main source of information for the nearly all later writers on the Djadjawurung, it was obviously going to be difficult to find out more about the lower Loddon. All that I picked up were incidental scraps left by the first of the white settlers in the area: Aborigines worked for squatters around the homesteads and out on the runs by washing sheep and mustering; Frederic Godfrey, one of the brothers who took up Boort Station, employed 'Jackie Logan' as a groom and Jackie travelled all the way to Melbourne with Godfrey and his horses; there were no accounts of violence as the runs were taken up and sheep and cattle ate the grass that had once fed the game consumed by the Aborigines; but there was one story from 1849 of a Boort Aborigine being killed by a marauding group of traditional enemies from the Murray, and of warriors from Boort leaving to take revenge. Amid dispossession and imposed revolution, old enmities survived.

By a strange irony my thesis on the attempts to educate the blacks of Victoria was typed by a black woman. In 1966, with a draft of my thesis in my luggage, I went to Port Moresby to teach at the Administrative College of Papua New Guinea. Jessie, the secretary at the Admin College at Six Mile, typed the final copy for the examiners, pausing now and again to talk to students in any of the several languages that she casually commanded.

Preparing courses on new topics at the Admin College and the University of Papua New Guinea, and absorbing and being absorbed into a frontier Australian town transforming itself into a sprawling city and a capital of a foreign country, I rarely had time to think about Aborigines. I prepared nothing from the thesis for publication.

When I returned to Australia I sometimes thought about returning to the history of the people who had once owned the land that was now being worked by the fourth and fifth generation of my own family. But some other task always seemed to be close to, or just past, its deadline, and my experience in Papua New Guinea among peoples who were numerous, and retained their lands, their languages and the stories of their own past made me reluctant to write about Djadjawurung from fragments written by outsiders.

In Papua New Guinea I had walked with people on their own lands, and each rock, river bend, old garden site and sago swamp provoked its own story. At a red cliff they said this was where Wada made the commitment. One tribe had long been dominant, and the lesser and surrounding tribes were trying to put together an alliance to challenge it. But that was difficult and dangerous. If the dominant tribe learnt that another tribe was trying to bind others to an alliance it would be attacked immediately; and any minor tribe could curry favour by denouncing the new alliance to the dominant tribe. All the minor tribes were cautious when they met. And it was then that Wada called for a boy of the dominant tribe. Wada took the boy, spoke to him kindly, turned the boy's head away and split it with an axe, killing him instantly. All knew that the dominant tribe would learn what had happened and who was present, and take terrible revenge. Now all the minor tribes were committed, and would have to act quickly. They did, and that was how the dominant tribe was defeated and new alliances were formed.

At a clump of flowers and bright-leafed plants that stood out against a wall of rainforest, people said that was where an angry husband waited and killed his wife's young lover. It was the wife who had made the garden, and the plants kept reseeding. At a rock they showed me the teeth marks of the giant who had once roamed the area and eaten the slow and careless. Over there, they said, was the site of the village before the big flood swept through the valley; here were sago palms first planted by people now driven from the area; and that woman sitting outside her house was the descendant of the one of the few to survive from the tribes who had previously owned these lands.

To walk across the paddocks in Boort is to move within a known farming history. In the 1944 drought the dry grass was blown against that fence, drift sand piled against the barrier of grass, the fence was buried and the sheep just walked over the top; over there we felled the oak trees and the grain was so straight we split fence droppers from them; those laser-graded lucerne bays looking like lush billiard table tops were once lignum swamps; that bit of rusted iron now used to mend a sagging gate once fitted a bullock yoke; and over there Dad had yarded the draught horses and fed them before dawn so they could work all day. But just a hundred years before I was born that same country had other markers evoking other peoples' histories. Wars, ambushes, defeats, victories, escapes, acts of courage, births, jokes, love, times of hunger and plenty, marriages, quarrels, alliances were all evoked by old camp sites, creek beds, stands of timber, open spaces, sand hills and even by what was transient – the smell of bush honey and the chilling sound of a curlew in the night. What could be learnt in much of Papua New Guinea with all its frustrating complexity of different perspectives and the joining of the remembered and the mythical left me reluctant to try to write a history from loose generalizations and with almost no names of particular people and without memories that mattered to them.

Queen Jerrybung's picture continued to hang on the wall near the headmaster's office long after I had left the area. I wonder if any later teachers tried to explain who she was to children who had just travelled across ground that had meant so much to her. Then a new headmaster in a general clearing away of the old tossed her out. Fortunately there were other copies of the picture of Jerrybung, and her name and image survive. But that is about all of her that survives from the past so close. I regret that I have not tried to give her a history, but that is partly because I know it would be so much less than I would want and she deserves.

My thanks to Paul Haw and John Nelson who aided my recall.

14. A Village School

Nation *(15 Oct. 1966), pp. 5–6.*

Written on the blackboard with that neatness of hand practised universally by primary school teachers was the poem:

Goodbye to the roar of the busy street and the dusty pavement that scorches the feet

The holidays are here!

What significance had the poem for the children of Lea Lea where the school ground is the lee slope of a dune with sand soft to ankle depth? The roar of traffic is never heard at Lea Lea: the twenty-three-mile road from Port Moresby ends at the river immediately before the village. Travellers have to leave their cars or trucks under the scattered coconut palms and make their way into the village by one of the outrigger canoes which lie on either bank of the river.

If the poem was alien to the culture of the Motu people, it has not caused them to reject the school. Deputations made by the villagers to the Department of Education in the 1950s were representative of their desire to obtain schools as the means to knowledge and better paid jobs. Before the establishment of the Administration's school, the LMS Mission had conducted classes in Lea Lea; the teacher was the pastor assisted by his wife and children – if they were sufficiently well-educated. The mission only went to standard (grade) 4, and few students completed the fourth year. The language of instruction was Motu, but some simple English was taught. Sentences such as 'Henao goes to the garden' were read from English primers by the better students. Some of the parents of the present students at the primary school are literate in Motu only. But, of course, apart from 'The New Testament' they possess little written in Motu on which they can demonstrate their literacy.

The mission did not resent the establishment of the Primary T School, – the 'T' standing for Territory, indicating that the school follows a Territory-oriented syllabus as opposed to some of the schools in the town which follow 'A' or New South Wales courses. From a total village population of approximately 700, it has 179 students, the enrolment being slightly inflated by students from the neighbouring village of Papa. In some age groups there would be close enough to one hundred per cent attendance at school. Only five grades are being taught in 1966, standards one, two, four, five and six. The preparatory class and standard three had to be abandoned because there were neither teachers nor classrooms available.

Figure 3: Hank Nelson (holding camera) at Lea Lea Village, 12 August 1966. Bill Gammage (holding a green coconut) is left of him, then Ratu from Rabaul, a Primary T School teacher at Lea Lea, and his wife, also a teacher, from Lea Lea.

Source: Photo by Chris Gammage, provided by Pacific Manuscripts Bureau, Canberra, PMB photo 46-097.

What opportunities will be open to the thirty-three students completing standard six at the end of the year? Perhaps ten will go on to higher education at Sogeri Secondary School (a boarding school for boys) or at Kwikila (a co-educational boarding school). Another handful might find places at Idubada Technical School or at some other vocational training centre. Few of the girls will have any opportunity to continue their education. Generally the villagers are reluctant to allow their daughters to wander among strange men at distant boarding schools; and some parents are anxious to have their girls earn a cash wage as soon as possible.

For those who remain in the village, the chances of entering the cash economy are limited. When orders for wood are received, bundles are cut and sold in Port Moresby to the Papuan householders who depend on wood for fuel. Some fish, shell-fish and crabs, also, can be sold in Port Moresby. There is little possibility of developing cash cropping in the sandy soil, low rainfall conditions of Lea Lea. Cattle could be grazed on the land at the back of the village – land traditionally used for hunting – for the country is covered in coarse grass, is only slightly undulating, and is lightly timbered. That cattle can be run is demonstrated on the nearby Steamships Trading Co. lease. A cattle industry requires skills and capital. The skills could be acquired, but in a community which at present lacks the funds to run a motor vehicle, the accumulation of finance to purchase stock and run a fence will be a long task.

For some time to come the basic means of entry to the cash economy for the villagers will be through employment in Port Moresby. The construction industries in particular offer opportunities for the men. Lea Lea has disadvantages for the commuter. The two trucks which leave each day for Port Moresby charge three shillings for a one-way fare, to the fifty or so daily travellers. For a workman receiving perhaps ten dollars a week, sixty cents represents a high percentage of his earnings. The cost of fares largely explains the absence of women travellers. Girls in wage employment (frequently as shop-assistants) live in employers' hostels in Port Moresby.

The trucks are run by the Pako brothers, sometimes referred to as the only Motu entrepreneurs. It seems unlikely that the villagers will be able to purchase a truck of their own in the near future, although by their donations of ten dollars per person, the villagers raise approximately 6,000 dollars a year for the church.

The newcomer to the Territory who receives perhaps ten or twenty requests for a job from hopeful 'houseboys' is immediately aware that he is in a country with an excess of population demanding urban employment. Even more depressing are the figures given by the World Bank report on New Guinea: it gives a figure of 80,000 indigenes in employment in 1963, an increase of 10,000 over the past decade. Relative to the total number employed that growth rate may be reasonable: seen against a population increasing at about three per cent p.a. it means a consistent decline in the proportion of the population in wage labour.

It has become a cliché to speak of New Guinea as a land of villages; but it is against a background of innumerable villages like Lea Lea, some with superior resources, some with inferior, that the problem must be seen. Half of the children from the villages have no schools to attend. Inevitably the villages without schools see the first step towards meeting their rising expectations to be the opening of educational opportunities for their children. The questions put by Mr Sinake Giregire (Goroka) on the first day of the recently completed ninth meeting of the House of Assembly were representative of a number of similar demands:

Is it intended to establish a primary school in the Yonki area in the Eastern Highlands district?

If so, when?

If not, why not?

And the reply given by Mr FC Henderson, the Assistant Administrator (Economic Affairs), did not contain any heartening euphemism which could be taken back to the voters.

> *Mr Henderson: The answer to the Honourable Member's question is as follows:*
>
> *A primary school will be established in the Yonki area of the Eastern Highlands District.*
>
> *Not in the foreseeable future.*
>
> *Lack of trained teachers and insufficient funds.*

Later in the session John Guise summarised the demand for education: 'There is a shortage of teachers and I think that every member coming here, including myself, will always ask for teachers. This pressure is coming from the people and also from local government councils everywhere'.

The Administration's policy, as Mr Henderson made clear, no longer aims for universal literacy in the immediate future. Rather than dissipate limited resources in the dispersal of education, funds are being directed towards the previously neglected secondary and tertiary levels of training. Resistance to the Administration's policy is apparent in two areas – from those places at present without government primary schools and from villages (like Lea Lea) where there are still inadequate opportunities for students leaving the primary T schools. 'Balanced development' in education is desirable as long as you don't live in one of those areas which have to be neglected to create 'balance'.

It has been said that the revolutions in the African States were revolutions of school teachers. Being an educated and urban class, they have not always been content to work in the villages on relatively low wages. There was no evidence of intense dissatisfaction likely to lead to militant action among the five staff members at Lea Lea. Satu, the fifth grade teacher, originally from Rabual, married a local girl and stayed on in the village. One of the other teachers also came from outside the Central District, and the apparent acceptance of the two outsiders by the villagers may be evidence against the fears of regional and tribal fraction fighting in an independent Papua New Guinea. The housing provided for the staff by the Administration – except for the small aluminium house provided for the headmaster – is not greatly superior to the general level of village dwelling. Relative to Australian standards (admittedly an unfair comparison), the staff were not well educated. Satu, for example, had completed standard nine before doing a one year teacher's college course. He is currently attempting to improve his qualifications by taking a Queensland correspondence course.

14. A Village School

The economic basis of life in Lea Lea will be changed very slowly. The value of Territory exports might be rising, but the figures reflect little change in the majority of the villages. The capacity of the schools to open wider opportunities is limited. But the aspirations of the village people for education and ultimately for a greater share in the cash economy, are rising fast. The crucial thing will be the political effects of frustrated villagers demanding more opportunities for entry into the glittering cash economy.

15. Pictures at Tabara

Overland *109 (1987), pp. 6–14.*

Along the north bank of the Gira River in the Northern Province of Papua New Guinea the walking track winds through sharp changes of deep shade, half shade and bright sunlight. Even with our eyes full of sweat we were conscious of the condition of the light. Near Nindewari Village, in an open area of shimmering heat, there was a patch of swept earth, white stone border, bright crotons, fenced square, and in the centre a peaked corrugated iron roof supported by stakes. Although not a grave, it looked like a memorial of some sort. We wanted to cross the intense heat of the open space and escape into the dark heat of the rain forest; but we asked what it was.

Many of the young people of the area know a little English, and they speak it with a distinctive, clipped carefulness. Five or six of them answered, each giving a quick rush of words. Perhaps they were translating from their own language, and while one was talking another was choosing the foreign words to push the story along its well-known track:

> *A young man. He was only fifteen or sixteen. He was making love to a married woman. They used to meet very often. Then the husband found out. He came back to the village in the early afternoon. He sat there sharpening his bush knife. For a long time. In the evening he waited here by the track. When the young man came along he killed him. He kept cutting and cutting. And he threw all the pieces away in the bush. Then he ran. He went to Ioma. He travelled all night. To give himself up to the police. The people gathered all the bits of the body. They found every piece except his cock and balls. They smoked the body to keep it so that the government men could look at it. This (and they indicated the fence, crotons, and roof) is the place where the young man was killed. He is not buried here. He is buried in the village cemetery.*

The story was dramatic and grotesque. Such stories are attractive to Australians who have just arrived in Papua New Guinea. The stories confirm what they hoped: they have passed beyond the Australian frontier to the exotic. And they are themselves unthreatened. They cannot wait to write home, or get home and talk about it.

We had flown in from Popondetta to Dodoima on a six-seater Islander, crossing the uniform pattern of oil palms, the mass of rain forest, the Kumusi, Opi and Mambare Rivers, and losing height over curve on curve of the Gira. Dodoima airstrip is a patch of vivid green where the Gira leaves the foothills of the central ranges and begins its north-eastward surge to the Solomon Sea. At Dodoima some Binandere saw their first wheeled machinery: on the undercarriage of an aircraft or on the Scott Bonnar mower used to help cut the *kiawa* (whiteman's) grass on the runway.

Chris Owen, Andrew Pike and I were going to Tabara village with John Waiko. John had recently graduated from The Australian National University in Canberra, the second Papua New Guinean to gain a PhD. Amid flowing robes, floppy hats, mortar boards and speeches, John had stepped forward to take his degree wearing a gown, feathered headdress and shell face ornaments. Now his Binandere people were to celebrate his doctorate. We three foreigners had come to take part, watch and record.

At Popondetta airport the Papuan clerk stated on the loading form that each of us weighed seventy-seven kilos. Was that the known average weight of white travellers in the tropics, or did we all look the same?

It was a four-hour walk from Dodoima to John Waiko's village of Tabara. After three hours the unpracticed walkers among us could not alter stride without feeling pain. We were fixed in mobility.

The track crossed a succession of steep-sided creeks feeding into the Gira. Some were bridged by heavy tree trunks adzed flat on top, and at other longer crossings the logs tapered to sapling, bending and whipping with each stride. All the barefoot Binandere, including those with awkward two-man loads lashed to poles, slapped their feet confidently on wood over space. At each creek we measured our agility and comfort against humility. We could follow the lead of the Binandere; bounce across on our backsides; or ignore the bridge, plunge into dense bush, wade through stagnant water and haul ourselves up the far bank. The Binandere watched closely and covertly. All hoped for a spectacular display of foreign ungainliness so that they would later mime, laugh, mime, and laugh again. We avoided disaster, but at the expense of pride, splinters, scratches and a soaking to the waist.

Less than an hour out of Tabara we were told to board outrigger canoes. Each time a white boot was placed in the main hull, a Binandere politely urged us, 'Watch the outrigger'. I thought this curious advice until I realised that it was the lightwood outrigger that gave the first sign that the canoe was tilting.

Strong current and intermittent deft poling from the Binandere took us quickly downstream. With Tabara still out of sight another canoe joined our quiet convoy. It took station on the left. The rainforest on the banks was darkening with evening, but low-angle sun still lit the eastern edge of the river, and it fell on a spectral figure kneeling just forward of the stern poler in the strange canoe. The spectre was in fact a boy of about seven painted in grey clay, and dressed in broad green leaves and white streamers of beaten fibres. He was, we were told, representing the spirit of John's uncle, the man who had first brought mission schooling to the area. John's uncle had since died, but the boy honoured his place in John's education. There could be no Binandere precedents on how to greet a returning doctor of philosophy. George Kandoro of Tabara, John's cousin, had choreographed a new village ceremony.

The canoes rounded the last bend and the polers thrust for the *papo*, the shelving bank of the Tabara canoe landing. The *papo* is still for the river people what the steamer jetty was to the white men in the tropics, and what the railway station was to Australian country towns. The *papo* is the point where the Tabara have met the outside world. Brides from other villages have stepped ashore on its grey sand, some surrounded by families displaying their strength, others as trembling captives. Men have arrived at the *papo* to offer feasting, fighting, trading, treachery, a new religion and a new government. Women have wept when young men left to work on plantations or enlist in the army or the police, and they have wept again on the *papo* for those who returned and those who did not. And now when village groups from downstream want to arrive in style, white leaf-pennants flying and canoes low in the water with pigs, taro and bananas, they battle upstream close to the far bank, pass the village, then turn and race into the *papo* with the current.

At the *papo* we were met by drummers, dancers and a chanted welcome that swelled and died. Headdresses and leaf streamers waved with the gusts of sound. Spearmen raced forward, retreated and charged again. All the time the spirit-boy stood quietly at John's side. He was both shy and assured. The welcome was a compressed re-enactment of many meetings with strangers: the shouting of 'Who are you?' the challenge, violence, a treaty, and an invitation to the men's house.

From the front platform of the house set aside for us we looked out on swept earth surrounded by some fourteen other houses, each with its own split-palm floor, vertical lath walls and shaggy sago-palm thatch roof. Each house sat on posts, some over two metres high. The only useful plant cultivated right against the houses was tobacco. Old men plucked leaves, cured them over the fire, and rolled themselves a cigar as they talked. Beyond the houses were betel and coconut palms, behind them rain forest and the curve of the river. The food gardens, extending over two kilometres, were across the river where they were protected from the foraging village pigs. Logs lying on the ground marked off ownership and gardens in different stages of production: newly cleared land with timber piled to dry for fuel, freshly planted taro, tangles of sweet potato vines spilling from earth mounds, mature gardens dense with maize, tapioca, peanuts, cabbage, pumpkin, beans and onions, and old gardens in which even the sugar cane and banana palms were disappearing in the secondary rain forest.

The Binandere led us through their gardens with pride. The obvious productivity does more than demonstrate that the Binandere possess fertile land and it works well: the constant harvest confirms for the Binandere the essential correctness of the way they organise their material and spiritual worlds.

The Tabara grow no cash crops. For a time Australian field officers tried to compel the villagers to grow tree crops, but economic laws were stronger than those of the government. Any harvest had to be carried on men's backs and in canoes to meet boats that did not come and for buyers who did not care. The Tabara found it cheaper to pay fines and easier to labour in gaol.

In the evening some women lit a fire in front of our house. We sat in the dark on our platform looking at other fires, trails of smoke, and people moving in and out of the shadows. A house, a young Binandere man told us, is not complete without its fire. Did we, he asked, notice a lone rock in the river? He took great care to remind us of the particular rock where the river was fast and shallow. That rock, he said, was once a house. No one lit a fire in front of it. Believing it had been spurned, the house left and became the rock.

At daybreak each morning there was a rhythmic swishing as Binandere women swept the *arapa*, the open space between the houses. When we first looked out on the *arapa* each day it was still patterned with the crescent strokes of the bush brooms. During the day fat pigs, healthy chooks and skinny silent dogs left one lot of shade, crossed the *arapa*, and found other shade. In Tabara the vegetarians and omnivores do well, and the carnivores struggle.

To a westerner the *arapa* could look like a street; but that is absurd for there are no vehicles, and no roads connect the village to anywhere else. And the Binandere do not see a space equally free to all pedestrians. They think of each house as having a claim to the *arapa* immediately in front of it. The Binandere feel more secure in their own section of *arapa*. The protective spirits of ancestors, they think, are more able to guide and guard them close to their own houses. A person suspicious of another does not lightly enter the rival's *arapa*, and a man wishing to make a strong speech stands before his own house.

We cooked some of our own food, but much of it came in leaf-covered bowls full of steaming taro, yam and banana. At the end of one meal I was asked if I wanted anything else. I said I wouldn't mind a small sugar banana. Someone, I thought, would just throw me one. In fact someone had to take a canoe across the river in the dark and walk to the gardens. About an hour after my request I was presented with an enormous branch of sprouting banana hands. While I tried to say that the bunch could be better used somewhere else, it was lashed to our platform. Next morning other branches were tied to our house. My suggestions that we could not possibly use so many bananas were met with cheerful indifference.

15. Pictures at Tabara

Our house was thick with the scent of ripe bananas, and insects swarmed around the oozing fecundity. Had the *kiawa* slighted his hosts by asking for more at the end of a generous meal? Or was the display to demonstrate to other Binandere the capacity of our hosts to feed guests a reckless excess? Andrew preferred a sexual explanation. In asking a woman for a banana (a phallus) I had shown my ignorance of metaphor and biology. The thousand bananas celebrated and sustained a joke. That was why the Binandere sometimes slapped their thighs and laughed as they looked on the decaying reminders. Or perhaps there were reasons beyond *kiawa* speculation. One of the first things that a stranger learns is that he is not the centre of events; he is temporary; events matter in the way they change relationships between Binandere.

In 1930 F.E. Williams, the Papuan government anthropologist, wrote of the plays staged by the Orokaiva, a neighbouring Northern Province people. They were, he said, 'valuable as a source of pleasure and amusement, and as an art that is its own reward'. That was an unusual judgement for the time, one likely to bring guffaws of contempt from the white-suited men in Port Moresby's Papua Club. Williams wrote of the dance dramas, but the Binandere also put on impromptu farces. Young men prepare during the day, and in the evening present a play of capering, distorted faces, funny dress and knock-about jokes. Children become so convulsed with laughter they verge on hysteria.

One midday the young men said that they needed a whiteman for the play that they were putting on that night. No, we said, we admired the plays but we had no ability as actors. The whiteman, they assured us, had nothing to say, just sit there. He was a *kiap*, a government field officer; and the Binandere wanted me, I looked right. Sensing their own escape, Chris and Andrew were immediately converted to enthusiasm for the play.

I asked was it certain that the *kiap* was just a prop. Yes, yes. Just sitting. In that case I would be in it. The players conferred. It would be better if I would shout out in English to a Binandere question, 'I don't understand'. I agreed to the one line. The players again went into Binandere pre-production discussion. There was one more thing. The second time I was asked a question I had to shout, 'Have you got a licence?' 'Licence' in this context meant a letter of authority from a government officer. So I was dragged deeper into Binandere farce.

The incident forming the basis for the play was well known to the Binandere. In the early days of Australian control a group of Tabara men, conscripted to carry for a government patrol, were released from duty in the Goilala mountains and told to make their own way home. At Ioma they had to report to the *kiap* and collect rations for the final walk to Tabara. Only one of the Tabara carriers had been away to work on a plantation. He often entertained the villagers with stories of the outside world, and he demonstrated the strange ways of the whitemen by speaking their language and imitating their behaviour. When the tired Tabara carriers reached Ioma he was nominated to tell the *kiap* who they were and what they wanted. But in reality the only foreign words he had picked up on the plantation were isolated commands in English, swear words, and a few disconnected phrases in Police Motu, the lingua franca of the Papuan coast. To the admiration of his fellow Tabara and the complete confusion of the *kiap* he produced his jumbled vocabulary.

Figure 4: The *kiap* play sequence with Hank Nelson in Tabara village.

Source: Frames from *Man Without Pigs*, provided by Ronin Films.

In my role as *kiap* I sat on a patrol box in the *arapa*. A 'cookboy', obsequious to the point of shivering stupidity, kept bringing me cups of tea. The 'carriers' in strange clothes, faces painted in absurd contortions, stumbled into view. Their spokesman was pushed forward and he gave forth a volley of English and Motu. I shouted my first line: 'I do not understand!' The apparently terrified Binandere fell over backwards, the men in front knocking over those behind in a domino fashion. From then on it was ad libbing, random action and general chaos.

15. Pictures at Tabara

The Binandere actors understood all that went on; the audience followed about eighty per cent; and with little warning of the plot and no comprehension of Binandere I understood about ten per cent. At what I thought an appropriate moment I came out with my second line and demanded a licence. Perhaps the timing was right, or perhaps I just added a further element of farce. With just two repeated lines from me the Binandere actors sustained over half an hour of sight gags, lewd asides, political satire and funny walks. The *kiap* was guyed, and so were the yokels and the pretentious of Tabara. The audience loved it.

Our planned entertainment for Tabara was the *asisi wasiride*, literally the moving spirit, the picture show. Nearly all the Tabara had seen pictures, but this was the first picture show in Tabara. To be able to throw pictures on to a sheet draped down the side of a house was logistically complex. We needed to have in the one place at the one time a two-stroke generator, fuel, a projector, and film. The compact Honda generator was also needed to recharge camera batteries so that Chris could keep shooting film. Under civil aviation regulations we could not take fuel on an aircraft that also carried passengers. Before we left Port Moresby Chris had arranged for the Papua New Guinea Office of Information staff – the travelling picture show men – to bring film, projector and fuel by boat along the coast, transfer to a smaller craft and come up the river.

On Thursday evening a man arrived from Manau on the coast. Through interpreters we learned that the Office of Information team had arrived at the coast, but had no outboard-powered dinghy to come up the river. After long discussions with other Tabara men John thought he could persuade them to take six outrigger canoes down to the mouth of the river, walk across to Manau, direct the coastal boat to stand off the Gira, load the canoes at dawn when the surf was down, and battle upstream through the next day. It would be a gruelling trip for the canoemen.

At about ten o'clock that night there was a cry, '*Dinghy gupeira, dinghy gupeira*'. The dinghy was coming. Excited groups hurried to the *papo*. Through the heavy humid air I thought I could hear a distant motor. At times I imagined I heard the sound I knew in another place as the drone of a tractor working through the night, the farmer desperate to sow while moisture still darkened his Mallee paddock. The sound faded and we began walking back. High cloud covered the sky, but the near full moon gave just enough light to walk without torch or lantern. Only a patch of bamboo was absolutely black.

Again there was the cry of 'dinghy, dinghy'. We went back to the *papo*, and now the sound of an engine revving and dying was clear. Suddenly we saw a torch flashing, the outline of a boat and the white churn of the wake. Keeping in the deep water close to the far bank, the dinghy drew level with the *papo*. The villagers on the bank were calling out, and we picked up occasional comments translated into English. 'It's not our boat'. But the engine slowed and it turned towards the *papo*. 'They haven't got the pictures'. Then the torches on shore picked up the shine of metal film cans lying among the cargo. Like victorious warriors home from battle we carried stores, projector and film into the village. The women already had mugs of tea and bowls of food ready.

While the boatmen ate on our platform, Tabara men and women drummed, danced and sang. One woman left the dancers, warmed a drumhead on the fire, tested it with palm and finger taps, and returned to the dance.

John spoke quietly of the tenacity of the small boy and six men on the dinghy who kept driving their boat upstream with just a handheld torch to give them warning of rocks and timber. The Office of Information men said that they wanted to show the films immediately. They had a sea-going boat waiting near the mouth of the Gira and had to meet it the next day. No-one seemed surprised at the idea of starting a picture show close to midnight, but John pointed out that people in nearby villages were expecting to see the films and they would be unable to come to a sudden showing. The travelling picture show men agreed to leave their equipment with us.

The Office of Information men and the boat's crew were up before dawn, and left at first light. Early on that same Friday afternoon we discovered that they had taken all the petrol with them. We could neither show films nor recharge batteries. But, we were told, another dinghy was coming on Monday and it was carrying a forty-four gallon drum of *bensin*, petrol.

A saga of confusion over the petrol had begun. For me the confusion was increased because I was never sure of the source of the many conflicting messages, and I did not know whether others were hearing the same contradictions.

The second dinghy came the next day, Saturday. The boatmen had no forty-four gallon drum, and, they said, only enough *bensin* to get back to Manau. At Manau they would store the dinghy until at some unknown time a coastal boat would drop off fuel. The nearest government station, Ioma, we were told, had no petrol. We wondered whether it was worth paying about $300 for a charter aircraft to bring fuel to Dodoima. But a runner would take a day to reach Ioma and we were uncertain of the speed and accuracy of any response.

Someone remembered the mower at Dodoima. If there was an engine, there was *bensin*. But, no, for many months bent backs, sweat and swinging grass knives had cut all the cursed *kiawa* grass on the airstrip.

We were then told about driftwood *bensin*. A forty-four gallon drum had been washed away in a flood and found stranded in a creek by some villagers living upstream from Tabara. When the owner claimed the petrol, the villagers said he could have it after he paid them compensation. The owner had no money, and the finders kept the drum. The dinghy men left by canoe to see if they could buy the come-by-chance *bensin*. They were back the next day: the villagers did have a drum, but it was small and it only had enough petrol in it to cover the first joint of one finger. They left drum and *bensin* where it was.

As we sat on the house platform in desultory conversation, the boatmen speaking Binandere and us English, John in one of his comments that linked the two groups told us that there was some spare fuel on the dinghy. One of the boatmen, John and I went down to the *papo* and collected two plastic containers of oil, an auxiliary tank from the outboard and another four gallon drum of petrol. We could run the two-stroke generator to charge batteries and for several hours of films.

Had the boatmen given us the fuel that they needed to get back to Manau? Would they now have to drift and pole downstream, leave the dinghy on the river and walk across to Manau? Later when I gave one of the boatmen antibiotics for a tropical ulcer on his leg I tried to question him closely and casually. He said they still had enough *bensin* to get to Manau.

Placed in sequence and isolated from other events the story of the petrol has a step by step clarity. Even the contradictions are precise; the dinghy would come on Monday and it arrived on Saturday. But at the time I often heard half statements, searched for another person likely to be better informed, and asked for someone to interpret. And all the time other things were happening that were of immediate interest. The sago palm was cut, the sago pulverised, washed and carried in an old canoe hull into the village; the rehearsals for the *ario*, the dance drama, went on in the bush; visiting village groups arrived; prolonged discussions took place on the distribution of pig meat and other commodities; and there were emotional accusations and counter accusations of sorcerers being paid to impede the ceremonies.

Our pursuit of the *bensin* told us most of all that we were outsiders. The petrol actually existed, and our need for it could be explained easily. We could ask simple direct questions. But if we struggled to find out about petrol, then what chance did we have of learning about the non-material? We could observe and record, but it was doubtful whether we could find out what it all meant to those directing and taking part in events. As on other occasions when I have been fascinated by what I could see and bemused by village talk, I wondered about all those travellers and anthropologists who write crisp certainties with no admissions of bewilderment.

We showed the *asisi wasiride* over three nights. People walked for several hours or came by canoe, they ate with those linked to them by kin or some historical debt, and joined various groups on woven mats in the *arapa*. Soon small fires glowed at the front edge of several mats. Smoke drifted through the projector beam. Young men stood at the back where they could hear almost nothing of the sound-track above the hammering of the generator engine. Dogs and pigs scavenged cautiously for discarded food at the edge of the crowd of about 400 people. Late in the night children slept in positions of contented exhaustion.

Among the films we showed were a documentary by Chris on the Gogodala people of the Western Province of Papua New Guinea, his Pidgin language feature, 'Tukana', shot on Bougainville, and a documentary, 'Angels of War', made by Andrew Pike, Gavan Daws and me. 'Angels of War' includes scenes in which John interviews Orokaiva and Binandere ex-serviceman, so the Tabara saw one of the few films in which their own language is used.

During the films the Tabara talked among themselves, and directed occasional comments at the screen. They were quick to comment on the way other villagers carried out everyday tasks and behaved towards each other. In 'Tukana' the Tabara applauded quietly when the wicked suffered, and they were quick to express their consternation when young men and women scorned their parents. This was an immorality so extreme that the Tabara could not look at it dispassionately. To countenance such behaviour was to accept the destruction of Tabara. All in the audience knew that the towns with other values beckoned the Binandere young. In 'Angels of War' there is a scene where an Australian kicks a surrendered Japanese soldier. Australian audiences are embarrassed by the incident; the Binandere approved of Australian violence.

When people gathered in the village in the evening the sounds most likely to rise above the general noise were the cries of greeting and bursts of laughter. But as the egalitarian and competitive Binandere prepared to celebrate John's doctorate there was tension about contributions in work and kind, who would be hosts, and who would be artists and entrepreneurs. The prominence of one man or clan was detrimental to others. All acts to advantage or disadvantage someone would eventually be repaid. When clan leaders discussed plans in the evening, or when the dance leader denounced the men who could not reproduce the movements of the hornbill, men shouted, and a disruptive brawl always seemed possible. John's immediate family were the book-keepers of intricate village balances. They met in frequent low-voiced conferences to calculate the debts paid and incurred. Some older clan leaders might have been offering aid which they hoped that John could not repay immediately. Then they would have the right to call on him to act for them in Port Moresby in that alien culture of cash, forms to be filled in, and government patronage.

15. Pictures at Tabara

Figure 5: Dr John Waiko with his mother in Tabara village at the time of filming *Man Without Pigs*.

Source: Image provided by Ronin Films.

Before 9 o'clock on the morning of the first of two days of festivity people began collecting at a clearing about the size of a small cricket ground. It was like show day in a country town. Families carrying net-bags of food and green coconuts took up positions against the boundary vine. There was much shaking of hands as groups met, and constant chopping. Nearly all men and many women carried bush knives or tomahawks. They cut leaves to sit on and to drape on heads and shoulders. By midday some had cut poles and vines and built shade houses; and the bush that usually pressed against the clearing was hacked into retreat.

The young men, the farceurs, acted out a story familiar to the Binandere about a crying baby. Their appearance in bulbous masks and bodies covered in black and grey clay was more elaborate than in the impromptu evening capers. Women danced in pairs. They were without drums, but kept the beat with their feet and pounded the ground with the flattened ends of ginger stalks.

The main troupe of *ario* dancers entered the arena, and pairs of men and women came in from four different points. The dancing ground was a swirling mass of colour. Red earth dye mixed with the beaten bark of the *simani* and the intensely bright yellow of the scraped root of the *nonda* were everywhere shimmering and flouncing in layers of fibre draped from shoulders to ankles. All the men wore full headdresses with small feathers at the front through to the bird of paradise plumes at the back. White shell and dog-tooth ornaments were hung on chests and held in the mouth. Red-brown tapa cloth hung from waist bands. All men carried hand drums. Palm frond screens were shifted from the centre of the arena to reveal five-metre high carved poles supporting a stepped ramp leading to a platform above the height of the headdresses. A man and then a woman danced on the platform and displayed the *yavetu*, the bone of the dance, the motif, a baby-sized wooden figure carved secretly by Reginald Oveva, an artist from a neighbouring village. Bodies glistened with sweat. An old man dropped out, short of wind, he said. Women arrived with metal boilers of water and handed enamel mugs to the dancers. Old women sang a lament for those who had once danced in splendour but were now dead. Other women danced at the side of sons new to the *ario*. A dome, representing a cave, suddenly raced across the arena. There were people crouched inside giving the dome an eerie mobility. It was a dramatic coup. The hornbill dance, the sago dance and the wallaby dance were completed, and the Binandere had acted out legends defining where they came from and who they were. We left the dancing ground with its trampled grass, slashed branches already wilting, and litter of peel and husks. Back in the village we sat on the house platforms, ate and talked.

The next day the pigs to be killed were paraded shoulder high around the *arapa*. Still with front and rear legs tied to poles, the pigs were lined up along the *dapamo*, a tree trunk fixed horizontally about half a metre above the ground. John, dressed in The Australian National University doctoral robes, emerged from a house. People expressed quiet admiration for the blue-and-black gown. Perhaps they guessed that this was the dress of declamation rather than dance. Escorted by men in headdresses and tapa cloth, John led a procession around the *arapa*. Suddenly there were shouts in the crowd, a thud as a round-house right connected, and a club arced through the air. Someone blew a whistle, men and women rushed forward, and the hotheads were pushed apart. The Binandere share the paradox of other cultures: warriors are heroes and the peace-makers are blessed. At the height of the melee John said calmly, 'Think of this in the School of Music', the scene of his Canberra graduation. He then spoke to restrain his wildest supporters.

The flare of violence died quickly. The young men of Tabara had clashed with those from another village. Someone had stood up, the young men at the back had shouted for them to sit, there were comments, then insults and a fight. In another country the beer would have been blamed; but in Tabara there was no beer, no trade store and almost no exchanges involving cash. The fight was another incident in a long-lasting rivalry between the two villages.

15. Pictures at Tabara

Figure 6: The graduation ceremony in Tabara.

Source: Frames from *Man Without Pigs*, provided by Ronin Films.

The procession moved on. John climbed a low platform especially built in the *arapa*. He addressed the people who remained close to their houses and shade. Nicodemus Kove, one of John's first teachers, spoke, and I tried to say what John had achieved in a foreign education system. I began, 'Ladies and gentlemen of Tabara *edo nasi berari de. Ositeraria butu da ainda …*' I had written a paragraph and John had translated it for me to read. I continued in English and John turned the talk. Women put shade leaves and cooling water over pigs they had just fed, pigs that were known by name and were accustomed to lie close to the family mat in the evening. Other Binandere men spoke, then John walked the *dapamo* log to nominate those to receive pigs.

In the evening the young people began their 'disco'. A string band played all night. The lead singer, a young boy, knelt to project his voice into the microphone of the one guitar hooked to a battery-operated speaker in a radio. Most of the songs were in Binandere, adaptations of those played by the string bands of the Papua New Guinea towns. On the first day of celebrations the old arts of Tabara had been displayed on the dance ground; on the second day John in his doctoral robes had inserted a glimpse of another culture into the village; and the night of the second day belonged to the *gita*, the instrument that was changing church, funeral and dance music on the Gira.

We left at dawn the next day and walked through flood waters to Dodoima. Our weather was clear, but storms in the ranges had sent a mass of swirling mud-coloured water down the river. We no longer had to worry about the log bridges; they had disappeared, and we swam in warm, opaque water. Our guide, Dudley, was a tall young Binandere of about fourteen. His English was the most fluent of those who were educated in the area and stayed there. At school he had been consistently around the top of his grade, but when the final primary school exam was held he was fourth, and only three Gira pupils were given places in the high school at Popondetta. John, in one of the services he could provide for his people, was trying to find a school that would take Dudley. At one creek Dudley made real what I had presumed was old *masta* folklore. He waded into the water, took a deep breath, held a bag of our gear at arm's length over his head, and kept walking. He had calculated correctly. The water rose to his wrists only, and he made the crossing in one breath.

Figure 7: Hank Nelson in a flash flood on the Gira River, Oro Province.

Source: Image provided by Ronin Films.

As the water on flat parts of the track rose above waist level we wondered what was happening to the carriers who were following. The film, in taped cans, would survive immersion, but the sound tapes had little protection. We joked about reviving the silent documentary, the film in which you learnt to appreciate Binandere music by looking at it. But as we rested on a rise at Peio village, John and the carriers came yodelling and splashing through the flood. When the Gira rose they had cut timber, made rafts and floated the cargo. All the tapes were dry. We missed our charter flight. It roared overhead as we waded beneath a thick forest canopy. We could neither wave nor hurry.

By the time we reached Dodoima the Gira was almost contained within its banks, but its surface was still riled and heaving, it roared like surf, and mud-stained foam hung on snags. The fall of the river was sharper here, and stones rolled in the stream. There were no more Binandere villages higher up the Gira. As we stood on the flood-washed bank looking at the river a man on a black motor tube swept into view. He went with such speed, the tube seemed to be skipping across the surface. Far out in the stream, he could not join a shouted exchange. He waved a relaxed arm and was gone. We could not ask whether he had long planned this day, how and why he got his tube to the Gira, did he have business down-stream, or was he a great opportunist. For us he was the man who took the flood, became the fastest man on the Gira, and for an instant gave us a share in his exhilaration. At the airstrip I wrote a note in case the pilot came back. It said we were in Usi village, just ten minutes' walk downstream. For a moment I thought about carving DIG into a soft-trunked tree, but decided that the Australian pilot might not have been instructed in the same repetitive explorer history as my generation. And nothing could have been more alien to Burke and Wills than the Gira and the rain forests where men became hornbills and danced in swirls of colour. I cut a stick and used it to pin the note to the split palm shed housing the no-*bensin* Scott Bonnar.

The charter picked us up two days later.

NOTES

Dr John Waiko obtained his Ph.D. in the Department of Pacific and Southeast Asian History at The Australian National University. As one of his supervisors I was invited to attend a celebration in his home village. I am grateful to John and the people of Tabara for their courtesy and generosity. Andrew Pike and Chris Owen were initiated as friends of John and as film makers. In various writings John has recorded much of the history of the Binandere people. I am grateful to John, Andrew and Chris for reading a draft of this article.

16. Minimay: One of 6,000 Weatherboard Schools

Australian Cultural History 7 (1988), pp. 5–17.

At the western end of the Grampians in Victoria the slopes push the streams in many directions. The creeks feeding the Wimmera River flow north, Mosquito Creek drains intermittently into the lagoons of southeastern South Australia, and the Glenelg curves south. It alone has its secure route to the Southern Ocean. The watershed northwest in wet years spreads through chains of creeks, swamps and lakes: Lake Winter, Lake Charlegrark, Booroopki Swamp and Warm Swamp; and Neuarpurr, Minimay and Tooroot Swamps. The fall on the land is so slight that often it is only the height of the water itself that forces the frontier of the flood further north. Swamps and creeks disappear at the southern edge of the Little Desert.

In the early 1880s selectors were taking up 320-acre blocks in the Booroopki and Minimay area. They struggled to clear land so they could scratch in a few acres of hand-scattered crop; they extended their brush and dog-leg fences, and converted bough sheds into mud-plastered stringybark huts; and they went without to pay their debts to the storekeepers and the Lands Department. Most selectors were determined self-improvers. And they wanted schools for their children. As a group the selectors petitioned, and separately they wrote to their MPs and the Minister for Public Instruction. On 1 May 1882 Andrew McLaughlin listed nine Minimay families with a total of twenty-five children of school age. Chas Harris wrote five months later:

> *As the selectors of the parish of Minimay is badly situated with regards of a School We do humbly ask of you to try and see if we can get a school erected here for it is much needed there is between 20 or 30 children here growing up in ignorance.*

William McBean, a former teacher, said he was ready to take time from working his selection to open a school, but he was too poor to do so without more help than his struggling neighbours could give.

John Neilson, who had taken up a block north of Minimay Swamp, confirmed that the selectors could 'muster at least twenty (20) children'. Neilson had not then been to school himself, and the hand that pushed the pen was more accustomed to grasping an axe handle; but his sentences were clear and confident. The selectors used terms of gentility and formality as they 'begged respectfully' for attention; but at a time when few children in the world were educated by the state, they did not doubt that they had the right to ask the government to give them a school. The government agreed that the selectors' case was sound, and said that something would be done when funds were not so tight.

In 1883 the government reserved five acres for a school on the northwest edge of Minimay Swamp. A year later when a public works officer inspected the site he reported that this was one case where the surveyors had done what they were often accused of doing: they had chosen 'the worst site they could find'. There was no house in sight, not even a fence, the land was low-lying, and it was cratered and warped with crab-holes. Workmen, trying to unload a portable school from a bullock wagon, had to take their boots off and wade through water. They cut timber to keep the dismantled school above flood level. The Minimay parents petitioned the Minister to shift the school to a new site on a dry bank half a mile to the east. In the face of the righteous indignation of the selectors, the district school inspector wondered why local people had not previously pointed out that the site was unusable for half the year. He agreed that the school, one classroom and two small rooms for the teacher's quarters, be erected at the new site.

When the selectors first asked for a school they were uncertain what name it should be given. For a while they assumed that their school would be Lemon Springs, but in 1885 the Education Department designated the new building, Minimay School No.2600. The next year another school about six miles to the east was given the name, Lemon Springs. Soon there was a Minimay store and wine bar, a post office and a sportsground. The schools were important in defining communities, and fixing their centres.

Minimay had a building, but no teacher. John Neilson, who had already written twice to point out that there were 'a number of children here that [would] soon be beyond school age', wrote again to ask why there was no teacher. He was right to worry; the nine-year-olds had turned fourteen between the time the selectors made their first request, and the opening of the school.

After several teachers refused appointment to Minimay, the Education Department sent nineteen-year-old Norman McLeod to open the school. McLeod had not been to teachers' college, but he had served four years as a student teacher at Beaufort in western Victoria. He arrived by coach at Minimay on 6 May 1885 and opened the school; and he began work without 'the necessary furniture' of a blackboard and a teacher's desk. McLeod left Minimay three months later suffering, the examining doctor said, from pains in the chest and general debility 'brought on by work and want of proper food'. The school stayed shut, and the children were left to work or roam.

Again the selectors wrote their letters of complaint: 'the children [were] going back daily'. A relieving teacher, James Groutsch, arrived after a month, stayed two months, and was replaced by Donald Schultz. Within a few weeks of the start of 1886 Schultz was posted to Tallengower. Groutsch hired a buggy at Department expense and came back briefly until Margaret Brennan took over. But Brennan, home with her mother over Christmas, died suddenly; she had no will and no assets but for the few pounds still owing from her annual salary of $128 plus results. The staff changes continued. Groutsch made a third brief appearance before the children of Minimay. In the first three months of the school's existence the relieving teacher spent more time in the Minimay classroom than any of the other seven head teachers.

The Minimay parents, sick of the traffic in head teachers, held a meeting and E. Jelbart wrote to the Secretary of the Education Department saying that they wanted a permanent male teacher. The Department, constricted by its own regulations, continued to appoint according to the staff lists, and its instructions to teachers to go to Minimay 'without delay' were met with letters of anguish and inventiveness. Annie Forbes said she had made careful enquiries and had learnt on reliable authority that the school was near a tract of swamp. She was sure 'were I to go there, that my health would break down in a very short time … owing to the constitutional weakness of the chest and throat'. Also, she wrote, she was supporting her aged mother. W.B. Newton, already serving in the Mallee, said that his health was 'undermined by want of a proper diet' and as he was trying to do further study he 'would like somewhere nearer civilization'. Miss S. Halligan wrote from her isolated school at the mining town of Walhalla in Gippsland:

> *I beg most respectfully to point out that the school is situated in a most extremely wild and remote district, and my friends contest it is utterly unfit for the residence of an unmarried female who would have to live entirely alone.*

The Department accepted the pleading of most of its teachers: few suffered any penalty on the promotions list.

Miss Mary Dennis, certain that she would suffer 'hysteria' from loneliness in such a distant part of the colony, made an extra plea for sympathy by pointing out that she was an orphan. When Jelbart wrote her a soothing letter about Minimay and told her of the 'respectable family' with whom she could board, Dennis wrote to ask the Department if the offer was still open. The fact that she was an orphan then became a reason why she was 'eager to get on'. She took up duty at Minimay on 24 October 1887 and left at the end of the year.

Miss Isabella Strachan applied to be sent to the Minimay area; but soon after she complained about the place and her lodgings. Rose Jelbart, who had taken Strachan into her home, suppressed her hurt, and made a strong reply. It was true, Mrs Jelbart wrote, that Miss Strachan had to share a room with a girl paid to work in the house, but she was 'treated more like a daughter than a servant. I would not think', Mrs Jelbart said, 'of putting anyone in a room with a lady teacher that was not thoroughly respectable and *very well behaved*'. If Miss Strachan insisted, then Mrs Jelbart would at great inconvenience remove her own sister from her room and give that to Miss Strachan, 'for our school is our great anxiety, and we always try to make teachers comfortable'. Mrs Jelbart ended her defence of her hospitality: 'The best way I can put it is – we make them one of our family'. It was not enough: Miss Strachan did not complete the year at Minimay.

In February 1889 Miss Sarah Bradley arrived to take over the school. The first teacher willing and able to stay more than twelve months, Miss Bradley was not to retire from the Education Department for another forty years. But in the two winters she taught at Minimay the floods came north, seeping, wind-blown and sometimes rushing into low land. Attendance dropped. In June 1890 the average attendance was seven, it was six in July, and five in August. Even in November there were still two families cut off from the school by swamps. The Department reduced the status of the school to 'temporary' and therefore Miss Bradley had to shift.

No teacher arrived at the start of 1891 and the parents renewed their protest against neglect. Then Edward Hayes arrived, he won the support of the community, the swamps dried, and the enrolment went to over twenty. The Department instructed Hayes to be ready to shift as the school was to be re-classified and he was not qualified to hold his position in a larger school. One group of parents objected: they were, they said, 'most unwilling to lose our teacher'. But other parents wanted their school returned to its old level; they thought that would be to their advantage in the long run. The school was re-classified, Hayes left, and numbers fell again. When the inspector arrived in mid-1893 there were only four children present, and the teacher thought that the monthly average would be only three. Minimay closed in September 1893. The parents enlisted the aid of a member of parliament, and Minimay was resurrected in 1894 as a half-time school with Lemon Springs. The teacher taught three days at Lemon Springs and two at Minimay. In 1901 Minimay again became a full-time school. It continued until 1951 when it was transported once, and the children daily, to become part of Goroke Consolidated School.

Besides the basic problem of getting both a teacher and enough pupils together in the one room, there were other and briefer disruptions to education in Minimay. Dependent on the one teacher, the school was always vulnerable to the vagaries of personal illness or family bereavement or any other of the random impediments likely to afflict someone trying to do a job. James Groutsch arrived by coach from Horsham on 20 January 1887, he opened the school, but no children came because they did not know that a teacher had turned up. Sarah Bradley missed a day in June 1889 because she lost the school key. The Department reluctantly accepted her explanation, and told her to be more careful in future. A Department officer also reprimanded Groutsch when he stayed home on a day of constant rain: wet weather and impassable roads were 'not sufficient reason for not opening the school'. Groutsch missed another day when he went to Goroke to celebrate Empire Day, broke a buggy pole on the way back, and could not reach Minimay in time for school the next day. Bradley's horse fell with her on the way to school; and the Department accepted her absence without comment.

The school's tin chimney with its lean to the east sometimes drew smoke upwards, and sometimes rolled it back into the classroom. The children escaped into the yard, dried their eyes, the teacher put the fire out, and the children eventually went back to a room that was 'horribly cold and cheerless'. The Departmental officer in Melbourne noted that as it was already August, the worst of the winter was over, and the repairs could wait. Early the next year the chimney was altered, but smoke still billowed into the classroom, and children were absent with sore eyes and colds.

The 1887 school year began with the children from six families gasping and racking with whooping cough. On some days no one went to school. At least it was not diphtheria. If the 'dip' struck a small school the teacher might have to write 'deceased' two, three or even four times in the right hand column of the Pupils' Register. When the school re-assembled a fifth of the spaces at the long forms could be empty.

The history of the Minimay school has much in common with other bush schools built on corners reserved from the lands of cockies and blockies. The small farmers, storekeepers and the local government officers such as policemen persisted until the Education Department agreed to provide a building; distant officials despatched blackboards, desks and 'notes of moral lessons', alphabet cards and a manual of drill; and a young man or woman arrived, reluctant, apprehensive or enthusiastic, to teach. Unlike a church the school belonged to everyone. Unlike a post office or a railway station which also provided a service, the school was taking some members of the community and trying to influence what they knew, what they did, and what they could become. Like Minimay, other schools of the area that started in the 1880s – Booroopki, Bringalbert North, Neuarpurr and Lemon Springs – were all at some time closed or reduced to half-time. The schools suffered when drought, floods or bad prices forced selectors off their blocks; and they suffered from the random effects of family sizes and teacher competence and stability. As in other early rural schools many children at Minimay were old for their grade. In 1890 one fourteen-year-old was in grade four. In grade three the children varied in age from eight to twelve.

Minimay was different from the other schools because of one pupil who went there. When John Neilson wrote repeatedly on behalf of those children passing from days of play to a lifetime of work before the district had a school, one child he had in mind was his own son, John Shaw Neilson. Before the Neilsons left Penola in South Australia and drove their wagon and cattle to the selection pegged at Minimay, Shaw Neilson had gone to school for about fifteen months in 1880 and 1881. He was just over thirteen when the school opened at Minimay, and by the time he left the next year he had watched at least three teachers – and Jas. Groutsch on a second stint – stand at the blackboard and easel in the narrow classroom, the sun a shaft of yellow air in the small north window. The only reading books in the school in Neilson's time were Thomas Nelson's Royal Readers; and perhaps just before he left there were three geography books, and wall maps of the World, Australasia and Victoria to be gazed at by the curious or dreamy or indolent. Shaw Neilson was remembered by one of the younger boys at Minimay as 'quiet ... spare and tough with that haggard look common among "grafting" bush boys'. He was a boy of no 'outstanding characteristics'; just another country kid in 'clodhopper boots', broad hat and pants at half-mast. He is known now by other Australians as one of the nation's finest poets, the singer of delicate songs. He began writing verse the same year that he left school.

Neilson, so sensitive to the music in words and to colour, could have taken little from the Minimay school. Groutsch who taught him for the longest was asked by the Department why he taught no singing or drawing. He explained simply: 'I am not skilled in drawing, and have no voice for singing'. The Royal Readers, dense volumes of over three hundred pages, provided the rhetoric and sentiment of empire: the Great Siege of Gibraltar, the Battle of Trafalgar and the Death of Nelson, the Balaclava Charge, and the Relief of Lucknow. But the Readers did contain the best known poems of Browning, Byron, Goldsmith, Scott, Shelley, Tennyson and Wordsworth.

Neilson's lack of schooling narrowed his art. He admitted: 'When a critic says ... that I have a very limited range of words, he is not far from the truth'. And sometimes his bush pronunciation led him into faulty rhythms. His evening became 'even-ing', and remembrance became 'remember-ance'. He accepted correction quietly. He was not a man of anger or excuses.

Most of Shaw Neilson's education was at home. His cheerful father, whose life was endless hard work and a cycle of debt and foreclosure, wrote verse and treasured his few books. He knew Adam Lindsay Gordon by sight, and his poetry in detail. Shaw Neilson's mother taught a 'hard, hard religion' of a God whose blue rage was always about to fall on the unwary. She cooked no meals on Sunday and left the cows to bellow as their udders swelled and milk oozed from their teats. But it was to his mother that he took his first verses. In 1889 the Neilson family, the parents and Shaw, the oldest of five children, crossed floods and the Little Desert to take up a rented farm four miles out of Nhill. It was a continuation of what was to be another thirty years of failed farms, contracting for bush jobs, and wage labour.

Late in life Shaw Neilson said that his poems came pressing into his head 'too thickly, like a lot of cabbages in a bed'. Another time he said they were like 'puppies all pushing and battling for their mother's teats'. Neilson lost many poems and part-poems; they were jostled from his mind by other ideas and rhythms before he could fix them in writing. He wrote his first published poems at fifteen or sixteen, before he left Minimay, and in his later poetry returned again and again to that land of red gum, stringybark, she-oak, creek and floodway. Minimay gave him his images of both wealth and poverty. He built his ideal land from fragments of good times and good years. It was a place where: 'The lakes shall be many and gentle'. A time when:

The oats they were over the fences, and seven feet high!

Our own little creek, it was flooded a dozen times over;

And water-birds came without warning to blacken the sky.

Neilson's good land was rich with wild honey and birds: cranes, plovers, wrens, mallee fowl, native companions and the smoker parrot with 'Moonlight and sunrise' running on its wing and 'Lightning and sundown, every joy in yellow' in its coat.

The 'poor, poor country' was there too. It was where 'the thin wheat and the brown oats were never two feet high'. It was where:

The land is all buckshot and sorrow,

It cries like a prayer;

The rubble it writes in the cutting-grass;

Famine is there.

When he wrote those lines he had in mind, he said, the iron-stone gravel country south of Minimay, patterned with stones forced up by the roots of the sword grass. In the poor country Neilson, the gentle dreamer, saw people made hard: 'Men with their dreams burning out' and 'wasting worn-out women too,

Praying for death ...' Women who saw their children die, as Neilson's mother saw one of her sons die, turned in their anger and said that the 'God of love' was 'A foe to me and mine'.

Neilson was a 'homemade instrument'. His delicate craft owed most to his own abilities, the harsh and beautiful lands where he lived, and to his family, rather than to the weatherboard school. The succession of teachers that passed through Minimay probably had little idea of the talent being nurtured in thin, silent Shaw Neilson. But all teachers in one-teacher schools faced the possibility that on their own they might have to tend a talent able to speak to a world scarcely glimpsed in Royal Readers or on wall maps.

Other places, distinguished by a particular teacher or pupil, provide an equally good opening to an investigation of bush schools. In 1878 a nineteen-year-old Englishman was 'flung into the wide sea of Australian bush' to teach at the half-time schools of Sparkes Creek and Junction Creek in the Liverpool Range west of Scone in NSW. His name was Havelock Ellis. Later he was to write that 1878 was the 'loneliest, the most isolated' year of his life. It was also, he said, 'the most seminal and even the most ideal', 'the most fateful, the most decisive', 'that wonderful year', and 'the most eventful of my life'. In 1878 Ellis began writing serious prose, decided to study to be a doctor, 'gained health of body' and resolved the discord in his scientific and spiritual response to the world around him. Back in England and with his reputation established as one of the learned men in the arts and sciences, Ellis kept a photograph of Sparkes Creek beside his bed. Some of the teachers who stayed in the bush, starved of intellectual stimulation and tempted by farmers' nubile daughters, may have thought they knew why Havelock Ellis devoted so much of his life to writing his seven-volume *Studies in the Psychology of Sex*.

Bulby Brush public school on Bunya Creek in northern NSW was opened in 1920. All of the twenty-two families with children at the school were dairy farmers; two were share farmers and the rest were on their own or rented blocks. Bulby Brush was Standard Plan No 3; an eighteen-foot weatherboard square with big windows on the south, a verandah on the north and west, a tank stand on the shady southwest corner, and steps leading to the western verandah and the tiny 'hat room'. The interior was crowded with eight desks, each able to take four pupils. In 1935 Inspector D. Hayes said that a 'competent teacher' ought to be able to find 'satisfactory' accommodation for forty-five children. But in the following year the Department extended the school by seven feet and put in four more desks. Les Murray, born in 1938, went to Bulby Brush Standard Plan No 3 plus seven, and he saw it again as it is, and as he remembered it, when he drove to the nearby town of Gloucester:

> *... the pines round my one-teacher school*

With its zigzag air raid trench and morning flagpole;

From there I remember birthdays, and how to shin

Fast over fence rails: You're last! – I'll be first in Heaven!

At Pioneer in northeast Tasmania the rough board school with its shingle roof and ramshackle chimney was held nearly upright by poles bracing the walls. In 1906 the teacher was Joseph Lyons. Trained under the monitor system, he was soon to be one of the first teachers to enter the Hobart teachers' college. Lyons was to become premier of Tasmania in 1923 and prime minister of Australia in 1931. In the mid-1920s John Tonkin was the teacher at Group Settlement No. 6 in the extreme southwest of Western Australia. Big timber towered over the corrugated iron roof and in winter water lapped at the stumps of the school and the tank stand. John Tonkin became premier of his state in 1971. In Gippsland, Victoria, at the Tarraville school, easily mistaken for a church with its brick walls, high ceiling and vestry entry, Ada Crossley did her lessons. But it was her singing which took her to Melbourne, then overseas, and to command performances before her Queen. Her voice had an extraordinary purity and 'the luscious richness of a Carlsbad plum'.

In 1914 the Commonwealth Government asked the South Australian Education Department to supply a teacher to open the first government school in Alice Springs. A Commonwealth official wrote on the file: it was 'no place for an unprotected young woman'. The South Australian Department appointed Mrs Ida Standley. She went north by train to Oodnadatta, and the police were given the task of escorting her over the 600-kilometre track to Alice Springs. She retired as teacher to the white children and teacher and matron to the mixed-race children fifteen years later at age sixty. She is one of the few, perhaps only, bush school mistress to have her name on the map of Australia: Standley Chasm in the MacDonnell Ranges is named after her.

It is no surprise that distinguished Australians learnt and taught in the rural schools. After all, when the one-teacher schools were at their most numerous in the 1930s there were over 6000 of them. Over half were in New South Wales and Victoria and there were four in the Northern Territory. Assuming an average enrolment of twenty, then over 120,000 Australians were in one-teacher schools.

Small rural schools were common elsewhere in the world. What made the Australian system different was that the schools were part of highly centralized systems, the state met nearly all costs, in any one year some of the best young teachers were posted to distant country schools, and the number of children needed before the government provided a school was low. In South Australia just six children were enough to keep a school open. In the berry and apple growing valleys of Tasmania there was a school every four miles or so, and children walked to school.

A study of one-teacher schools opens many tracks into Australian history. The teachers can be seen as coming out of one community or sub-culture, going to an institution and then travelling to another community with the specific task of training the young. Under the pupil-teacher or monitor systems some teachers may not have been to any training college. Unlike teachers at large schools who had numerous colleagues and could select a particular group to mix with after school, the bush schoolies were in direct and constant contact with the community they served. A young woman who went into a dairying district in the 1930s might well be trapped in that community. Her board would be provided by a family tied to seven days a week of hard work. The only time members of the family could get away from the farm was in the middle of the day. The teacher might go for over a month before she could get to a bank and cash a cheque. Even the bicycle, the young teacher's means to independence, was of little value on wet hills and roads of black mud cut hock-deep at cattle crossings.

Seen as the setting for thousands of rural schools, Australian geography and social history become diverse. All teachers in training were aware of the dramatic differences between the suburbs of Brisbane and the islands of Torres Strait, or between an Italian cane-growing community near Tully and a centre on the Darling Downs dominated by the descendants of German settlers, or between the Huon Valley and the Bass Strait Islands. And practising teachers were quickly aware of other differences: the style and frequency of entertainment varied, expectations about the school differed, and the sense of cohesion and easy familiarity within communities changed markedly from one district to another. Teachers in their writings and memories are able to comment on many ordinary homes with the hessian walls recently whitewashed, and the wash basin carefully placed for the visitor; and they are able to say a lot about the communities that came together at the school Christmas concert.

At some schools all children came from similar homes. Out of the first sixty entries on the pupils' register for Minimay school kept from 1904 all parents are listed as farmers except three: a grazier, a farmer and grazier, and one home duties. But at Wee Jasper in the 1930s the list of occupations covered the full range of rural occupations: grazier, station manager, boundary rider, policeman, storekeeper, teacher, dingo trapper, road worker and simply 'dole'. All the children from those diverse homes met in the one small classroom, were taught by the same teacher and played under the giant gums on the bank of the Goodradigbee. How they acted towards each other, and what that schooling in common did to them should tell us much about wealth, behaviour and attitudes in Australia.

Some women recall their bush school with delight: the one time in their lives of uncomplicated equality between the sexes. Others have less glowing memories. Several have said that in the playground the boys dominated. The biggest boys decided what game they would play and whether or not the rest of the school was needed. If the boys wanted to have a football match, one woman recalls, then it would be her job to be boundary umpire. She was not, however, allowed to say when the ball crossed the line. That was a decision for the boys who were playing. Her task was merely to retrieve the ball when told. With small numbers, the character of a school could change quickly. Cliff Green says that at one stage at Wilton all the older children were girls and they ran an efficient matriarchy.

The various education departments provided an incidental gene exchange. Men took wives from rural districts and young women married into the communities where they taught. From 1926 until the neighbouring schools at Kapinnie and Brimpton Lakes on the Eyre Peninsula of South Australia closed, eight women teachers married and settled in the area, and two women left as teachers' wives. Throughout Australia women ex-teachers became presidents and secretaries of the CWA and the hospital auxiliary; and their children were likely to go on to higher education.

The woman teacher fresh from the city was assessed by all the single young men; and with different intent and equal intensity she was inspected by the young girls sitting in the desks. The teacher's clothes, manners and her escape in the holidays to distant places made her much more like the women of the magazines. There was an unfair comparison with the mums who did the milking in bran bag aprons. The teachers by their very appearance beckoned bright and ambitious girls; and the school and a scholarship was one means to escape the narrow life on the farm. Shaw Neilson's sister, Maggie, took a job as part-time sewing mistress, and tried desperately to become a teacher by correspondence studies. Her nervous intensity drained away her cleverness, and she failed.

In 1910 W.H. Smith BA (Lond), the inspector for southwest Queensland, travelled over 11,000 miles by train, coach, buggy, sulky and motor car to visit all but two of the 115 schools in his district. Just the physical problems of surveillance in a centralized system covering such vast areas were immense. The inspectors' reports, with their comments on the trivial and the fundamental, are records of what mattered to the senior men and the centres of the state systems. The change over time in the inspectors' concerns and vocabulary are marked. In 1929 an inspector at Stradbroke in Gippsland wrote: 'The young children's lead pencils are not long enough. Much of the blotting paper should be destroyed; much untidy work is due to dirty used-up blotting paper'. In 1970 a successor wrote: 'Attempts to create an appropriate social & emotional climate are being quite successful. Firm, positive relationships are being established'. An authoritarian interest in the insignificant had been replaced by a guess at the fashionable and intangible.

The punishment books are one record of what happened in the classroom and the playground. Successive entries from a NSW school in 1923 say something about the teacher's attitude to those who carried out crimes and those who benefited from them: 'stealing biscuits', two strokes with a cane; 'receiving biscuits', one stroke. And there is an ambiguity in the delinquency of a boy aged nine: 'Kissing a girl after two warnings', one stroke. The reasons why pupils were punished changed from general deficiencies such as 'gross laziness', 'idleness', and errors in classwork to specific crimes such as 'kicking a girl and lying', to no corporal punishment. To the 1940s girls were caned infrequently; after that their punishments were rarely corporal, and their crimes went unrecorded.

Inspectors' reports and the pupil registers document the changing function of the bush school. In 1910 most pupils in the one-teacher schools had all their formal education in that one school, and not many were reaching the eighth grade. Inspector Smith in southwest Queensland noted that only two per cent of scholars were in grade six and nine per cent in grades five and six. There should have been a total of thirty per cent in grades five and six. At Minimay about half the children enrolled between 1904 and 1920 completed eighth grade and gained their Merit certificate, and only two, both girls, were said to be going to high school. A teacher remembering his time at Kiamal north of Ouyen in Victoria, said, 'the Merit was the BA of the Mallee'. But by the 1940s it was very rare for a pupil to leave Minimay for immediate 'home duties' or 'farm work'; nearly all were going on to high or technical school.

Most of the one-teacher schools were utilitarian rectangles of weatherboard under a corrugated iron roof. Early in South Australia galvanized iron walls were also common, and chapel-like stone schools were built in the Adelaide hills and beyond. The granite schools at Faraday, Sutton Grange and elsewhere in central Victoria made good use of the local quarries and local skills. The scholars at Boonmoo in north Queensland began work in July 1910 in one of several 'tent schools' then in use. The iron sides were five or six feet high, then calico continued over the wall plates and across to form a ceiling below the iron roof. There were no windows and 'the heat was intolerable'. Railway carriages were used as classrooms at work camps, and indigent governments sometimes hired community halls or other buildings. Between the wars Bob Allanby taught at a school housed in a surviving section of the Port Arthur convict settlement. The thousands of tourists who now tramp though the stone building are told of only its first public function.

16. Minimay: One of 6,000 eatherboard Schools

What went on in particular buildings is worth knowing because it can make a page, perhaps more, in biographies. But general research into the experiences of those who taught and those who learnt in the one-teacher schools is important for the access it gives to a distinct part of Australian educational history, and to what went on in many rural communities. Two final observations. Where once the basic groups among parents were based on race, nationality, religion, wealth and pretensions to position, by 1970 some rural communities were divided between old farmers and timber workers on one side and alternative life-stylers on the other. In 1930 children got themselves to school; in 1980 their parents drove them in the car – or the four-wheel drive.

17. From Wagga to Waddington: Australians in Bomber Command

Delivered at a conference held in Lincoln, UK, 26–28 May 2000.

The main train line from Sydney to Melbourne runs from Central Station south through the Southern Highlands and crosses the high bleak grazing lands of the Great Dividing Range just west of Goulburn. From there the creeks drain into the Lachlan and the Murrumbidgee, and like the train line the rivers make their way west.

At Junee the train line branches, with the Melbourne line going south through Wagga and the Hay line curving away to the west, a straight line alongside the twists and loops of the bed and billabongs of the Murrumbidgee. Just west of Junee at Marrar the country opens out: the southwest slopes become the western plains – 'the sunlit plains extended'. The first of the towns on the Hay line, Coolamon, Ganmain, Matong and Grong Grong squat in rich, red, gently undulating farm land. Spreading box and neat white cypress pine line the fences. Creeks such as Smoky, Dead Horse, Boggy and Frying Pan – names that recur across the Australian landscape – follow wandering depressions south and west towards the river. Wagga, twenty-five miles from Coolamon, is the dominant town of the eastern Riverina.

When Arthur Doubleday was just old enough to be a useful wood-and-water joey, he went with the horse-team and wagon carting wheat to Ganmain. 'Anglia', the Doubledays' home block, named after the area that Arthur's father had left as a child, was thirteen miles out of Ganmain, and it was midday before the ten-horse team brought the wagon around the football oval, through the trees along Boggy Creek and joined the queue of carters waiting to dump their bagged wheat on the lumpers building the giant stacks at the railway siding. There was only one tough pull for the Doubleday team on that thirteen miles, a sharp rise on the Dulah road that tested the trace chains and the couplings, but it was a long way to cart. On their return journey the Doubledays camped in a paddock and came home the next morning. They could not afford to exhaust the team because they had three months' carting to do, and then the team had to be fresh for the cropping.

Arthur Doubleday, born in 1912, the second son in a family of five girls and three boys, went by horse and sulky or rode to the one-teacher Methul school, five miles northwest of 'Anglia'. Having completed his primary schooling, he went as a boarder to the new Yanco Agricultural High School. With its long drive bordered on one side by river red gums and on the other by lush irrigation country, Yanco Agricultural High occupied the imposing two-storey red brick homestead built by Samuel McCaughey, the man who had once controlled over 3,000,000 acres and owned more sheep than anyone else in Australia. Those familiar with Yanco's exposed timber interiors, the 'cathedral size stained glass windows', the artificial lake and orchard, were not likely to be intimidated when they entered the most affluent RAF officer's mess. In his three years at Yanco, Arthur Doubleday responded to the work in the paddock, sheds and classrooms, and 'loved' the cricket and football.

Just after Arthur Doubleday left school to work on the family farm, William Brill, another boy from the red soil of the eastern Riverina, went to board at Yanco Agricultural High. 'Clearview', the Brill farm just south of the Ganmain–Matong road, was well named. From their home at the top of a gently curving slope, the Brills could see the wheat silos nearly three miles away in Matong. The seven Brill children walked downhill to the weatherboard school of Derrain, and although there was twenty years from oldest to youngest, they all had the same teacher, Charles Banfield. He ruled, Fay Brill said, not with a rod of iron, but with a 'switch of the pepper tree'. And when Vic, who was younger than Bill, went on to Wagga Wagga High, Mr Banfield had taught him so well that he learnt no new maths for the first three years. Bill Brill left Yanco in 1930 with his Intermediate Certificate: he had failed Geography and passed with honours in Agricultural Chemistry and Botany.

On 3 September 1939 the Doubledays had all gathered for shearing, and they were sitting around a roaring fire when they heard on the wireless that Australia was at war. They decided that Harry, who was the oldest and had a crook back, would stay home and run the farm, and Arthur and the youngest boy, Jim, would go to war. There was, Arthur said, a 'lot more of the Mother Country attitude' in him, and he thought he was going 'home to fight'. By 1939 the Doubledays were farming the home block and two others, 'Dulah' and 'Hopewell'. The horse teams were gone, and the Doubledays had tractors, and their wheat went down the road in a cloud of dust. They owned the first semi-trailer in the district. The Brills too had switched to tractors in the early 1930s, and Ken the oldest boy had married and taken up his own block at Landervale on the Grong Grong–Ardlethan road. Bill went north to work with Ken, and while there he met and courted Ilma Kitto who was the head (and only) teacher at Landervale.

'Anglia' was less than twenty miles from 'Clearview', and Arthur Doubleday and Bill Brill knew one another, in the way that country people knew about each other. They sometimes saw each other, or heard talk when they were at dances, or sheep sales, or waiting at the wheat silos. And the people of Coolamon and Matong were brought together by one of the few significant cultural forces that divide white Australians by place: they were within the northeast frontier of Australian rules football that stretched south through Victoria to Tasmania and

17. From Wagga to Waddington: Australians in Bomber Command

west to the Indian Ocean. Bill played in the black and white of Matong and Arthur in the green of Methul. Matong and Methul were in different leagues, but Arthur and Bill could read about each other in the *Coolamon–Ganmain Farmers' Review*, and they certainly would read about Ken Brill, one of the stars in the strong South Western District League. By 1939 Arthur no longer ran onto the clearing in the trees that served as the Methul oval: a damaged knee had ended his football days. On the mechanised farm, Arthur had retained his interests in horses – he did some horse-breaking around the district and rode in buck-jumping shows. Bill, too, was still interested in horses. He had joined the local militia unit, the 21st Light Horse, and he was proud of his mount, Peanut.

On 19 April 1940 Brill was tested to see if he was a suitable candidate for aircrew training. The men on the interviewing panel pencilled in their impressions: 'rather slow chap but is intelligent', 'neat and respectful', and 'not striking. Quiet country chap'. They noted that he was a 'grade' footballer and was interested in cricket and swimming. They thought he would not be commissioned, but decided he might make a wireless operator/air gunner, and put him in the Air Force reserve. About the middle of 1940 Arthur Doubleday was also passed medically fit and satisfied his interrogators, and he too joined the Air Force reserve. Bill and Arthur both said that they were Methodists, Bill said he was a farmer and farm labourer, and Arthur located himself a shade higher on the rural ladder, he was, he said, a 'farmer and grazier'. Bill was twenty-four and Arthur twenty-eight. Both were of medium height with Bill at five feet ten inches slightly taller and more barrel-chested. Bill was, Arthur said, 'strong as a Mallee bull'. As they waited for their call-up, the air force supplied them with exercises in trigonometry, mechanics, theory of flight and Morse code. Bill was eager to show Ilma his work when he solved a difficult equation, and ready for private tuition when the answer was elusive.

Bill and Arthur were called up for service in November. The farm calendar helped Arthur recall the time. It was, he said, just before the 1940 harvest. When Arthur got on the train at Coolamon on Armistice Day, 11 November, Bill was already on board. He had bloodshot eyes and Arthur was suffering from pains in the stomach. Arthur said that if the Germans could see them they would think they didn't have too much to worry about. Bill and Arthur stayed together on the train to Sydney, and on the bus to Bradfield Park Initial Training School. Bill Brill became Leading Aircraftsman 402933, and Arthur Doubleday 402945, just a dozen numbers separating them. When they left Bradfield Park both had been selected for pilot training, and both were sent to do their elementary flying at Narrandera, just a few miles from Yanco Agricultural High, and less than twenty miles by Tiger Moth from Landervale. Arthur and Bill could check their navigation by glancing out of the cockpit and seeing how Ken and Harry were getting on with the harvest. From the end of January and into February the novice pilots tested themselves with side slips, steep turns, instrument flying, forced landings and aerobatics. After just two months both left Narrandera, having satisfied their instructors that they should continue to train as pilots. Brill had gone solo after just seven hours of dual instruction, and he had logged twenty-five hours as a single pilot in the Riverina's summer turbulence.

As applicants were numerous, those selecting aircrew could afford to set a high standard. The instructors could continue to be tough as the trainees went through a succession of schools, each about three months in length: Initial Training School, Elementary Flying Training School, and Service Flying School. During every course there was a strong chance of being 'scrubbed', of failing and being re-mustered to navigators', wireless operators', bomb aimers' and air gunners' schools, or to ground duties. The failure rate, for example, at Uranquinty Service Flying Training School for the 74 trainees who entered 26 course in September 1942 was 21 out of the 74 (28%). It was higher later in the war, up to 50%. And all who went to Uranquinty had already done about sixty hours on a Tiger Moth. That is, they had passed the initial demanding tests.

Those who qualified as aircrew could believe that they had joined the elite. They were going to do something that continued the traditions of the aces of the Great War and they knew it was going to test to the utmost their skill and courage. In 1941 Pip Beck, an eighteen-year-old wireless operator in the Woman's Auxiliary Air Force arrived at Waddington, a Bomber Command airfield near Lincoln. As she went to the Waafery she passed a group of sergeants: 'I knew from the brevets that they wore that these were aircrew, the fabulous beings I admired and hero-worshipped … they were young gods … and I blushed for the purple prose of my fancies'. They almost certainly knew how they looked to her.

Brill and Doubleday were about to join that elite, but by age, education and background, they were different from most Australians selected for aircrew training. They were older, they were country boys, and they had completed just three years of high school.

Early in 1941 Ilma Kitto left her school to make a rush trip to Sydney to see her fiancée, but she was too late. Bill Brill, Arthur Doubleday and other Australians had sailed for Canada on 19 March. At No 3 Service Flying Training School at Calgary, Brill and Doubleday learnt to fly the twin-engined Anson, added another fifty hours' solo to their log books, marched in the parade at the Calgary Stampede, graduated with almost equal marks, and were awarded their wings and commissioned as pilot officers. Arthur Doubleday said 'my whole experience in Canada was memorable and pleasurable'. The supervising officer, asked to comment whether there were any points in flying or airmanship that Brill should watch, simply wrote 'Nil'.

In August 1941 the Australians sailed in a 100-ship convoy from Halifax in Nova Scotia north through thick fog to skirt Greenland and Iceland, and into the Clyde. They came south by train to Bournemouth Personnel Reception Centre, before being posted to 27 Operational Training Unit at Lichfield. By October 1941 Brill and Doubleday were flying Wellingtons across the English counties; it was less than a year since they met on the train that took them to Sydney and Initial Training School. At Lichfield Brill and Doubleday selected their crews. Or perhaps their crews selected them.

Doubleday says it was a 'roundabout thing'. He met a gunner in the mess, and the gunner knew a wireless operator and the wireless operator knew a navigator. Brill's crew was Les Shepard, a bank clerk and another Wagga boy, as second pilot; Hugh Thompson, MA, BSc, an English biologist concerned with the human brain, the 'cool, calm navigator'; Dave Wilkinson, a professional golfer from Yorkshire, radio operator; Kevin Light, an aeronautical engineering student from Sydney, rear gunner; and Fred Lofts, a London salesman, front gunner and bomb aimer. Others who flew at least four operations with them were Tom O'Donohue, a clerk from Brisbane, Peter Gome, an art student from Birmingham, and Ned Walsh from Gympie in Queensland.

Exactly a year after they took their first flights at Narrandera at the height of summer, Brill and Doubleday flew a 460 Squadron Mark IV Wellington on a circuit and landing exercise at Molesworth, just west of Huntingdon. Within days, 460 shifted to Breighton in southern Yorkshire. A new airfield, Breighton in January 1942 was mud, snow, Nissen huts, and three intersecting runways on a high, windswept plain. The Australians soon found the compensation of Bubwith, a village within easy walking distance and with two pubs, the Black Swan and the Seven Sisters. They were known to the Australians as the 'Dirty Duck' and the 'Fourteen Tits', or slightly more decorously, the 'Fourteen Titties'.

Imagine Breighton in January 1942 and the Australians praying for a hard frost so that they might walk on top of the slush and not knee-deep in it. Imagine the crowded mess and Bill Brill takes a couple of gum leaves from an envelope. We are not sure who sent them to him, perhaps his youngest sister Fay, or perhaps his fiancée, Ilma. He lights them and then walks through the mess leaving behind wisps of smoke and the sharp, distinctive smell of burning gum leaves. That smoke was sufficient to transport every Australian, those from the city as well as bush, halfway around the world.

By March 1942 460 Squadron was ready to go to war. Brill and Doubleday were among five crews selected to fly on the first operation. The 'rest of the crews' Brill said, 'were envious'. The waiting crews were briefed four times, increasing the tension, before the weather cleared and there could be no more delays. Brill and Doubleday were keen to fly but uncertain how they would perform. Doubleday said that before an operation he never felt much different. There was just the increased tension felt by a batsman waiting to walk to the centre, but, he added, the fast bowler always looked more dangerous from the fence than the crease. Brill admitted more anxiety. He wrote about his feelings before another operation:

> *I wandered around with a feeling of having a half pound of lead in the pit of my stomach ... Perhaps it was fear ... How could I get back from this when others who are better than I'll ever be, have fallen on such targets? Will I funk if I'm in a tight spot? Will I let the rest of the boys down? Who am I to hold the lives of five other men in my hands?*

It had taken Flying Officers Brill and Doubleday sixteen months from the red-soil paddocks to war in the skies of Europe.

Brill and Doubleday followed a common pattern of Australian airmen going to war in Europe. Nearly all were part of the Empire Air Training Scheme linking the men of the dominions to Britain. The first Australians to train in Canada had gone in July 1940, so Brill and Doubleday were early, but not pioneers: the traffic of Australians in their bright blue uniforms reached its peak in 1943 and early 1944. Some 10,000 Australians completed their training in Canada, just over 647 went to schools in Rhodesia, and most of the 27,000 Australian aircrew who served in Britain had their wings before they left Australia. But they too went by sea across the Pacific, crossed North America by train, and then waited for the convoys that took them into the Mersey or the Clyde.

Among pilots Doubleday was an exception: he wanted to fly bombers, 'the bigger the better'. He had a rational argument, the bomber was the weapon that could hit back, but also his experience with trucks, tractors and harvesters gave him familiarity with heavy machinery. Brill had the same interest and confidence with machinery. At the start of his reflections on his first tour he wrote of the Wellington with its two eighteen-cylinder, twin-row Wasp engines; its slow cruising speed and high fuel consumption; the trouble they had starting it in cold weather; the fact that when they first arrived at Breighton they did not even have a plug spanner; but that during his time on the squadron there was not one case of a Wellington on operations suffering from engine failure. These were the comments from someone who knew a lot about starting International and Bulldog tractors on frosty mornings at Landervale.

For Brill and Doubleday the first operation was greater in anticipation than in reality. They flew as second pilots on a short flight to Emden, one of the closest German ports, and they bombed through cloud. Brill thought they might have 'frightened a cow or two'. On all of his first six operations Brill crossed the North Sea to bomb ports, or to drop leaflets telling the French that *'La Liberation n'est plus un espoir. La Liberation est en marche'*. He did not see flak until his third trip and did not fly as first pilot until his fifth. And then it was, as he said, 'only poor old le Havre, which every crew in Bomber Command has visited as a "fresher"'. But there were moments of danger. On one mission Brill had a 'torrid time' in flak, and while he could not remember chewing the gum he had with him, on landing he found that repetitive chomping had left his jaw muscles so exhausted he could not open his mouth. Arthur had a more exciting early leaflet raid when he was suddenly 'grabbed' by a radar-controlled searchlight, and he desperately tried to remember all he had been told about evasion. He dived and flattened out as low as he dared, but took a 'hammering' from the flak. The rear gunner, who quite reasonably thought all the enemy fire was directed at him, yelled advice in his Lancashire accent, and they escaped out to sea. Through the first six weeks of operations just one crew in 460 Squadron was shot down.

On 5 April 1942 Brill flew to Cologne, the first mission requiring him to cross extensive occupied territory and attack a defended target. They were given 'quite a reception' crossing the coast, and the 'target itself was an amazing sight'. There was a light flak – 'all colours' – heavy flak and at least a hundred search lights 'holding some poor johnny and plastering him with everything they had … The haze, the flares, the dozens of dummies and dozens of incendiary loads made the whole place bewildering'. Through the rest of April he flew another six times to Germany: to Hamburg, Essen, Dortmund, Hamburg, Rostock and Kiel. Over Essen, Ned Watch, who had flown with Brill as second pilot, went to close the flare chute just as the flak gunners opened up. Brill said, 'The first burst was rather close, and the blast gave the plane such a kick that it tipped old Ned off his feet. From then on, what with flak bursts and evasive action, Ned was rolled around the fuselage like a pea in a whistle'.

By his eleventh operation Brill was 'beginning to get a little accustomed to being scared'. It was just as well, because Dortmund was a 'cauldron of flak':

> *Never have I worked so hard, or have I done so much evasive action. The poor kite stood first on one wing, and then on the other, on its tail, and on its nose. The sweat poured off me, half from exertion and half from fright. And still those beams played across us, until I prayed for them to shoot us down and finish it all. Sometimes I wonder if I was a bit mad during part of that show. Can remember looking at times and seeing a big blue beam cutting a track in the sky a few feet above. I screamed laughing … and cried, 'Ha! Ha! Missed again'.*

Brill flew through some thirty miles of 'candles' and, short of fuel and holed with shrapnel, landed at Swanton Morely in Norfolk.

On his first tour Brill flew eighteen times to Germany, but a raid on France was probably his most hazardous. In May the crews watched anxiously as the moon waxed and the night shortened leaving little darkness to hide a bomber. These were the conditions that Bomber Command needed to make an attack on the Gnome and Rhone works at Gennevilliers, a suburb of Paris. To prevent civilian casualties, the attacking aircraft had to be able to see their target. Only experienced crews were chosen, and those now included both Brill's and Doubleday's. On 29 May seventy-seven bombers took off into cloud and rain squalls. Brill flew at just 175 feet across the Channel so that he was under the cloud and could see exactly where he crossed the French coast. By the time Brill's apprehensive crew reached Paris the weather was clearing, and as they ran in towards the target they were immediately picked up by searchlights. With the bomb doors open they were hit by flak, shrapnel exploded through the aircraft, and cut the hydraulics. Brill 'put in some pretty hard work at the controls' and brought the Wellington over the centre of Paris at about 1000 feet. They were under constant fire as Brill again came over the target, and released the bombs. Flak put the rear turret out of action, and one 1000-pound did not release. They swung for home, as Brill said, with the bomb doors flapping in the breeze, and with a precarious hold on a 1000-pound bomb. They made an emergency landing at White Waltham near Windsor, a short strip, but it did not matter as a flat tyre slowed them on landing. Of the four Wellingtons that had taken off from Breighton, Brill's was the only one to bomb, and his and Arthur Doubleday's were the only ones to get back to England. Brill's Wellington was beyond repair. Brill was given an immediate DFC, the first in 460 Squadron.

When the Wellingtons of 460 Squadron returned from a raid and joined those circling above Breighton waiting for the controller to bring them down, the crews were discouraged from calling each other on the radio. But often they would hear a cheerful Australian voice call, 'How are yer, mate?' And they would know that Brill and Doubleday were checking on each other.

Doubleday finished his tour with a raid on Saarbrucken at the end of July 1942. He was the first in the Squadron to complete a tour, and was awarded a DFC. Brill finished a few days later on 11 August after thirty-one operations. They had taken five months to complete their tours. During that time 460 Squadron had lost twenty-two aircraft, more than its total of eighteen when it began operations. But of course that is the number of aircraft lost on all raids, and is not a measure of their chances of survival. Brill and Doubleday had flown frequently, and that meant that they flew on half of the squadron's operations. Brill had flown on six raids when five per cent or more of aircraft from all squadrons had been destroyed, and on three of those – Essen, Hamburg and Warnemunde – it was seven or more per cent. The average loss per raid over the five months had been about three per cent, and that gave a forty per cent chance of survival over a tour. On raids in which Brill had flown, twelve 460 Squadron aircraft had been destroyed.

Don Charlwood, a navigator who completed a tour with 103 Squadron and served as an instructor at 27 Operational Training Unit, Lichfield, wrote:

> *A few outstanding men recognized that the Command needed their leadership and expertise. Their presence on a squadron lifted morale enormously – provided they stayed alive ... Epitomising such men at Lichfield were two former Riverina farmers, Arthur Doubleday and Bill Brill. They were squadron leaders, each commanding a Lichfield training flight.*

It is a fine tribute, yet a senior officer wrote at Lichfield that Brill was just a 'good steady plodder' and gave him four out of ten for initiative. That judgement was in sharp contrast to those who knew Brill as 'charismatic' and a leader of 'outstanding personality'. Perhaps Brill manifested those qualities of leadership only when they were needed – on an operational squadron – but it seems unlikely. In volunteering for a second tour, Brill and Doubleday had committed themselves to another twenty raids.

After eleven months instructing novice crews Brill and Doubleday went to a conversion unit at Wigsley, and there they trained on the Halifax and the Lancaster, the four-engined heavy bombers that had been demonstrating their superiority over the Wellingtons by the time that Brill and Doubleday ended their first tours. Both picked up most of their new crew while still instructing. Ron Fuller says that they were having a beer in the mess at Lichfield when Brill said that he was going back to operations, and he wanted Bob Curtis and Ted Freeman to fly with him. Ron said that he would go with them, but Brill thought there was no chance that he would be allowed to go as he had already done fifty operations, nearly all in North Africa. Fuller insisted he was going anyway, so Brill asked for his release, and to everyone's surprise it was granted. When Doubleday arrived at the Conversion Unit, he still did not have a navigator, but Bob Murphy who was a navigation instructor there was already a friend of Arthur's. Bob said that going on a second tour was 'normally a voluntary job, but they asked me and I couldn't knock 'em back'.

Brill was posted to 463 Squadron, Doubleday to 467. Both had the rank of Squadron Leader, both served as flight commanders, and both squadrons were operating from Waddington. As a re-introduction to war, Brill flew as 'second dickie' to Stettin on 5 January 1944. On the long nine-hour flight there was much more to observe and much of it was disturbing: the density of the bombers in the stream, the use of flares at the turning points, the bombing on coloured marker flares, the efficiency of the German night fighters, the increased use of radio and radar for navigation, the demands for precision in navigation and timing, and the intensity of the light over the target area. It was a contrast with Brill's first tour when he had often nosed his way around the target then selected his own bombing run. He decided he would never cross a track marker – the chance of collision was high and the markers attracted the night fighters.

Imagine the mess at Waddington in the winter of early 1944. Outside the cloud is low, and mist and sleet are scudding across the runways. There have been no operations during the day and the forecast means that there will be no air war in western Europe that night. Suddenly there is a cry among the drinkers, 'Clear the runway! Bill Brill will do the impossible'. An indoor runway is cleared of furniture, a sofa is placed across the far end, and beyond it a fine, leather officer's chair is laid on its back. Brill in his socks runs flat out down the runway, grips the top of the sofa with his hands, somersaults, lands in the chair and his momentum turns it upright, leaving Squadron Leader Brill sitting comfortably in the chair. The act is a challenge to other airmen, especially those misled by drink-induced confidence. Soon the end of the runway is littered by pranged airmen who had crash-dived into the wall and floor. The challengers retire to the bar.

Brill and Doubleday returned to operations at the height of the Battle of Berlin. During the first three months of 1944 Bomber Command lost 763 four-engined bombers. The loss rate was greater than the replacement rate – this was a battle that could not be sustained. In those three months both Brill and Doubleday flew on eleven raids, nine of them into Germany, and on those nine raids the average loss rate was 5.5 per cent. At that rate less than one crew in five would complete a full tour.

Brill and his new crew flew their first operation together when they went to Berlin on 20 January, and they went to the 'big city' again on 27 January. As flight commander Brill thought he ought to fly 'R' for Robert: it was said to be a jinxed aircraft, a 'chop kite'. On its last flight it had come back with a dead rear gunner – he had died when the oxygen failed. At other times its crew had claimed an engine had lost power, but no faults had shown when the ground staff had tested it. The take-off for the long flight to Berlin was in daylight and Brill flew northeast out over the North Sea and then came south with a tail wind. But one engine did indeed give trouble and Brill was lower and slower than normal. Over Berlin the bomb aimer, Bill McMahon, had just released the bombs when the Lancaster was hit in several places. Brill had been watching gun flashes from below and counting the seconds from the flash, ready to exploit the few seconds that he had to take action if he became the target. So Brill thought they had been hit by flak, but in fact another bomber above them had released its incendiaries on them. One had gone straight through the perspex in the nose of the plane, but McMahon had the presence of mind to pick it up and throw it straight back out again. Other incendiaries hit the navigator's table, severed the rudder controls, jammed the rear gunner's escape hatch, and destroyed most of the aircraft's electrical system. As Brill was struggling to regain control, the mid-upper gunner, Tubby Fuller, said there was a plume of flame coming from the port wing, and it was so long it was streaming way past the tail. Brill told the crew to stand-by to bail out, and he put the Lancaster into a dive, a standard way to try and blow a fire out. But he could still see the flames and told the crew to jump. McMahon jettisoned the front hatch and sat with his legs dangling. The navigator, Bluey Freeman, was next in line to jump, but neither was eager to plunge into the inferno of Berlin. Fuller, unable to open the rear door, kicked a hole in it, put his hand through and opened it from the outside, but before he jumped he pulled the emergency hatch in the roof to release the dinghy so that he could have a last look outside. He too decided to stick with the plane, but the wind gripped him and almost sucked him out. The rear gunner, Bill McDonald, said he could not open the rear turret, and so he had no choice: if the plane went down he went with it.

Then Bob Curtis, who had gone up into the astro dome, said that the fire was nearly out. As Brill had levelled off and almost had the plane under control he told Len Smith, the flight engineer, to go around and tell the crew not to jump. On his way back to his turret Tubby Fuller pressed past Curtis whose parachute released, and yards of silk 'spewed out'. Knowing that at any moment his life might depend on his parachute, Curtis tried to stuff silk and cords back into its pack. By this time 'R' for Robert was down to 14,000 feet and no one was sure where they were or where they were heading. Holding a torch in his teeth, Freeman worked out their position and gave Brill a course. With limited control, freezing wind streaming in hatches and bomb holes, and bits of aeroplane threatening to tear in the wind, they set off for home. Brill climbed in spite of the cold and in spite of the fact that Smith passed out because of a lack of oxygen and Curtis was vomiting. Curtis kept working on the electrical system, and had some of it repaired before they got back to Waddington. They landed after a nine-hour flight, the second last home. Thirty-three Lancasters did not get back: that was 241 airmen. In Berlin about 700 people were killed, and 20,000 had their homes destroyed. When Brill's crew inspected their plane on the ground they found that seven or eight incendiary bombs had hit them, and the fire in the wing, just missing the fuel tanks, had been caused by a bomb penetrating the wing, burning its way through and falling out.

In a letter home written on the day that they got back to Waddington, Curtis began: 'Dear Dad, Phew! Have I got some news for you …' He ended: 'Every time I tell this story in the mess or nearby pubs I get a couple of free drinks'. Brill wrote, 'it was not my idea of an evening's entertainment'. They flew again to Berlin three nights later. The Waddington squadrons lost six Lancasters, three from each squadron.

On his second tour Brill faced extreme danger on two other raids, and both Brill and Doubleday flew on the Nuremberg raid in March, Bomber Command's most costly attack. Nuremberg, Brill said, was the most frightening. He flew through the fragments of a Lancaster that exploded in front of him. One engine was put out of action, another stopped briefly and the rear gunner reported that his turret was not working. Again Brill told the crew to get their parachutes handy, and again they kept flying, and arrived at Waddington an hour after the other crews. By then the weather was closing in, and landing was dangerous. Arthur Doubleday, who was waiting for Brill, said, 'He always caused me some anxiety'. Brill agreed. He told a reporter, 'I am always getting into tight spots'.

As flight leaders Brill and Doubleday deserve much praise for sustaining the morale and efficiency of the two Waddington squadrons through those bleak nights of long flights and high losses during the Battle of Berlin.

From April 1944 Bomber Command switched much of its destructive power from Berlin and other major German cities to preparations for the Normandy landings. The operations against gun emplacements, ammunition dumps, marshalling yards and ports took half the time of the flights to eastern Germany and losses were lighter. Brill flew as deputy controller on the raid to Sable-Sur-Sarthe on 6 May, and saw the bombs turn the ammunition dump into a 'bubbling boiling mass'. The cascades of sparks and the explosions were, Brill said, better than the fireworks he had seen at the Calgary Stampede three years before. No attacking aircraft was lost and a 'good time was had by all'. Arthur Doubleday flew twice on D-Day, 6 June, attacking coastal guns and returning to bomb the railways at Argentan. At the end of his second tour, Doubleday flew twelve successive raids on targets in France.

Brill and Doubleday flew as deputy controllers, and then as controllers. That meant that they had to arrive early, check that the marker flares were correctly located, calculate the wind speed and direction over the target, and redirect those aircraft bombing in the wrong place. Having to stay longer in the target area was not always appreciated by the crews. Before a raid on Cherbourg, Bob Curtis wrote on his route map, 'Controller again – what a bastard'. As controller Brill also felt an increased obligation to bomb accurately. On 8 May over Brest all the defences were alerted and other aircraft were turning for home by the time Brill came in to bomb. He was picked up early by the searchlights but he was determined to hold the plane steady and he refused to look away from his instruments. The Lancaster was 'plastered', but he did not dive and twist until after the bombs were dropped and the confirming photograph taken. As they came away the rear gunner warned that 'odd pieces' were falling off the starboard elevator, and one engine stopped, but they made it home with 140 holes in the fuselage.

On 11 May 1944 J.R. (Sam) Balmer, commander of 467 Squadron, was killed in action, and Brill was named as his replacement, and he and his crew transferred to the sister squadron at Waddington. It was as Wing Commander that Brill completed his second tour on 4 July 1944. Bob Curtis, the wireless operator and gunner, had actually finished his tour one trip earlier, but volunteered to go on one extra raid so that the crew could stay together. McDonald was not with them. He had filled in with another crew and been killed. Len Smith and Bill McMahon, both on their first tour, had more trips to do after 4 July. Both survived, Bill as a prisoner of war. He had parachuted out over Germany and landed on the roof of a farm house.

Arthur Doubleday was also promoted, but he went to command 61 Squadron, a RAF squadron at Skellingthorpe. He was, he said, the only Australian who had enlisted during the war, and who had acquired his skills through the Empire Air Training Scheme, to command a RAF squadron. Given short warning of his appointment, Doubleday and his crew arrived at Skellingthorpe to find that 61 Squadron had suffered high losses over Berlin, and had just had three aircraft shot down on the Nuremberg raid and another two damaged in crashes. Bob Murphy, Doubleday's navigator, said that they walked into the mess, and 'you could hear a pin drop'. On their second night at Skellingthorpe Doubleday's crew tried to lift morale:

> *we decided to put on a party ... Got the beer flowing, blackened a few bottoms and put the impressions on the ceiling of the mess – generally livened the place up and within a few weeks we had a tremendous spirit going in the squadron ...*

Doubleday, who brought a quieter, more deliberate style of leadership to the mess, saved his flamboyance for the air where he flew his aircraft to the extremes of its capacities. Later he said that his six months with 61 Squadron were the most satisfying of his air force career.

Both Brill and Doubleday continued to fly after they completed their second tours. Normally they flew with new crews, or crews they thought needed guidance and encouragement. Doubleday ended up flying fifty-five missions, and Brill fifty-eight. To fly with strangers whose behaviour in air battle was untested added to the risks. On one flight Doubleday heard his bomb aimer say in a matter of fact voice, 'Flak on the port skipper'. It was the sort of statement that normally warned of distant danger, but suddenly shrapnel hit between the inner and outer port engines and Doubleday learnt that he had an unflappable bomb aimer whose voice showed not the slightest trace of excitement even when flak was about to explode a few feet from his nose. On 31 May the crews of 467 were selected for an attack on the railway junction at Saumur in France, but the weather was so bad that Brill told a 'sprog' crew to stay home and he and his crew took their place. A month later a new pilot flying 'second dickie' was killed, and the members of the now headless crew faced being sent back to training and again going through crewing-up. Brill took over as pilot and took them on an attack on the railway yards at Limoges in France. He said the 'excitement and enthusiasm expressed by the crew members repaid my small effort'. The excitement was understandable: they nearly collided with another Lancaster on the way in to bomb and had to make another circuit. Below them they could see the opposing armies 'blazing away' at each other. Having been twice briefed to go to Konigsberg but never having made the long flight to the Baltic Port, Brill made a special application to the base commander and was allowed to take a new crew there on 26 August 1944. With the novice pilot acting as flight engineer, they flew the long leg along the Swedish coast looking at the lighted towns below, and the Swedish flak coming up a considerate time after they had gone. It was all, Brill said, 'uncommonly pleasant'.

Brill's crew also say that one night the bombers were moving around the peri-track waiting their turn to take-off when one plane stopped. Brill, who was not flying, drove down to see what was causing the delay. Expecting to be told about a mechanical or electrical fault, he found a traumatised pilot who said he was not in a fit state to fly and, if he did, he would simply kill the rest of the crew. Brill said, 'I will bring you home'. He got his flying kit, and flew the aircraft. Later he arranged for the pilot to be sent to Hugh Thompson, his navigator on the first tour. Thompson, then living in Surrey, provided rest and advice, and the pilot returned to the squadron.

When asked about Brill and Doubleday, a fellow Riverina airman, Reg Bain, said, 'They were mad. They would turn around and have a look'. Where most crews wanted to get in and get out of the target area as fast as possible, both Brill and Doubleday several times made more than one bombing run, and sometimes chose to have a look at what they and others had done. It was not simply a result of responsibilities as flight or squadron commanders or as master bombers. On the twentieth raid of his first tour Brill bombed Emden, went out to sea and then:

> *I turned the kite around to have a look at the show. It was an unforgettable sight. Must have been seventy or more flares hanging over the centre of the town, with the usual searchlight cones and more than the usual amount of coloured light flak weaving its way up. Fires and gun flashes on the ground and flak bursts in the sky made the picture complete. And the whole issue was reflected in the water.*

At other times he wrote of circling low over the target to have a 'looksee'. When the bomb aimer had difficulty locating the target in a raid on Hamburg, Brill said on the intercom that he would 'stooge into the centre of the flak' and see what they could find, but 'The suggestion was promptly greeted by "Drop the damn things and go home" from every corner of the kite'.

Historians, or all concerned with human behaviour, need to ask why it was that some men who were aware of the casualty rates volunteered to fly a second tour, or to fly the extended tours required in Pathfinder squadrons. The equation that measured life against death was inescapable: the chances of completing a tour of thirty missions when the loss per raid was three per cent was forty per cent – less than an even break. As one said, 'we all knew we were "juggling with Jesus"'. By the time Brill and Doubleday went back to operations there was not a shortage of aircrew – in fact there was a waiting list. The fact that both were to serve as flight and squadron commanders was no comfort: six 463 and 467 Squadron commanders were killed in action, and Rollo Kingsford-Smith and Brill were the only commanders to survive the tough years before the D-Day landings. Yet forces within some men compelled them to go back again. They were uncomfortable about instructing young men to do what they had learnt to do and could do better. Those who survived the trauma of operations often suffered depression, and one way of lifting that depression was to go back into the cycle of the build-up, the intensity of the raid, and the exhaustion of post-operation. Adrenalin, Kingsford-Smith says, 'was God's gift to aircrew'. But adrenalin could come at the cost of dependency and depression. A high-minded sense of duty, guilt, the boredom of instruction, a rational belief that those who were best at operations ought to do them, the lure of the intensity and sense of purpose in life on an operational squadron, and escape from post-trauma depression led men back to operations.

Another puzzle is why Australian aircrew were prepared to fight in a war so far from home, even after Australia was in its own war in the Pacific. But the images that had lured many into the air force – from Biggles to the Battle of Britain – centred in Europe. Australians believed that the great events of the world had their genesis and their resolution in Europe, so to fight there was to be at the determining point of Australia's fate. It was also true that the most advanced aircraft and the best material conditions for aircrew were in England. As Ivan Pellas said, he didn't want to be sent to the back end of nowhere, living in a tent without grog and girls. And Australians now presume a distinction that most Australians did not make in 1939 or 1944: Australians then were both Australian and British. They could be aggressively Australian and critical of much that they saw in England, and still be proudly British. To be absorbed into an Empire Scheme and dispersed into British squadrons was not in conflict with their personal sense of identity. Generally airmen do not regret the combination of policy and chance that took them from Wagga to Waddington – or Bendigo to Breighton. And into a RAF rather than a RAAF squadron.

The Boy from Boort

In the Australian casualty lists of World War II, two figures stand out: the 8000 who died as prisoners of the Japanese, and the 4000 who died in Bomber Command. In 1945 and into the early 1950s both ex-prisoners and aircrew were accorded national recognition, but by the 1970s both groups had declined in public consciousness. From the early 1980s the ex-prisoners were rediscovered, and Changi, the Burma–Thailand Railway and the Sandakan death march re-entered Australian popular history. The men of Bomber Command have remained in relative decline. They have in part been victims of Australian history serving Australia's present.

While neither Arthur Doubleday nor Bill Brill was a national hero when he came home in 1945, there were stories about them in the press, and Arthur was offered pre-selection for two safe seats in Parliament. But when Arthur brought his young English bride back to the farm at Coolamon, there had been prolonged droughts, and the light red soils were on the move. Storms left the house and everything in it veiled in fine dust. Farming and parliament did not seem attractive, and he went into civil aviation, was appointed Regional Director for Queensland in the Department of Civil Aviation, shifted back to New South Wales as Regional Director, and then became Director of the Department of Transport in New South Wales until retiring in 1977.

Bill Brill came home, and married his fiancée school teacher in the Ganmain Methodist church, and stayed in the RAAF. Group Captain Brill died of a heart attack in 1964 when he was just forty-eight years old. Was the officer who in 1940 said he would not make an officer or a pilot at his funeral? Outside their old comrades from Bomber Command, few Australians now know about Brill and Doubleday, the flying farmers from the Riverina.

18. Observing the Present: Writing the Past

Pacific Lives, Pacific Places: Bursting Boundaries in Pacific History, edited by Brij V. Lal and Peter Hempenstall, pp. 22–33. Canberra: Journal of Pacific History.

On Monday 27 March 2000 I landed at Jacksons Airport, Port Moresby. I shuffled off Qantas flight QF95 through the covered tunnel, into the new air-conditioned airport, and went by air-conditioned car to the Airways Hotel with its grand entrance, polished wood floors, silent lift and blocks of air-conditioned rooms clinging to the slope.

It was almost exactly thirty-four years since I had first landed at Jacksons. I had then flown all night on the TAA Bird of Paradise Electra ('Big. Powerful. Fast. Smooth. Slice two hours from the Territory/Australia trip'), arrived just after dawn, walked across the tarmac through air so dense it was like wading through a cappuccino, presented my entry permit to the Australian official, waited in the open-sided shed that catered for all passengers from Kieta or Lae or Sydney, and went by car, windows down, shirt sticking to the seat, past Four Mile and down the dusty, gravel road to the isolated Administrative College housing in Waigani.

The change in the speed and ease of travel, and the fact that it is possible now to move within a protective cocoon, is significant. But other changes are obviously more important. TAA (The Friendly Way) was an Australian domestic airline. In 1966 the customs officers and airport officials were all Australians. Banks were branches of Australian banks – the Commonwealth, the Bank of New South Wales – the currency was Australian, and the tellers and the customers were all Australians – except perhaps for a nervous group of Papua New Guineans waiting for the most literate among them to join the queue, and wait for a turn to enter the alien world of commerce. In 1966 all members of the First Division of the Public Service were white, and in the Second Division (where the minimum entry was three years of secondary schooling) Papua New Guineans were outnumbered twenty to one. The senior police were all white, but in 1964 the first two Papua Guineans were appointed as sub-inspectors, so the old barrier that had stopped Papua New Guineans rising above the ranks of sergeant and warrant officer had ended. Even so, a newly arrived Australian going into the Port Moresby police station to change a State to a Territory driving licence was more likely to be served by a white woman office worker than a Papua New Guinean policeman. The 'Pacific Islands Regiment' was a unit of the Australian Army, controlled by the Australian Defence Act, and over 600 of the 3000 personnel were white.

All senior officers and technical staff were Australian. As in the police the first officers had recently been appointed: Second Lieutenants Ted Diro and Patterson Lowa had been commissioned in 1963.

At the top of Hunter Street, the House of Assembly, the archives and the museum shared the modest building that had once been the European hospital. In the Assembly the debates, both for and against, were dominated by Europeans. The radio station, 9PA, was run by the ABC, and most of its announcers had careers that considered a shift to Port Moresby as not much different from one to Launceston or Townsville. The news services in Motu and Pidgin and the broadcasts to schools presented by Papua New Guineans did at least give the ABC a local distinction to balance its familiar Australian accents and 'Blue Hills', with its evocation of a past Australia. The daily newspaper, the *South Pacific Post*, had just come under the control of the *Herald and Weekly Times* of Melbourne and was later to become part of the growing empire of Rupert Murdoch. It was written by and for Australians, the advertisements were directed at the Australians, the sporting teams most reported were dominated by Australians and a few were exclusively white.

In 1966 an Australian travelled in an Australian Territory and was carried, directed, serviced, protected, punished and entertained by Australian institutions. It was not even clear if or when Papua New Guinea was going to end its constitutional association with Australia. The Minister, Charles Barnes, had been to Port Moresby in January and declared that when the time came, the people of Papua and New Guinea could choose for themselves what they wanted. In February *Pacific Islands Monthly* said that if the 'majority of Papua-New Guinea's moderate, not very ambitious leaders then had to choose they would opt for close ties with Australia'. But among general uncertainty it did seem that Mr Barnes had made it clear that there was no chance of the Territory becoming a seventh state of Australia. A report, just made public, reminded Australians that there were still parts of the Territory where government, exploration and adventure were one. Assistant District Officer R.I. Barclay and Cadet Patrol Officer K. Taylor had walked for eighty days through the headwaters of the April and Leonard Schultz Rivers where they were the first government officers to contact several hundred people. Simply the appearance of the people with their bark topknots and cane waistbands – not their aspirations for statehood –was news. Barclay, Taylor, five policemen and over fifty carriers had crossed a river forty-two times in one day and gone without food for four days as they penetrated the deep gorges at the divide between the Sepik and Western Districts to meet timid, suspicious peoples. The Territory was still an Australian frontier, and the land recently described by McCarthy and Souter (and about to be described by

Sinclair) was still out there. In 1966 Australians were discovering Papua New Guinea as they were trying to change it more rapidly than ever before, but the extent to which they were preparing for complete separation was unclear.

When I arrived at Jacksons airport in 2000 I joined the queue for foreigners entering the country. I presented my Australian passport and visa which allowed me a single entry, prohibited work and required me to have a return ticket. It was checked by a Papua New Guinean immigration officer and my luggage was inspected by Papua New Guinean customs officers. A young Papuan woman asked me, 'Have you been to our country before?' I thought about explaining that I had been many times before, and that the first time I came it was my country, but that at some time it had become hers. The formal date of transfer was 16 September 1975, but in fact over time I had observed the country going from 'ours' to 'theirs'. Perhaps I should have said that the country had always been hers, but when I first came to Papua New Guinea Australian institutions had been imposed across the surface of a small part of the country and this had made it possible to travel from Brisbane to Boroko within a familiar Australianness. I simply said, 'Yes'.

Historians write from a particular present. For historians of Papua New Guinea that present has changed radically. The visible changes are most obvious to me as I drive through the suburb of Boroko – from the Hubert Murray Highway, down Boroko Drive and then back along Vaivai Avenue. In 1966 Port Moresby had a population of just over 40,000 and 10,000 were expatriates. About one third of the expatriates lived in Boroko. All those louvre-windowed bungalows, on high concrete posts, all those cars parked underneath and in the driveways, all those neat Sogeri grass lawns, all the bauhimia, allamanda, ixora, bougainvillea, hibiscus, tanket and travellers' palms bought from Sheedy's at Six Mile, all the blue-lined Clark swimming pools, all were possessed by Australians and reflected Australian aspirations for the good suburban life. The Papua New Guineans who washed, cooked, cleaned and gardened in many of the Boroko houses were scarcely visible, although they numbered just a few less than the Australians.

In 2000 Port Moresby has a population of about 400,000 and in that city ten times greater what were once called 'expats' and now 'non-citizens' are fewer, and the Australians are the tiny minority – perhaps 3000. In Port Moresby less than one in a hundred is an Australian. Boroko and Korobosea, so obviously white suburbia in 1966, are now home to over 25,000 Papua New Guineans.

Suburbs in other cities change their ethnicity. Parts of New York went from being Irish to East and Southern European to African–American. Richmond in Melbourne changed from Tigerland to Little Saigon. But what happened in Boroko is more significant. The Australians have not moved to another more spacious, leafier suburb with higher real estate values and lower crime rates – they have gone altogether. Boroko was the leafy suburb. It did not compete with Airvos Avenue and other streets on Touaguba with their views of the harbour or reef and Coral Sea; but it was a suburb of privilege and power. This has been a shift of people in terms of power as well as a shift in space, and it has been almost complete.

The change in the present is also apparent in the extent to which people feel at ease. Questions of 'law and order' constantly intrude on all peoples' daily activities; much ordinary activity is curtailed or conducted at risk. Crimes of outrageous bravado capture headlines. On 17 December 1999 a gang hijacked a helicopter and tried to rob the Port Moresby headquarters of the Papua New Guinea Banking Corporation. Intercepted by the police, four were shot dead and a fifth died on the way to hospital. Using a Toyota Landcruiser stolen in Lae, five men drove into Lalibu in the Southern Highlands, held up the bank, and left with K22,000. In November 2000 hijackers armed with rifles and hand grenades ordered a light aircraft on a regular run between the Morobe goldfields and Lae to divert to Graraina. There they unloaded $262,000 worth of gold and disappeared into the bush. Equally audacious, but more profitable and less dangerous, have been the misappropriation of funds. The assets of the Motor Vehicle Insurance Trust, Post PNG, the National Provident Fund, and the Investment Corporation of PNG had, the Prime Minister Sir Mekere Morauta said, been 'raped and plundered'. The Motor Vehicle Insurance Trust had shrunk from a value of K150 million to K3.89 million. Monies have moved through accounts in Australia, Hong Kong, Switzerland and the Cayman Islands and individuals have – sometimes deviously but legally – rewarded themselves with payments in the millions. People die in acts of careless and wanton violence. A six-year-old girl was shot dead while travelling with her parents on the Magi Highway just outside Port Moresby. An Enga man in the suburb of Morata was blown to pieces by a hand grenade and in revenge three men were chopped to death. In March 2000, I was parked outside the National Archives, just off Independence Drive. The archives close at lunchtime, and as I waited a few minutes for the reading room to reopen I sat in my car reading the *Post-Courier*. A member of staff immediately came out and told me to come inside and wait. To sit in a car with the door open, I was told, was to invite someone to steal it, and I might be injured in the process.

When I returned to the Archives and began reading the District Commissioners' *Annual Reports* the present dominated. I could not stop thinking about the questions of law and order; they arise from immediate conversations, and from ordinary and extraordinary events. Were the crimes related to particular values and ways of behaving in Melanesian cultures? What had happened to those opposing forces in Melanesian cultures, those that restrained the hot heads and ensured peace and harmony? To what extent had Australian institutions been inefficient or inappropriate? Why had the values proclaimed by governments and missions had so little apparent impact? What was the relationship between the resurgent tribal fighting, armed robbery and fraud and corruption? Where should Papua New Guinea government and foreign aid agencies direct their aid to obtain immediate and long-term benefits? How should we interpret those post-war years of apparent peace, low levels of crime, and the dominance of Australians and Australian institutions? Were these superficial and ephemeral impositions, coming under increasing strain even before the Australians handed over power?

The District Commissioner for Kieta District reported in 1948 from Sohano that as a result of recent patrolling the estimated decline in population on Bougainville during the Second World War was between twenty and twenty-five per cent. Losses had been heaviest in the Kieta and Buin areas. Patrol officers listed the losses from the direct and indirect results of war people shot for presumed aid to the enemy, killed by strafing aircraft, deaths from deprivation, and from other New Guineans who took advantage of the turmoil of war to attack old enemies. Particular cases were referred to Crown Law Officers to see whether war damage compensation should be paid. Korovei, a man aged about twenty-two from the Reboine area south of Kieta, had taken refuge with the inland Nasioi when air strikes increased against the Japanese occupying his village. He had died of exposure and malnutrition. Onaba Bora of Keveri was in Abau in 1944 to give evidence in a court case. Two Americans asked him to provide a woman who would have sexual intercourse with them. Onaba refused and they bashed him with pistol butts, leaving him paralysed. He got around the village in a sitting position, lifting himself with his hands. Both cases merited compensation.

When I first read post-war patrol reports, I had sat in a room at Konedobu at the headquarters of DDA – the Department of District Administration, at the very source of Australian imposed peace. From that place at that time, the violence of war seemed a terrible aberration: the violence of a world war had fallen on a people who had both accepted and appreciated peace. In 2000 I was entering the Archives to escape a dangerous world. It was then possible to see some parts of Papua New Guinea as being engaged in persistent tribal warfare, the Australian rule having been imposed with force and the threat of force, the war suddenly introducing vastly greater and less predictable violence, and by the early 1970s these areas were again places where armed men solved disputes and redistributed wealth. In March 2000 peace could be seen as an aberration. Of course the present influences all historians, but in one generation in Papua New Guinea the transformation has been so great in where people live, who they are, what wealth and power they have, and how they behave, that the questions historians might ask and the answers they suggest have taken an equally sharp turn.

Soon after first arriving in Papua New Guinea I began to write about it. The immediate social and physical landscape was so dominant it was impossible to write about anything else. It was presumptuous of me to comment so soon on a place that I knew little about, but I was writing from and on those dominant Australian institutions. To write critically about policies in education, economic development or constitutional change was in most cases to pass judgement on fellow Australians. The easy targets were those in high office who were blind to impending change, the planters who sat in exclusive clubs and railed against lazy and unreliable workers, and the Governor-General Sir Silas Atopare outlining the government's program for the next year. Three days later I made the short journey down Independence Drive from the Archives to the new national parliament and took a seat in the public gallery. The government faced significant issues: an agreement with the International Monetary Fund for emergency funding to rescue the economy had just been announced, half the K267 million contributions to the National Provident Fund were found missing, in the Eastern Highlands fighting in the Kofena and Kainantu areas had resulted in eighteen deaths and there were reports of high powered rifles being used, and the Loloata agreement had just been signed by central Government and Bougainvillean representatives. But my interest was in people as much as the topics causing debate.

When I began teaching at the Administrative College in 1966 the Australian government had recently accepted that it had to force the pace of Papua New Guinean advancement in the public service. The course in which I was teaching, 'Stage 2', was designed to take Papua New Guinean public servants and increase the standard of their general education to the level of fifth year in an Australian high school. It attracted some of the most able of the young Papua New Guineans then working for the government. At the same time I was assisting with the teaching of the fifty-eight students enrolled in the University of Papua New Guinea's first preliminary year. Gathered from the few students who had completed four years of secondary education in the Territory, or been to teachers college or Australian schools, six of the students were twenty-five or more, six were seventeen or less and four were women. In a country in which there had been almost no secondary education in government schools, the students reaching the Administrative College and the University in those early years were exceptional either by ability, chance or family background. As they graduated from the university from 1970 right when rapid localisation was taking place, many were soon in positions of power in the public service. Less predictable was the fact that nearly all chose to stand for election to parliament – even those who were heads of government departments.

As I listened to question time and the debates in Parliament I took particular notice of the Prime Minister, Sir Mekere Morauta, the ex-Prime Minister, Sir Rabbie Namaliu, and the Minister of Transport, Bart Philemon. All were from the first preliminary year of the University of Papua New Guinea. Dr John Waiko spoke, and he arrived in 1967 to join the second intake. Paul Pora, formerly Minister for Finance, was there, and he was in Stage 2 at the Administrative College in 1967, and later transferred to the University. There were others whom I had known as young men around the campus or Port Moresby, but who had not been in my courses. Later I lunched in the members' dining room with two ex-students and Ministers. In the lively conversation the frequent jokes came from reminiscences, many detailing misunderstandings and failings of naïve young teachers fresh from Australia. By the coincidence of finding a job in Port Moresby when the University was starting (a fact scarcely known to me) I had come to know some of the generation that would assume positions of power in Papua New Guinea. I had seen them grow from the tentative young men of nineteen who had knocked on my door in Waigani to explain that the bus had not come to take them to their breakfast to confident grey-haired men who direct the affairs of the nation. What they do was inconceivable to their grandparents, scarcely comprehensible to their parents, and astonishing to me – although I had gone along with all the glib statements made at official ceremonies about the opportunities and responsibilities that were soon to be theirs.

As a student of human behaviour, I am conscious of the privilege of having been able to observe those profound changes in lives. I appreciate the fact that the ex-students talk frankly with me and in front of me. And when I come to write about recent events in Papua New Guinea I use insights taken from watching and listening to them, but there are some things that I make oblique or leave out altogether. My advantage can be in generalisation, but not detail. Sentiment does not always lead to moderation. The brutal attack on a friend may result in an immediate desire for a tougher police response. Personal relationships need not lead to favouring one side over another. Ex-students oppose each other in parliament. In the civil war on Bougainville they were on both sides and in the middle. Ex-students have turned out to be rogues, likeable, but rogues. Thirty years of living in, visiting and thinking about a nation means accumulated sentiment attaching to people and places, and that has its impact on what can be known, what can be said, and what one wants to say.

At the first meeting of the Interim Council of the University of Papua New Guinea held in Port Moresby in October 1965 it was decided to start teaching in February 1966. As the University had neither teachers nor building this was a decision dependent on quick and temporary solutions, and it meant that there was little time to think about the content of courses. The history course had to be one familiar to teachers and with books readily available. Bill Gammage had just a few days in February 1966 to find stocks of text books in Sydney and get them consigned to Port Moresby. Bill had a course in modern European and overseas expansion underway by the time that I joined him at the showgrounds. The foundation professor of History, Ken Inglis, did not begin teaching until the start of the undergraduate courses in 1967, but during 1966 he was planning for the new courses. He had no doubt that the history of Papua New Guinea was going to be taught, it was just a matter of when and in what way.

At the Administrative College Peter Biskup, Cecil Abel and Brian Jinks were already teaching some Papua New Guinea history. Jinks was using Papua and New Guinea examples in his politics and government courses, Biskup and I had both written about Aboriginal history, and I was teaching the economic geography of Papua New Guinea using the World Bank Report as the class text. Much of Elton Brash's English was *Another Country* by black American novelist (called a 'Negro writer' on the dust jacket), James Baldwin. The visit by Tom Mboya, then Minister for Economic Planning and Development in Kenya, had stimulated interest in the history and current events in the new nations of Africa. For me, and I presume others, one compelling factor when thinking about the content of courses was daily being confronted by classes of Papua New Guineans (and one Samoan at the University), and it was in that context of trying to teach Papua New Guineans about Papua New Guinea and often settling for makeshift and parallel texts that Jinks asked Biskup and me to join him in writing a history of Papua and New Guinea suitable for high schools and the Administrative College students. We signed a contract in October 1966. Determined not to begin with European discovery, we were pleased with our first sentence, 'Man has been in New Guinea for a long time'. That sentence was soon to look both mundane and sexist.

The first *Handbook of the University of Papua New Guinea* was published in October 1966 and Inglis committed the new Department of History to teach the history of Papua New Guinea in the second semester of 1967. The only reference book listed was Charles Rowley's *The New Guinea Villager*. First published in 1965, it was subtitled *A Retrospect from 1964*. Significant as Rowley's book was, even more surprising in terms of its date of publication and its emphases was Stephen Reed's *The Making of Modern New Guinea*, with its concern for a 'Kanaka revolution', the emergence of a new society from the meeting of Europeans and New Guineans. But Reed's book had been published in 1943, it was out of print, and he could not, of course, foresee the impact of the war and the direction of post-war policies. Other anthropologists had written numerous monographs and several of them contained much history. Margaret Mead's *New Lives for Old* was a study of the war on Manus; Peter Lawrence's *Road Belong Cargo* not only followed cults through time, but included a rare, detailed biography of a New Guinean – Yali; and Richard Salisbury, who had written *From Stone to Steel*, was talking about his coming book which would give both a European and a village perspective on history. On a visit north in 1966, Inglis had brought with him a copy of K.M.Panikkar's *Asia and Western Dominance*. It was, Panikkar had claimed in 1953, the first time an Asia student had attempted to 'see and understand' 450 years of European activities in Europe. Panikkar was set as text for the first history undergraduate course to be taught at the University of Papua New Guinea.

As we prepared to teach Papua New Guinea history in the second semester of 1967, then, we were conscious of the way Asians were bringing Asian perspectives to their history, and that Africans were being put into African history; we had several books on white endeavours in Papua New Guinea (such as those by Souter, Mair and Legge); we had the lonely *New Guinea Villager*, and much other material that was fragmented, coming from several disciplines, and varying in its quality and purpose. The outside men in the government service, the missionaries, and Sir Hubert Murray had written extensively about what they did, and sometimes they were illuminating about those that they wished to govern or convert. Ken Inglis demonstrated what we might do in a lecture on the Russian traveller and scientist, Nikolai Miklouho-Maclay, who had first landed on the Madang Coast (he left his name on the Rai Coast) in the 1870s. In the writings then available Inglis had sufficient information available to name individual New Guineans who had met Maclay and say something of their immediate and long term-responses to his visit. That set a pattern of not trying to present a Papua New Guinean perspective or a history of Papua New Guineans, but of giving two sides. This also worked effectively where we were dealing with topics other than those that were obviously meetings. For example, it was simple enough for us to look up the labour regulations governing plantation workers and talk about hours of work, rates of pay, ration scales, rules governing recruiting, and changes over time. The Territory's *Annual Reports* provided generalised information on the numbers of recruits, which districts they came from, which industries they worked in, and how long they signed-on for: but in tutorials there were students who had lived alongside plantations and those whose fathers had worked on them. Similarly when teaching about the Second World War, missions, village officials, and patrol officers, the history staff could present the official policy, the legal framework, how the literate claimed they behaved, say something about what was said about Papua New Guineans in the written record, obtain limited testimony from those involved, and then invite discussion in tutorials. Many of those tutorials were rich occasions for me, and I hope of some interest to those Papua New Guineans and Australians who were there as students.

Later when I was writing about Papua New Guineans – such as Papuan medical assistants and those who served in the Pacific Islands Regiment – I was continuing what had seemed effective in teaching. I was certainly concerned about the experience of Papua New Guineans and I talked to them, but the articles were saying at least as much about policies and prejudices of Australians who managed and commented on Papua New Guineans employed in Australian-dominated institutions. The book on gold mining, *Black, White and Gold*, was more obviously about meetings; for each goldfield had a very different history: white miners with the same inclinations and presumptions simply behaved differently on Misima to what they did on the Yodda or Keveri or the Lakekamu. Bill Gammage, who had not learnt the approach from me because he and others were already talking and writing in a similar way, made this form of history richer in detail and more elegant in presentation in his article on the Rabaul strike and in his recent book *The Sky Travellers*.

In the early years when we began teaching the history of Papua New Guinea, I would have written about Papua New Guineans, trying to see experiences from their point of view, paraphrasing what they thought about what had happened to them, and assessing the impact on Papua New Guinean communities. But by the time I may have known enough to attempt to do that, circumstances and attitudes had changed, and I was saved from presumption. Australia was handing powers to Papua New Guineans and they were rapidly taking control of institutions – from parliament to the post office – and making them their own. It was reasonable to think that they were about to shift behind the desks once occupied by foreign historians, re-read old sources, exploit new ones, and write their histories. Also, where in 1966 we had been on the end of the movement that was putting Asians and Africans into their own history, by the time Papua New Guinea was becoming independent, various people around the world were saying that they owned their own past and they resented outsiders telling them who they had been, what had happened to them, and why they were who they were. That movement to claim group histories was probably strongest among minorities crowded out of national histories by those who were more numerous and had greater access to power, education and the media. Aborigines, Afro-Americans, Hawaiians, Maoris and Native Americans have all suffered exclusion and made strong claims for both recognition in the national history and for a another history – one that was different from that of the dominant groups. Those arguments were put less frequently and less stridently by Papua New Guineans, who had retained languages and land, were numerically dominant, and now had their own nation. For peoples who possessed the present, history was not as important as it was for those who felt dispossessed of both past and present. The few Papua New Guineans wanting to lay claim to the past by argument or by putting forward an alternative view, did little to diminish the inhibitions felt by foreigners who may have wanted to present Papua New Guineans with their own history.

The restraints on writing about current events – sentiment, the sense of being an outsider, personal considerations – were paralleled by the factors that help persuade historians to choose one topic over another. In 2000, based in Canberra, I like to take a perspective from somewhere in the Coral Sea, looking north and south, explaining Papua New Guineans to Australians, Australians to Papua New Guineans, Australians to Australians, but not completing the reflections by trying to tell Papua New Guineans about Papua New Guineans. The young Papuan woman at Jacksons International Airport had indeed asked a complex question, 'Have you been to our country before?' I had, but it had been different then, and it has been different on every arrival since. This time I even got confused trying to drive across Gordons to the university. The new Poreporena Freeway blocked my way; but then visiting historians are likely to find the signs hard to read.

19. The Joke in History

Delivered in Coombs Seminar Room E, ANU, 26 April 2006.

It was 1965. The travelling salesman got off the train in Wycheproof, and walked into the draper's shop. Now, for those of you that don't know the area, that is not a long walk. The Bendigo–Sea Lake train runs down the middle of Broadway, the main street in Wycheproof. The salesman slung his case of samples on the counter. He was smartly dressed, but not too smartly. He wants to show he is from the city, he knows good clothes, he is not a failure, but he is not a city-slicker. He says, 'Hullo, Mr Cuthbert. Still busy. Still running the best business in town?' He is friendly but not too matey. It's 'Mr Cuthbert'. He flatters, because that is expected, but not excessively. He pauses, smiles and he says, 'Did you hear about the newly married couple? They couldn't tell the difference between Vaseline and putty. You guessed it, Mr Cuthbert. A tragedy. First windy day, all their windows fell out'. Again he has to get it right. He brings the latest joke and it has to be on the edge of outrageous. It will be overheard by a woman sitting on a high stool turning over the pages of Butterick's thick pattern catalogue. It has to be at the level where Mrs Williamson will later say, 'You'll never guess what I heard in Cuthbert's. I could never repeat it'. But, with just the right amount of encouragement, of course she does.

I told that story because I want you to have three points in mind: jokes have a context – they are told in a particular place to a particular audience; jokes have a function – and that is obvious in the case of the salesman; and there can be a fine line on whether the teller has got the joke right – because jokes often deal with sex, race, religion, nationality, politics, abnormalities and grossness. There was this Anglican vicar, a Catholic priest and a Jewish rabbi who were called upon to bless the mayor's new car … but you all know the joke.

A senior travelling salesman took a young colleague to his first annual salesmen's dinner. It was a fine occasion, and after the entrée and the formal toasts, various guests finished a mouthful of rack of lamb, stood up, gained attention, and called out a number: '75' or '17' or '38'. Each number was followed by thigh-slapping, uproarious laughter. The young salesman asked his older mentor what was going on.

'Oh', said the older salesman. 'I'm sorry. I should have explained. You've got your travelling salesman's joke book? Well all of us know the jokes in there so well, we save time by just calling out the joke's number'.

'Great idea', said the young salesman, 'Can I have a go?'

'Of course. Of course'.

So the young salesman pulled out his joke book, flicked through, put it back in his pocket, stood up a bit self-consciously, and said, '26'. There was no laughter, not even a snicker. Deflated, he sat down.

'What went wrong?' he asked.

'Well', said the older salesman, 'It was the timing'.

There is a craft to the writing and the telling of jokes. Same jokes and different tellers get different responses. Context, function, edge and craft.

When Tim Bowden and I were collecting material on the experiences of Australian prisoners of war of the Japanese, many of the ex-prisoners told us the same joke. Soon after they surrendered in Singapore on 15 February 1942, many Australian prisoners were sent from Changi into Singapore City on work parties. There they cleaned up the debris of battle, worked on the wharves and – just to rub it in – built a memorial shrine to the Japanese dead. Soon the men were short of food, in fact short of everything, and they began 'scrounging'. That is, they began thieving. They felt justified in doing this because they were taking from the enemy; they thought that by international law they were being short-changed; and they soon learnt that either they stole or they died. Men took pride in the art of scrounging. But the penalties were often arbitrary, immediate and horrific. One day a Japanese guard walked on to a work site, called the men together, took a digger's slouch hat and casually dropped it over a tin of condensed milk. He then said 'You Australians think I know fuck nothing. I tell you I know fuck all'. Then, with exaggerated casualness he walked over to where he had left the slouch hat and went to pick up the hat and the tin. But his hand closed on the limp hat. There was no tin. Some digger had pinched it while he was talking.

If the incident happened at all, then at most forty or fifty prisoners saw it, and later Tim and I were to say that we had spoken to eighty of them. It was a story that spread rapidly and widely among the prisoners, and Australian prisoners wanted to claim it as their own. The story raced nearly all the ex-prisoners home. Able Seaman Arthur Bancroft, he was called 'Blood' Bancroft because of his red hair, was on the cruiser *Perth* when it was sunk in Sunda Strait. Blood was one of just half the crew that survived battle and drowning. He was imprisoned in Java, shipped to Singapore in October 1942, and became part of 'A' Force that went to Burma to work on the Burma–Thailand Railway. Having recovered a little of his strength, Blood was selected to go to Japan to work in shipyards and mines. The Japanese brought him down the Mekong to Saigon, but by this time Japanese shipping was being disrupted by Allied bombing and American submarines. Blood was sent back to Phnom Penh by river ferry and then by train across Southeast Asia to Singapore. In September 1944 he went on board the Japanese transport *Rokyu Maru*, and was soon at sea in a convoy on its way to Japan. American submarines attacked in the South China Sea sinking several ships. The *Rokyu Maru* with about 1250 prisoners crammed on board was one. After a few days the American submarines came back through the wreckage they had wrought. They picked up Blood after he had been six days in the water. He was one of eighty Australians taken to Saipan and from there to Australia. In collaboration with R.G. Roberts, Arthur Bancroft wrote his account of being a prisoner of war, *The Mikado's Guests*. The austere war-time edition of Blood's account came out before the end of the war, and obviously before there was any pattern of how to characterise the behaviour of captors or captives. Early in his memoir, Bancroft takes delight in the Australians' skill as thieves: he says, 'Ali Baba and his Forty Thieves were mere amateurs'. He returns to the theme near the end of the book and tells the story of the hat and the disappearing can of milk.

Blood's was the first of a long line of reminiscences. They still come. Rowley Richard's *A Doctor's War* was published in 2005 when Rowley was 88. So that's sixty years of reminiscences. And the tin disappears often. Rowley skipped that story, but the bold claim 'I know fuck-all' was used in Alan Hopgood's play 'Weary' which had its premiere in Canberra in February 2005. I was probably the first to put the 'fuck-all' line into print (that was in 1985) so I was pleased to hear it get a good laugh in the Canberra Theatre Centre.

We can speculate about why the Australians liked the hat and disappearing tin joke and wanted to appropriate it. It's one of the weapons of the oppressed and the threatened with no chance to speak openly to have jokes in which they triumph and the oppressors are shown to be stupid. The hat joke is also one in which there is no horror and the Japanese are not shown to be brutal. The teller often begins, 'This Jap wasn't a bad bloke but he knew just enough English to get himself into trouble …' In Blood Bancroft's account, at the end of the day an Australian pulled the tin from his pocket and threw it to the guard with a cheerful, 'Here's your can of milk, Nip'. The surprised guard recovered, laughed and threw it back saying, 'Australia Number One'. The hat joke is one that presents the Australians as winning and taking the initiative when they had suffered defeat and were humiliated and smarting at their own impotence. It presents them as they want others to see them – displaying a casual larrikin indifference to authority and being winners; and it's a story that (with some moderation of the 'fuck-all' line) can be told anywhere. There is no starvation, no brutality, and no deaths. The Australians are the worthy sons of Ned Kelly and the Anzacs and the Japanese are generous in their acknowledgment.

The Boy from Boort

The hat joke may well have been first told in Australia by convicts at Sydney Cove. If people know of any record of this joke circulating among light-fingered slaves working on Hadrian's Wall or the Hanging Gardens of Babylon they can let me know.

But the point I want to make about this joke is that it has a history. Jokes are in our history and they themselves have a history, a provenance. So context, function, edge, craft and history.

Three different things provoked me into thinking about jokes. The first was reading Michael Young's first volume of his biography of Bronislaw Malinowski (*Malinowski: Odyssey of an Anthropologist 1884–1920*, Yale University Press, New Haven, 2004). This is a book based on wide and detailed research, assessing a leading social scientist of the twentieth century, presenting it to a world readership and requiring sustained scholarly writing. The need to write well is all the greater because Malinowski was himself a fine writer who engaged a wide range of readers and exposed them to a new discipline and the frontiers of scholarship about human behaviour. Young succeeds. His prose is always sharp and clear, and he has a consciousness of structure that goes beyond ensuring that there is an orderly sequence of narrative and analysis. Here is Young's summary: Malinowski 'could be moody, irritable, hypersensitive, self-absorbed, vain, petulant, foul-mouthed, sentimental and melancholic. But he could also be gregarious, emotionally generous, deeply courteous and scintillatingly eloquent. He was a demonically hard worker whose zeal galvanized those around him' (p. xxv). While reading this book, I found that I was often amused by the incidents described, the author's touches of irony and the occasional joke. After having introduced Borenius, a Finn who was a friend of Malinowski's in London, Michael Young has the single line: 'Malinowski liked to pun: "I supply the polish and Borenius the finish"' (p. 176). Other historians would have put that line in a footnote; or left it out altogether, but told it often in conversation.

The second stimulus to thinking about jokes in history was reading Alan Powell's *The Third Force*, a history of Angau, the Australian New Guinea Administrative Unit, the army unit that took over the administration of New Guinea during World War II. This is a book dense with detail. But just occasionally, there is an arresting anecdote. The American 1st Marine Division landed on Cape Gloucester in west New Britain on Boxing Day 1943. The 1st Marines had fought on Guadalcanal, rested and retrained in Australia. They were experienced and tough. They were supported by aircraft and a massive naval bombardment. On that first day, they put ashore over 12,000 troops and 7,600 tons of equipment. A few Australians in Angau went ashore with the Americans. Two of them were Keith McCarthy and Mark Pitt, both had served in the prewar administration in New Guinea and they knew each other well. Alan Powell quotes Keith McCarthy:

19. The Joke in History

'How goes it?' I shouted in Mark's ear, amid the fantastic din. 'No good', growled Pitt. 'The natives are completely out of control. They deserted their villages and won't obey my orders to come in'. 'Good God, man! You wouldn't expect them to do anything else with a bloody war all around them, would you?' 'It's no good', said Mark. 'They're ruined. The native sense of discipline is gone'. (Powell, p. 248)

In his introduction to the incident, Powell says that it could serve as a 'requiem for the pre-war social relations'. And at the end of the incident he makes no further comment. It is nicely used. It arises easily from what has gone before, and it is both evidence and illustration of the point that Powell wants to make about the dramatic and terrible disruption of war and the nostalgia of some of the whites for the prewar order. And it's funny.

The third thing that provoked me to think about jokes and how they are told and used was last year's reunion of the Boort football club's fiftieth anniversary of its 1955 premiership. I got an invitation as I had been a teenage member of the second eighteen. We did not win anything – except a few fights. We did a lap of honour when our captain won the toss. The reunion spread over several events. One was a lunch for about sixty people on the Saturday before that afternoon's game. After a formal welcome and the guest speaker, people were invited to the microphone to say whatever they thought appropriate. Many spoke. And many of them chose to recount incidents. The stories came in a style familiar to me, but I had forgotten how well they could be told. Strawb wandered up to the microphone. His real name is Aubrey, but that rhymes with strawberry which was reduced to 'Strawb'. Strawb began, 'We were playing the "Burn"'. That is Wedderburn. 'Wind and showers were blowing across the ground, and like a mob of cattle looking for shelter, many of the "Burn" had mobbed up on the half-forward flank. Redda and the ball were somewhere in the middle of the pack. Now as you know', Strawb said, 'Redda had more courage than sense'. Everyone turned and had a look at Redda. Stawb continued: 'So finding himself completely surrounded by red and black jerseys Redda knew what he had to do: retaliate first. So he clouted the closest bloke. All hell broke loose. In between swinging desperate punches Redda called to me. I was the only team mate within seventy yards: "Come on Strawb. Back-to-back and we'll have these bastards"'.

Strawb paused here and that gives me a chance to explain that before he began to talk Strawb had to lower the microphone. He is about 5 ft 7", standing on a box.

Strawb continued, 'So I said to Redda: "I see your predicament, Redda, and I appreciate the way you have selected me. But I wonder, Redda, if you could see your way clear to call upon one of the others"'.

With that Strawb left the microphone and returned to his seat and another of the old team mates wandered up.

It was one of many well-expressed and carefully crafted anecdotes. No doubt it had been through several edits during its many retellings. It was now sharp, concise and effectively underplayed. I realised that there were not many of my colleagues who, equipped with a better vocabulary and with the advantage of having dissected many a literary text, corrected a thousand student essays and worked long and hard on their own prose, could have told their stories as well as the country footballers at their fiftieth reunion. One difference is that those country footballers live within communities where the ability to hone and tell an anecdote is appreciated. Not all attempt to do it, but those who do it publicly had better do it well. Criticism of the failed anecdote may be short on detail, but it cannot be misunderstood. It may come in words such as, 'Bert, if I hear you mangle that yarn again, I'll spilt your head with a tyre lever and personally remove the defective bit of brain where good yarns go in and crap comes out'. That's shearing shed lunch-time lit crit.

It was at about this time at the reunion that Wychitella Byrnes said that we needed to problematise the definitional relationships between modes of mirth evocation. Wyche used to be the Jacques Lacan of the Buckrabanyule watershed; but after the drought broke in the spring he shifted to selling off Dorset-Merino first cross fat lambs. Wyche had a point. The price of lambs went up. But not forgetting the nuanced discourse space he had once adumbrated, Wyche led us in a chorus of that hymn: 'Oh what a friend we have in exegeses'.

Had any of that ever crossed Wyche's mind, he would have been right about the need for some sorting out of what we mean by 'joke'. I have, as should have been obvious, been laying out examples of a formal joke, wit with words, anecdotes, and the send-up which itself may range from gentle irony to sarcasm and to the absurd. I will try and illustrate some more about the differences, and say something about the utility of each for writers.

William Manchester the American novelist, biographer and historian wrote one of the most quoted, but not most reliable, biographies of General Douglas MacArthur: *American Caesar*, 1978. Manchester himself had fought as a marine from Guadalcanal to Okinawa, and the marine corps was navy, and MacArthur was army. Manchester and the marines were fighting close to MacArthur's army and competing with it for supplies and on strategy, and post-battle they competed for recognition and glory. Manchester's story of his war is told in *Goodbye, Darkness: A Memoir of the Pacific War*, 1980. The easy-going friendly Admiral Chester Nimitz, commander-in-chief of the Pacific fleet, was the man who was the direct competitor to the egocentric MacArthur. They met before the invasion of Hollandia and Aitape in 1944. I think they met in Australia, and not New Guinea. Here is Manchester writing of the encounter between the competing commanders:

> *Addressing their two staffs, Nimitz said of himself and MacArthur that 'the situation reminds me of the story of the two frantically worried men who were pacing the corridor of their hotel. One finally turned to the other, "What are you worried about?" The answer was: "I am a doctor and I have a patient in my room with a wooden leg and I have the leg apart and can't get it back together again". The other responded: "Great guns, I wish that was all I had to worry about. I have a great-looking gal in a room with both legs apart, and I can't remember the room number"'.*

That's a joke, but Manchester can get away with it because Nimitz told it, and it says something about the contest between MacArthur and Nimitz, and the style of Nimitz. Generally, I am not keen on the sorts of jokes that get into the commercial travellers' handbook of numbered jokes for all occasions.

For historians the anecdote often works better. When we were collecting material for *Taim Bilong Masta* we heard many superb anecdotes, some of which we could not use. This is another story from Keith McCarthy, the author of the incident on Cape Gloucester quoted by Alan Powell.

In the late 1930s Keith was Assistant District Officer at Talasea on New Britain. On one of his inspections of plantations on the coast east of Talasea, he arrived on the same day as the Burns Philp steamer. The planters had had a tough time during the depression, and the price of copra remained low at the end of the decade. The planter, I'll call him Axel because he was a Scandinavian, was desperate to get his copra loaded. He knew that the Burns Philp captain would give him little sympathy. If weather or schedule demanded that he pull away from the plantation jetty, he would, and there was not likely to be another boat for six weeks or so. Keith had no chance of inspecting labourers or records and he settled to watch the activity. The copra was being carted to the jetty by bullock cart. The bullock was moving with the slow, steady tread of the good working bullock, and the somnolent New Guinean driver sat on the shaft. Axel rushed up and in furious pidgin demanded that the driver give the bullock a hurry-up. The New Guinean gave the bullock a casual flick with his long cane, and the bullock's tread did not change. Axel abused the New Guinean, hauled him off his seat, snatched the cane, and belted the bullock. Disturbed by all this the bullock stopped and turned its head to have a look at what was going on. Axel, with increased fury, grabbed the head of the bullock to make it face in the direction of the jetty, and gave the bullock a round arm clout. Now a bullock's skull is heavy bone. Axel's fist rebounded, and from this point on you must imagine Axel with one bruised hand and a near-paralysed arm tucked into his side.

Axel seized on a plan to both punish the bullock and force it into plenty of hurry up. He grabbed some dried palm fronds, stacked them under the bullock's belly and with great difficulty with his one good hand and one half-paralysed arm, lit a match. As soon as the bullock felt the heat it moved forward, and as soon as the heat stopped so did the bullock. But the fire was now under the dray. By this time an audience of plantation labourers had gathered. All looked solemn and concerned. Not a flicker of a smile crossed one face. Axel screamed abuse and a few labourers went off, not too quickly, to get buckets of water, and others gathered around the smoking dray, but to the fury of Axel they were doing more looking than fire-fighting. Suddenly dray and copra burst into flame. With heat and a crackling fire behind it the bullock took off. It dashed down the slope, dragging its flaming chariot, clattered on to the end of the jetty, failed to run a straight line, plunged over the side, and stood with waves breaking along its heaving sides and the smoking copra bags drifting away from the dray.

The war came, passed and Keith McCarthy returned to New Britain. Keith was easily recognised. He was big and he had sandy red hair. He came back to Axel's plantation. But Axel was not there; the plantation had been regenerated by a new owner. He saw an older New Guinean looking at him, and after a while the New Guinean said, 'Macarti?' – as Keith was always known. '*Bipo taim bilong pait long ol man bilong Japan*'. 'You were here before the war'.

As the two began to talk, other New Guineans gathered around. The man who first spoke identified himself as the driver of the bullock dray for Masta Axel. All the New Guineans knew the story of steamer day and the great *hariap*. They began a familiar narrative with familiar actions. '*Wanpela bulamakau tanim pinis het bilong en, isi isi*'. 'The bullock turned his head, slowly slowly'. And several of them turned their heads slowly. '*Masta Axel paitim het bilong bulamakau*'. They flung the punch, suffered jarring pain in the hand and arm, and tucked the injured wing against their sides. They rolled with laughter as they said how the bullock moved forward and the fire was then under the dray. As some did Masta Axel's shouted abuse others rolled their eyes, said sorry many times, clicked their tongues and generally played the role of those who want to look like they are worried and trying to help, but are unable to understand and have no initiative. They described the last mad dash of the bullock, and all pretended to look over the side of jetty before falling over each other in an explosion of laughter.

Steamer day at Axel's plantation is a great anecdote. It tells us much about the desperation of the planters who were in debt and dependent on the trading companies' steamers. Some of them were then leaving coconuts uncollected on the ground, and many were malarious and lonely, the family having shifted to Australia. But most of all it reveals how those who are poorly paid and on the lowest rank in a racially segregated society retain dignity, have fun, and keep alive something of their own history. It is also a good anecdote because it is not dependent on the final punch line, but has a sequence of accumulating incidents, all of them interesting, all illuminating and all funny.

But while I have chosen to use steamer day and the great *hariap* as an example of an anecdote, I have not exploited it in a published form. It is too long. It is hard to fit into history on radio or on the page. It dominates by its length and in its hilarious imagery. It means a long separation between the introductory setting and the conclusions that might be drawn from it.

Other great anecdotes from Papua New Guinea and from the prisoners of war bring with them the same merits and problems: they have become beautifully constructed, they offer numerous delights of image, incident and side-track, and they tell us much about the history of a particular community, but they are difficult to use in the history that historians publish. I think of a story that I have heard Slim DeGrey tell and which he included in his reminiscences of Changi, the story of the eight-man dog. The historian wants a concise and immediately relevant anecdote – like Alan Powell's use of the despondent Mark Pitt and the lack of discipline in the villagers of war-torn Cape Gloucester.

While steamer day at Axel's is still fresh, I want to draw attention to another characteristic of jokes. They come out of particular cultures and they draw their type of humour and style of telling from those cultures. Steamer day has many of the characteristics of jokes told in Papua New Guinea. Often Pidgin, *Tok Pisin*, is the language of jokes. Everybody knows the story, it has many incidents, often slapstick, often violent, there are many laughs along the way, the repetitions in Pidgin seem to work so well – '*isi isi*', '*planti planti*', '*longwe longwe moa iet*' – and the accumulating incidents may end in chaos. That style is different from that influencing Strawb: he was expected to be concise, be clever in his use of language ('retaliate first'), have a fine control of the narrative, and be understated. All of you will know the New York Jewish loser style that Woody Allen uses – the stories in which he is going home from analysis and is beaten up by Quakers. Or the jokes of the late Dave Allen in which he talked of the triangular relationship between Irish parishioners, priest and God. If – as is obvious – the style of a joke is influenced by the culture of origin, then equally obviously jokes can be used to tell us much about those cultures. Historians who must always enter another culture, a culture separated from the researcher by time and usually by both time and place, ought to believe that they can make comprehensible the jokes of others. If they can not do that then neither can they say much about the religion or politics or social relations of other communities.

The Boy from Boort

I mentioned a third category of what we might broadly think of as a joke, and that is wit in words. We have had the example from Michael Young in which Malinowski provided the polish and his Scandinavian mate the finish. But historians have a great advantage in their writing because they can and should take those words and phrases that are so evocative of time and place, and also are compressed jokes. To take a simple example: the Hagen overcoat. In the highlands of New Guinea it sometimes gets cold, and on higher slopes there may be frosts. People do not wear clothes on the upper part of the body, so in the cold they can be seen with arms across their chests, hugging themselves. It is a common sight in the morning around Mt Hagen where there may be frost on the high slopes. So to have hunched shoulders and crossed arms to keep out the cold is to wear the Hagen overcoat.

The prisoners-of-war were inventive with language. To be 'Jap-happy' was to be too friendly or obsequious to the guards. But as the prisoners' uniforms wore out many found they had to adopt Japanese clothes, and often they worked or knocked around camp in the length of cloth that wound around the waist and between the legs. That also became known as a 'Jap-happy'. Men found that they could steal food when out on work details and smuggle it back to camp in a Jap-happy. That was called crutching. One of the most resourceful Jap-happy crutchers managed to carry a live chook back to camp. His record as the champion Jap-happy crutcher was challenged by Snow Peat – he crutched a pineapple, rough end and all. Now, not all communities have vocabularies with the sophistication and subtlety of that example, but all have words that are loaded with values, that are evocative of time and place and are often witty. They are there to be exploited – not too often, but often enough to help a reader enter that other time that we have researched.

When writing history, irony is an excellent tool. Gentle, subtle irony works best. If we use heavy sarcasm or lapse into the absurd, it is too hard to bring the reader back to serious revelations. We risk losing control of genre and purpose. But too often historians and other social scientists deploy irony against the easy targets. Many of us cannot avoid irony when we describe and quote a nineteenth-century missionary, a colonial official instructing villagers on hygiene, a planter sitting on his cane chair being served a drink by a black servant, a British army officer on the Northwest Frontier or in the Boer War. We send up the stereotype. That has all been done too often. But again I think that Michael Young gets it about right. He admires and is sympathetic to Malinowski, but after Malinowski has flattered a fourth or fifth attractive woman by seeming to want her judgment on complex issues, encouraged her to work with him, gone to bed with her, then quickly tried to untangle the relationship and written a profound and lengthy analysis of his own psychological state and morality, Young does employ restrained, effective irony.

19. The Joke in History

I have mentioned that jokes have a history, and I wanted to say something about collections of jokes that circle among particular groups of people and what they tell us about those people. Communities and cultures not only cultivate jokes of a certain style, they also have jokes with elements in common. The ones that I know most about are the racist jokes that were told by Australians in Papua New Guinea through much of the twentieth century, and the jokes that circulated among Australian servicemen. Both are rich historical sources, tell us much, and are under-used. Peter Stanley wrote a brief paper on Bluey and Curly cartoons. Bluey and Curly spent a lot of their black and white penned war in New Guinea. They were drawn by Alex Gurney and first appeared in the Melbourne *Sun News Pictorial* in February 1941. Amirah Inglis in her book *Not a White Woman Safe: Sexual Anxiety and Politics in Port Moresby, 1920–1934*, ANU Press, Canberra, 1974, used the story of the white woman and the towel story very well. And there are a few others who have drawn on jokes. But a rich field remains. Those who glean in that field have an obligation to both tell and analyse the jokes – both demand high skills.

There is one digger joke that I have always liked. It is from World War I, from the Great War. General William Birdwood, the Englishman, commanded the Anzac Corps, and by mid-1916 the Anzacs were in action on the Somme. You can imagine the trenches, churned mud, duckboards, and shell-holed no-man's land. Two diggers are leaning against the side of a trench, smoking and holding their .303 rifles casually in one hand. They watch a senior officer followed by an attendant junior officer pick his way along the trench. The diggers don't take their eyes off the two officers, but they don't shift to allow a wider passage and they don't salute. After the senior officer has passed the junior officer spins around and comes back. He says, 'Don't you who that was?' The diggers consider the question. One answers: 'Nope'. 'You ever met him, Barney?' 'Nah, not me'. 'That was General Birdwood'. And the first digger says, 'Well why doesn't he have feathers on his arse like any other bird would?'

This did not happen. It's imagined. But again it reveals much about the way some Australians want to see themselves. I reckon it's a great joke.

But my judgement of jokes has been known to be faulty. I once left a university meeting rather pleased with my profound and witty intervention. One of my more perceptive colleagues came up to me, and I was ready to receive his compliment on my wit. He said, 'Hank, there is a distinction that eludes you: that is the distinction between being smart and being a smart-arse'.

How many empiricists does it take to change a light globe?

We don't know. They just keep coming up with more anecdotal evidence.

20. Have You Got a Title? Seminar Daze

The Coombs: A House of Memories *(2006), pp. 235–42.*

When I arrived at the Coombs Building at the end of 1972, I reported to my new head of department, John La Nauze, in the Research School of Social Sciences. An Australian who had been at Balliol College, Oxford, in the 1930s, La Nauze seemed reserved and English. 'And what are you going to do, Nelson?' he asked. I told him that I was going to write a book. I was just about to launch into a summary of the astounding soon-to-be book, when he said, 'That's good, Nelson. Some people come here and they just go to seminars or do photocopying. I'm glad you're writing a book'. With that the meeting ended and I was out in the still unfamiliar Coombs corridors. I thought, he has lived up to his name, 'Jack the Knife'. Later, I was to appreciate La Nauze's scholarship and generosity. As I should have known, his learning, craft as a writer and understanding of his fellows were all apparent in his two-volume biography of Alfred Deakin.

La Nauze was right to warn of the time-consuming danger of seminars. In an ordinary week there are about 55 seminars in the six seminar rooms of the Coombs. On Mondays there might be eight or nine; they peak on Tuesdays, Wednesdays and Thursdays in a flush mid-week harvest of a dozen-a-day seminars; and decline to nine or ten again on Fridays. In most weeks the Coombs seminars spill over into University House, where departments sponsor one-or two-day conferences, and the Chancelry, where they exploit executive meeting rooms. Before the opening of the annex, Coombs academics were holding some 65 seminars a week. That's well over 2000 in a year. During the 33 years that I have been around the Coombs, perhaps 50,000 nervous or confident, novice or experienced academics have presented seminar papers.

Seminars flourish in spite of doubtful utility. It takes longer to listen to 6000 words than to read them, and reading is more likely to lead to careful assessment. Most people going to seminars retain little. They have just a general interest in the topic, and they note details only when they are relevant to their own work. Beyond that, they might be stimulated by the scholarly method, the way material is organised, or sources of data. Two days after the seminar, they would be lucky to recall five out of 50 minutes, and in a week that might be reduced to two. The seminar survives as a social occasion, a test before peers, and a commitment to a date that forces production. The seminar paper will have a second life as an article or a chapter.

Like others, I remember more of the occasion and particular incidents than the content. It was always good to sit alongside Bob Langdon. Bob had no formal tertiary education, but he was not intimidated by real or pretended expertise. In his own search for learning, he asked frank and searching questions, and in reply he demanded clarity. He also had a special weapon. Having gone from school to South Australian public service and in 1942 into the Australian navy, Bob worked his way to post-war England as a merchant seaman. Down and out in London, he revived his school shorthand by pawning his watch and typewriter, took a course at Pitman's College and spent his time on lightening phrases and transcribing his *Concise Oxford Dictionary* into shorthand. Soon his shorthand speed was fast enough to apply for a job as a Hansard reporter. Instead he went to Bolivia, and later exploited his shorthand as secretary and journalist. In Seminar Room E, Bob always listened intently, but would appear to take down just a quick casual note or two. At the end of the seminar he would preface a question with a statement such as: 'When talking about Queen Emma in Rabaul you said …' The astonishment of many a stranger to the Coombs grew with each verbatim sentence quoted back. Suddenly, the presenter realised he might be held to account for every word.

It was different sitting next to Oskar Spate. He had come to the Department of Pacific and Southeast Asian History after a career as geographer and director of the Research School of Pacific Studies. As he listened to the speaker, he would draw a contour map. Gradually a landscape emerged: promontories, deep gullies and winding streams, the density of contours indicating steep slopes and much danger of erosion. He would also pen witty couplets and limericks. On the back of a filing card on which was typed 'Tate, Vernon, Spanish Documents relating to the Voyage of the Racoon …' he once scribbled:

A chesty young lass of Mount Hagen

Believed in straight talk and no jargon

'I want two hundred pigs

ten shells and twelve wigs,

and even at that I'm a bargain!'

A good listener and sharp critic, Oskar sometimes made it hard for those beside him to give full attention to the speaker. I kept the card on which he had written of the Mount Hagen lass, and later used it as a bookmark in his autobiography, *On the Margins of History*.

Derek Freeman could be a more disconcerting seminar companion. When new to the Coombs, I went to an Anthropology Department seminar and sat next to Derek. Even before the seminar began he had taken out the Oxford

University Press edition of *The Poetical Works of William Blake*, and was soon immersed in *Songs of Innocence and Experience*. As the speaker began, Derek turned away so that his shoulder and most of his back were towards the head of the table. Every now and again Derek demonstrated his commitment to the power and simplicity of Blake's lines by making a note in the margin. Distracted and uncomfortable at this display of apparent indifference to what was being said, I missed much of the seminar. But as soon as the chairman asked for any questions and comments, Derek put his book down, corrected a couple of points of detail in the presentation and then fluently and without rancour destroyed the basis of the paper.

In Coombs seminars, careers have been made and ended. I chaired two ends. In one, words that should have been seen to be empty in writing were obviously so when spoken. It was then clear that the speaker would never write a publishable book. On another day I chaired C. Hartley Grattan who had by then retired from the University of Texas. Grattan had first visited Australia in 1927, published his first work on Australian literature soon after, and in 1942 had written *Introducing Australia*, a significant book for its time and for the Americans who were to read it. In 1963 he had published his two-volume work, *The Southwest Pacific*. The Grattan that I ushered from the tea room to Seminar Room D had a fifty-year record of writing on Australasia, was carefully dressed, urbane, and while elderly still had an easy fluency in an accent that came from Massachusetts, Texas and much world travel. He had notes to carry him through the first part of the address, but when he had to speak from memory he lost his certainty of sentence construction, and at times wandered into endless clauses. He had the fluency but he was not conveying the scholarship that he had displayed so easily through a long career. It was very sad. In question time he recovered, and answered adequately. Afterwards one of my colleagues told me I should have stopped the presentation much earlier. I replied simply, 'I couldn't'.

In the same room and soon after, I chaired another seminar which was equally embarrassing but the cause less public and more comic. A colleague had encountered an ex-diplomat who at the height of his career had been – and I am now making up details – the Third Secretary in the High Commission in Apia where he had been witness to significant events. He was asked to come along and share his knowledge. Unfortunately I had not been able to get a clear idea of what he was going to talk about, and as we sat at the head of the table waiting for casual academics to wander in, tinkling their cups and saucers, I leaned across and said, 'Have you got a title?' 'No', he answered, with fierce enthusiasm. He then launched into an impassioned speech: 'Well might you ask. All the other members of the department have been recognised. None of them, I think I can fairly say, have my record of service. I thought that in the last Queen's Birthday List I would have been recognised'. At this point I belatedly realised that I had invited him to express his pent-up anger about his own lack of a title. That left both of us in need of a title. I commiserated with him, and turned to the audience and gave some lame introduction which went a little like: 'How fortunate we are to have Mr ... with us and, as we all know, he is going to talk about something or other and it probably happened in Apia or nearby ...'

One of the most tense and productive seminars that I have been involved in took place in August 1991. Gavan McCormack and I gathered together six Australian ex-prisoners of war, a Korean who had served in the Japanese army as a guard of the prisoners, Japanese historians and Australian and Japanese journalists. All the ex-servicemen had been on the Burma–Thailand Railway. Because we were uncertain about what would happen and we did not want to put excess strain on the elderly participants, we had given the seminar no more publicity than the internal reminders that normally circulated within the Coombs for a departmental seminar. We also wanted all the participants to sit around the central table and talk, rather than give formal papers to an audience on the other side of a lectern. Some of the ex-prisoners of war, such as Tom Uren, ex-cabinet minister in the Whitlam and Hawke governments, and Sir Edward 'Weary' Dunlop, already recognised as the heroic surgeon and leader, were experienced speakers, and while all the others were articulate, several were hesitant about speaking at a university at any time, and certainly before an audience including their ex-enemies. We had unwisely used the term 'colloquium' in one of the descriptions of what we hoped was to happen. Hugh Clarke, an artillery man who had worked on the Thai end of the railway and then been shipped to Japan, rang up and asked, 'What's a bloody colloquium? I can't even understand what the dictionary says'.

We wanted the ex-prisoners to be candid and detailed. They had to show what was concealed behind phrases in Japanese histories which referred to 'unfortunate' or 'regrettable' events, but did not say what they were. We need not have worried. The ex-prisoners were determined to say exactly what had happened. Tom Morris had enlisted under-age straight from finishing his New South Wales Leaving Certificate, and he was nineteen when he was working on the Burma end of the Railway. Having recovered from sickness, Tom volunteered to work in the 55 Kilo Hospital, and at great emotional cost to himself he now carefully, almost relentlessly, described the stench, the overcrowding and the 'putrid cloths that were washed over and over again to cover ulcers'. The only treatment available was crude curettage of the festering ulcers, done without any pain killers or sedatives. Tom said: 'It was not unusual for 80 to 100 patients to have their ulcers scraped and gouged ... each day. It was pathetic to hear the screams of these poor souls, whose shattered nerves could no longer stand the strain ...' The nearby Japanese hospital, Tom said, was then 'lavishly supplied with drugs and medicines'. The ex-prisoners answered questions from the

Japanese historians and journalists without any apparent anger or resentment, and again with evocative, disturbing detail. On that cold day on the shady side of the Coombs I sweated with the tension and out of sympathy for those suffering from heat and deprivation on the Railway.

The Korean ex-guard, Yi Hak-Nae, was in an invidious position. But as we learnt, much of his life had been spent in difficult circumstance, and the discomfort of speaking in a Coombs seminar in front of his victims' comrades was far from the worst situation he had faced. He too had a story that he wanted told. With single-minded concentration that seemed to add to the narrative, Gavan translated for Yi Hak-Nae. He wanted, he said, to apologise to the ex-prisoners. He had visited the graves of the 6000 prisoners buried at Kanchanaburi in Thailand, left flowers, prayed and was unable to restrain his anger and tears. He then went on to explain how he had been taken into the Japanese army, beaten every day, and sent to Thailand as a guard. There, he could not avoid 'absolute, unconditional and immediate obedience' to all orders. After the war he had been charged as a war criminal for not providing adequate food and medicines, forcing sick prisoners to work, and failing to control subordinates who ill-treated prisoners. He was sentenced to death, and after eight months' wait, his sentence was reduced to twenty years imprisonment. Released on parole after ten years, he could not return to his 'beloved home country' because he was branded a Japanese collaborator and war criminal, but in Japan he had suffered discrimination and been forced to 'live in the extreme poverty'. He had been trying to persuade the Japanese government to recognise that he and his Korean comrades had been compelled to work for the Japanese army, and that they should be given the same aid that the Japanese government has given its own ex-servicemen – including those convicted of war crimes. Yi Hak-Nae also wondered why those at 'the lowest levels' went to prison and so few of those responsible for that 'nightmare period' were punished by the Allies. The ex-prisoners, still with vivid memories of bashings and deaths, may not have been moved to sympathy, but they did emerge with greater understanding.

The book that came out of that seminar, *The Burma–Thailand Railway*, was published in English and Japanese, and remained available ten years later. The Japanese scholars engaged by Gavan used their access to living and archival sources in Australia to increase their knowledge and publish further material in Japan. It was interesting to see the trust that developed between the Japanese historians and the ex-prisoners: both sides recognised the mutual desire to get the record straight. On return to Japan, one of the Japanese historians received a death threat from an extreme right wing organisation.

Nearly every week, scholars give seminars in the Coombs in what for them is a foreign language. They win admiration for battling through a written script, struggling with the inconsistencies between English spelling and pronunciation, and trying to interpret questions that come in a variety of accents from the Mallee and Maine to Manchester. On one occasion a speaker came to a halt, went red in the face and then emitted a word, a cough or sneeze. He went back to the start of the sentence and again halted and exploded. He tried a third time with the same result. Fortunately, a quiet, humane scholar sitting nearby looked across at the paper and said quietly, 'gonorrhoea'. The speaker had been attempting to begin a list of introduced diseases, and had been ambushed by an impenetrable collection of consonants.

My own experience of giving seminars overseas has scarcely been marked with success. When I spoke at the Cenderawasih University at Jayapura in what was then Irian Jaya, I was pleased to see a crowded hall. At the end of the talk I was given prolonged applause. For a moment I thought I had gained an international reputation. But the presence of uniformed Indonesian soldiers with pistols obvious in holsters should have alerted me to another explanation. The soldiers had rounded up the crowd to fill the hall, many of whom were neither students nor academic staff, few knew English, the language in which I had spoken, and of course they had expressed their pleasure when I had finished – they were at last going to be set free.

What makes a good seminar is elusive. An elderly actor, asked to say what separated the exceptional actor from the good and ordinary, said he had no idea, but when some actors walked on stage an audience looked, listened, and was provoked to feel and think. It is similar with seminar givers. Some scholars begin to talk and the audience listens: if others were presenting the same material the audience would think about whether they should buy bread on the way home – or mentally or actually begin to write their own next presentation. Those who have given the best seminars that I have heard (among the historians that includes Gavan Daws, Donald Denoon, Ken Inglis and Bill Gammage) spoke without rhetorical flourishes and they used plain English with a sparkling clarity, sometimes investing simple words with grace and power, and they shifted easily between particular cases, shrewd insights and generalisations. They were also saying something significant, evidenced by the prizes given to their subsequent books and the many translations of Daws' work. (Both Inglis and Gammage won Premier's Prizes and *Holy Man* appeared in seven languages.)

It has intrigued me that two of my colleagues can on different days give either a good or mediocre seminar. But most of us probably operate at around about the same level every time. This was brought home to me early in my career when I asked my wife if she was going to hear me give a seminar paper. She said, kindly, 'No. I have heard you'. I think that it is probably true that while I might talk about different people in different places on different events, I always give the same seminar. My wife now says that I either misheard or misinterpreted what she said, and my misunderstanding of that distant conversation comes out of my repetition of the anecdote, not from her words. The raises such complex questions about memory and narrative, indeed about all oral history and autobiography, that it is worthy of a seminar – even in Seminar Room A.

21. Em Inap Nau

Inside Story: Current Affairs and Culture from Australia and Beyond *(21 Sep. 2011)*.

> *'Em inap nau ...'* ('That's enough now ...') – Lady Veronica Somare's plea to her husband, the PNG prime minister, Grand Chief Sir Michael Somare, before he left for a heart operation in Singapore. She went on to say in Tok Pisin, 'Let the young do the work' (*National*, 14 June 2011).

By the end of January 2011 the politics of Papua New Guinea appeared to have reached an impasse. For health, age and legal reasons, and because he was unwilling to stand again in the coming 2012 general elections, Michael Somare, the dominant political figure since independence, seemed unlikely to continue long in office. But among the contenders to assume the prime ministership, none had commanding personal authority or stood in an undisputed line of succession. Replacing Sir Michael was only one problem for a nation on the edge of billions in resource development income and with courts and a media struggling to make sense of parliamentary and party manoeuvres.

Nine months later, the situation was no clearer. Sir Michael, hospitalised in Singapore, 'was retired', the acting prime minister was displaced, the constitution came under close scrutiny and – at what seemed like the eleventh hour – an unexpected figure returned to parliament in a wheelchair. As is often the case in Papua New Guinea (as I wrote in my previous report for *Inside Story*), unfolding events have continued to unfold.

Endemic corruption and violence mean that Port Moresby is perceived to be one of the world's least desirable cities. One survey ranks the PNG capital seventh out of the worst ten, just above Caracas and Mogadishu. But the absence of a prime minister and the ambitions of the contenders circling for support and opportunity have provoked no demonstrations. In London, mob looting and burning led to a political crisis and the deployment of 16,000 police on the streets. In Port Moresby, a prolonged and nation-changing political crisis has left the streets – notorious for opportunistic violence – indifferent. Whether that separation of mobs and national politics will remain is another unanswered question.

Among all the known corruption and violence, PNG still retains some institutions fundamental to a fair and democratic nation. The government funds them and appoints competent officers not intimidated by the powerful and not themselves tainted by rumours of corruption. The Ombudsman Commission is one such institution that has consistently fought to fulfil its role as monitor of the integrity of those holding high office. In late 2010 and early 2011 it seemed that the greatest immediate worries for Sir Michael's son and fellow MP, Arthur Somare, resulted from actions the Commission had initiated.

Both Sir Michael and Arthur were said to have failed to lodge income returns; in Sir Michael's case this violation of the leadership code went back to 1992–93. Sir Michael had delayed facing a leadership tribunal for misconduct in office by claiming bias among officials, deficiencies in the drafting of powers assumed by officers and the injustice of being prevented from getting his appeal before a judge. Having almost exhausted his legal options, he became the first prime minister to be held to account by a leadership tribunal. Before the courts made a decision on Sir Michael's final appeal, the chief justice moved to have a tribunal hear the charges. The tribunal, appointed in February, was a trio of retired and distinguished empire judges: chairman Roger Gyles, formerly from the Federal Court of Australia, Sir Bruce Robertson (Court of Appeal and High Court of New Zealand), and Sir Robin Auld (lord chief justice of the Court of Appeal of England and Wales). They arrived in Port Moresby in March this year.

Within a fortnight, the tribunal had made its decision: Sir Michael was to be suspended from office for two weeks. Sir Robin Auld had made a harsher judgment: he ruled that Somare was guilty of 'serious culpability' and should be dismissed from office, but agreed to accept the view of his fellow judges. On 25 March the *National* newspaper pondered the ironies and the justice of the decision. Nearly forty-five years earlier, Sir Michael had chaired the constitutional planning committee whose provisions were now being used to call for his suspension. The *National* thought it reflected very well on the nation that the prime minister could be subject to the tribunal and found guilty without any unrest across the country. But it wondered if the penalty was adequate. It concluded that although Sir Michael had received a mere 'slap on the wrist', this was balanced by the fact that his previously 'unblemished record' was now blemished.

More criticism of the prime minister came in early July, with the Supreme Court's ruling on Sir Michael's action against the Ombudsman Commission:

> *These proceedings ... [have] been a total waste of the court's time. Besides, we find that these proceedings are a culmination of a history of unnecessary, improper and inappropriate steps taken by Sir Michael through his lawyers without having any factual and or legal foundation and merit. Clearly all the steps Sir Michael has taken in these proceedings amount to an abuse of process ... (Grand Chief Sir Michael Thomas Somare, Applicant, and Ombudsman Commission, Respondent, page 68)*

Over the four months to early August much happened but few conclusions and little clarity emerged. At the end of March, Sir Michael left for Singapore on what was said to be one of his 'regular medical checks', according to the *Post-Courier*, and he was due back in a few days. Just what his status was while initially in Singapore was uncertain. He had 'stepped aside' when referred to the leadership tribunal, but this was said to be a 'blunder' that was not required by the constitution; he could simply have said he was on 'holiday', it was claimed. In what appeared to be an official statement, acting prime minister Sam Abal said, with casual brutality, that Sir Michael was going 'under the knife' but assured his fellow citizens that it was 'nothing serious' and expressed the hope that Sir Michael would be back within a week. He even added – with an unnecessary flourish – that Sir Michael was 'well and jubilant'.

But already the assurances of routine procedures and a quick return to prime ministerial duties were looking to be wildly optimistic. The first reports to reach a wide public that Sir Michael was seriously ill and faced dangerous medical procedures came on the weekend of 9–10 April when Catholic congregations around the country were asked to pray for their fellow believer. On 20 April, Abal conceded that Sir Michael would 'remain on medical leave until further notice'. Over four months in early 2011 Sir Michael's status at any one time may have been 'suspended from office', 'voluntarily stood aside', 'on holidays' or 'on medical leave'.

Abal and the Somare family continued to send out reassurances: Sir Michael was 'recovering' and, in spite of being seventy-five and having more 'corrective surgery', he was not standing down as leader of the National Alliance party and it was 'premature' to talk about electing a new prime minister. As for the rumours that he had died, they were 'false, irresponsible, distasteful and disrespectful'. But the public – or at least that part of the 'public' the media claimed to represent – was beginning to resent the lack of detail about the health of Sir Michael, who was in intensive care in Singapore. In a commentary piece on 31 May, the *Post-Courier* claimed that Papua New Guineans were 'watching' and 'they do not like to be treated with contempt'. The paper went on to point out that Somare had now been in hospital for eight weeks and there were still more rumours than facts. It was obvious that the government had not expected the severity of the illness or the long incapacity of their prime minister. But they should have: Somare's precarious health had been 'an open secret'; long before he went to Singapore he had dozed off in cabinet meetings, had difficulty breathing when climbing stairs and had 'sweated a lot'.

Ambitious men who coveted the prime ministership were constrained. Some (including Abal) held their positions because of Somare, and if Somare went they went; some (perhaps all) were uncertain that there was a vacancy in the prime ministership; and Somare still carried such prestige that no one wanted to be among the first to say that Somare no longer had the capacity to lead the nation and that 'I am the man to take over'. Potential candidates avoided criticising Somare by claiming that they were in his line of succession.

If there was any doubt of Sir Michael's incapacity to intervene from afar it was dispelled at a media conference on 23 June, when Arthur Somare said he wanted to 'talk about my old man's health'. There was, he conceded, 'great uncertainty' about Sir Michael's recovery. Arthur said there would be no visitors other than family members – Sir Michael's wife, Lady Veronica, and his children Betha, Dulcie, Sana, Arthur and Michael – who had maintained a vigil. Lady Veronica, Arthur said, had been fixed at her husband's bedside and 'might as well be part of the Raffles Hospital furniture'.

Until early June, the acting prime minister, Sam Abal, was behaving as expected: sitting in Somare's leadership position but not making 'any major decisions to move the country forward', according to a *Post-Courier* report on 2 June. He was seen as 'the "chief's boy", a "political softie" … who will not ruffle feathers', commented the *National* on 8 June. But on 4 June he suddenly controverted that assessment of him among allies and opponents by sacking Don Polye and William Duma from his ministry. Both ministers were thought to be favoured by Somare, both held key positions in the parties keeping Somare, then Abal, in office – Polye in the National Alliance Party and Duma in the United Resources Party. In dismissing Polye, who represents Enga Province, Abal also angered many of his fellow highlanders. Abal and Polye were now in dispute over control of the National Alliance Party and positions in the ministry; both disputes could add to the political cases awaiting resolution in the courts.

The National *of Wednesday 29 June began an article with an unaccustomed prelude:*

> *Yesterday dawned an ordinary sunny Port Moresby kind of day – a little on the windy side – but before it ended, Tuesday, June 28, was propelled into the annals of PNG history.*

> *Shortly after 3 pm, an announcement was made that Prime Minister Grand Chief Sir Michael Thomas Somare was retired after nearly 50 years in PNG politics.*

'Was retired', not 'had retired'!

Arthur said that the family had made the decision three weeks earlier when Michael was in intensive care. He was in no state to make his wishes known, and the family had delayed any public announcement in the hope that he might recover sufficiently to be consulted. That had not happened. The *National* praised the Somare family for acting in the interests of the nation and of Sir Michael: these decisions truly make them 'our first family'.

At last the citizens had been given what seemed to be an authoritative statement on the severity of the illness of their prime minister. They were being told he was unlikely to resume office or even participate at any level of national or East Sepik politics. It had been a long three months' wait. The severity of Sir Michael's incapacity was confirmed by Arthur who claimed he 'had not talked to [his] father in weeks'. The public also learnt a little of the specific medical procedures Somare had undergone. His 'personal physician', Professor Sir Isi Kevau, reported that Sir Michael had developed complications after a second heart operation, forcing a third operation. In spite of the evidence, Professor Isi allowed the possibility of gradual recovery.

In Tok Pisin Arthur explained why the family had tried to open a path for the nation to escape the conflicting constitutional interpretations and personal ambitions: *'Taim femili ino toktok, banis istap yet. Nau mi totok, mi kliarim rot. Em samting bilong palamen, kebinet na pati long mekim disisen. Em bai ino mo sanap long rot'*. The *National* gave the following translation: 'When the family did not speak out, it became an obstacle, but now that I make that announcement, it clears the road for parliament, cabinet and party to make a decision'.

As grand and unprecedented as the family's gesture may have been, it was obviously of doubtful legality. Arthur's claim to be 'removing our father' from office had several effects on the leadership impasse.

First, it provoked lawyers in private practice, official positions and parliament to find out what the constitution – or an (unlikely) precedent from elsewhere – allowed in a situation where the nation had an ill and aged prime minister, hospitalised for two months in another nation and no longer capable of indicating whether he wanted to continue in office. The constitution provided no quick solution but its framers had anticipated the situation. Under section 142(5), the ways a prime minister 'shall be dismissed' are listed; at (c) comes the necessary procedure. If the national authority responsible for licensing medical practitioners has reported to the speaker that two practitioners have jointly determined the prime minister is no longer either physically or mentally able to carry out his duties, he can be removed from office. Section 143 added that where the prime minister was 'out of speedy and effective communication' the acting prime minister could exercise all the powers of a prime minister.

Second, under that reading of the constitution the office of acting prime minister (then held by Abal) had increased in importance, and its elevation might have opened another way to claim the substantive position of prime minister.

Third, Sir Michael was retiring ('being retired') from several positions: the prime ministership, as member for the regional electorate of East Sepik (the electors had known no other representative since 1968) and as parliamentary leader of the National Alliance Party.

Fourth, it now seemed appropriate to pass judgment on Sir Michael: the man who had been the elected head of self-governing PNG in 1973 and independent PNG in 1975, a position he retained until 1980. He subsequently served two more terms as prime minister, the last, beginning in 2002, being easily the longest any Papua New Guinean had held the position. The premature obituaries properly praised his longevity and his steering of the nation through its first years and regretted that the 'Great Unifier' would not be available to again lead the nation through a crisis. Muted criticism pointed to his failure to groom a successor; and the generous praise was on intangibles, not on what was practical and measurable: more and better roads, increased school attendances, more extensive health services, improved law and order, and job creation.

By the end of August, criticism of the failures of the Somare government were growing, but at first they were largely deflected by the charges of negligence and corruption being directed at ministers taking advantage of Somare's incapacity. Specific and strong attacks were also made on Arthur, with fewer attempts to distinguish between father and son. At a meeting in the capital of the Southern Highlands Province, Mendi, 'All speakers spoke generally of the concentration of power in the hands of a few, namely Sir Michael, his son Arthur and a few ministers who were also accused of failing to stay the advance of corruption in high places'. According to the *National*, Jamie Maxtone-Graham, the health minister, said: 'Decisions were dictated and bulldozed down our throats. Arthur Somare used the position of his father to dictate to us. There was too much concentration of power in one family'. Sir Michael was no longer exempt.

Fifth, in the search through the constitution's legitimate ways to replace a prime minister, another possible way – this time within the control of parliament – had been discovered. Under section 142(2) a prime minister was to be appointed after a general election or from 'time to time' by the head of state (represented by the governor-general) acting on the decision of parliament. One of those occasions that might arise from 'time to time' was when the prime minister was 'absent from the country' or out of 'speedy and effective communication' or 'otherwise unable … to perform' his duties. Section 142(4) strengthened the powers of parliament and its officers to fill a vacancy. If parliament was not in session when a prime minister was to be appointed then the speaker was to immediately call a meeting of parliament with the appointment of a prime minister 'the first matter for consideration'.

As a result, the lobbying intensified among members who thought they might be nominated for the fast track provided by the constitution. The *Post-Courier* of 20 June listed seven who were vying for support among their fellow members of parliament. When a candidate and his supporters thought they had built a majority in the parliament, they followed the tactics of others who had aimed to bring off a 'political coup': they gathered and isolated their supporters on an island or at a tourist resort to prevent their being seduced by greater counter-offers of positions and cash. On the eve of parliament resuming, they prepared for a dash through its procedures.

On 1 August the main opposition contenders, and many MPs from the government side who had now joined the opposition, gathered at former prime minister Sir Mekere Morauta's well-positioned house on Port Moresby's Touaguba Hill. A journalist who approached the house noticed about one hundred parked cars outside. The main aspirants at the 'haggling table' were thought to be Don Polye, William Duma, Francis Awasa, Sir Mekere Morauta, Belden Namah and Peter O'Neill. The AAP correspondent in Port Moresby, Eoin Blackwell, said that Morauta and Polye were 'instrumental in orchestrating' the leadership vote due the next day in parliament.

Parliament met the next afternoon. There was some confusion among members as they looked for seats following the various defections. The speaker, Jeffrey Nape, accepted the nomination of Peter O'Neill for prime minister by MP Belden Namah, seconded by William Duma, declined to hear all points of order or calls for divisions on the voices, and ruled that the nomination of O'Neill be forwarded to the governor-general, Sir Michael Ogio. Polye appeared 'stunned' at the few members supporting him, according to the *Post-Courier*. The swearing in was completed by about 4.30 pm. Parliament reassembled later that afternoon (*National*, 3 August 2011). The vote, seventy to twenty-four, was overwhelmingly in O'Neill's favour. To secure such crushing numbers, O'Neill had split the votes of the major parties previously supporting Sir Michael – the National Alliance Party, United Resources Party, Pangu Pati and People's Action Party. Only the party led by O'Neill, the People's National Congress, moved as a bloc to the new government. The fracturing of the parties may be as important as the end of the nine-year Somare regime in allowing a reshaping and new fluidity in PNG politics.

Abal was unhappy. 'I may not be a lawyer', he said in a written statement, 'but there is no procedure for the speaker to commence parliament and just presume vacancy of the position of prime minister when there is no legal documentation or substantiation of that move. The speaker hijacked the process and committed an illegal act'.

When releasing the names of those to hold ministries in his new government, O'Neill spoke of them as 'simple and humble leaders for the people of Papua New Guinea'. He said that he had consulted political parties and leaders and 'tried his best to cover all provinces in his cabinet'. It was a conciliatory statement that might be expected of a new prime minister. But, examined closely, it is clear that the distribution of ministries represented a sharp shift in power in personnel, parties and geography. The divided National Alliance had obviously lost its pre-eminence. Under Somare the East Sepik and West New Britain Provinces had been centres of power; now they were the only two provinces to have no representatives in cabinet. And there had been a marked change in representation from the north to the south. The highlands had secured the main economic portfolios: prime minister, finance and treasury, and petroleum and energy.

Peter O'Neill is himself the representative of a Southern Highlands electorate, Ialibu-Pangia, towards the east of the province. On the headwaters of the rivers flowing into the Purari, which makes its way to the Papuan Gulf, the electorate can claim to be both Papuan and highland. O'Neill, the son of an Australian father and a highlands mother, looks like a strongly built highlander. Fluent in English and with an accounting degree, O'Neill previously gained a reputation as an energetic and effective minister when he was in charge of several state-owned enterprises. His reputation was tainted by claims that he had fraudulently benefited from National Provident Fund transactions and, by creating the District Authorities, effectively given local MPs control over policies and funds, opening the way for them to 'buy' greater influence.

One attempt by the Papua New Guinean government to reduce the frequency of court intervention and bring greater stability to the political system has been to introduce more controlling legislation: for example, the Organic Law on the Integrity of Political Parties and Candidates (OLIPPAC) 2001. The legislation encouraged parties to register, provided government funding for parties, committed party members to vote as the party decided on votes on key issues – no-confidence, the budget and the constitution. The new rules may have increased the role of the courts as they play a part in the interpretation of party constitutions that are now of increased complexity; the Organic Laws themselves have been challenged; and clearly in the election of O'Neill, members of parties felt free to decide for themselves which side they supported. In addition, the rushed vote for O'Neill may have violated other requirements of the constitution, such as the need for a notice of motion and the restrictions on a vote of no-confidence close to the scheduled next general election.

Something like this now seems to be the state of play in the contests for the prime ministership of Papua New Guinea:

- Peter O'Neill is recognised as the prime minister by most people. He has a cabinet and ministers and he bases his claim on the fact that the prime ministership was vacant and he was elected by a majority in the parliament.
- Sam Abal says he was appointed acting prime minister by Sir Michael when as prime minister Sir Michael clearly had the power to nominate a deputy. That commission, Abal argues, has never been withdrawn.
- Sir Michael may never have resigned the prime ministership; if so, there was no vacancy to contest.

As of 1 September Sir Michael has been able to speak for himself. 'I am ready, willing and able to complete my term as the only legally elected prime minister of Papua New Guinea', he told the *National* in a blunt denial of the view that he is mentally and physically incapable of returning to the position. He returned to Port Moresby on 4 September and attended parliament on 6 September in a wheelchair.

The rumours about Sir Michael's ill health and the disputes about his replacement may not have excited the many unemployed on the streets or in the squatter settlements on the edges of the towns, or disturbed the rhythm of the women carrying home in the evening their heavy *bilums* (string bags) full of sweet potatoes and wood scrounged for a cooking fire, a little heat and a lot of smoke to ward off the highlands' chilly nights. But the political impasse also meant the neglect of national issues that needed attention. Nearly all the indicators of welfare (health and literacy, for example) were stable or in decline.

One characteristic of the many claims and counter claims about the failure of past governments to combat corruption and ensure government services reached distant communities was, initially at least, the absence of criticism of Sir Michael's many years in office. Coup leaders need to justify their actions, and when Peter O'Neill has done this he has condemned the interim government of Abal. O'Neill has found a convenient target; but given the brief regime of Abal and the fact that the system he took over was long in place, the criticisms have been unfair. The tribunal of eminent judges may have blemished Sir Michael's record, but the public, his colleagues and rivals have been reluctant to exploit that exposure of weakness in the Grand Chief.

Given the inescapable problems to confront any new government of Papua New Guinea, perhaps we should be trying to explain why there is such competition for the prime ministership rather than accepting that intense rivalry is to be expected.

Papua New Guinea has survived nearly nine months without its being clear who holds the prime ministership and without the benefit of a disciplined cabinet.

Given the lack of violence, the possibility of long delays of cases enmeshed in the courts and the need for time for new political alliances to stabilise, it might be desirable for the process of gradually acknowledging the end of the Somare era to continue for a little while yet. The last thing that the peoples of Papua New Guinea and of neighbouring nations (Australia, Indonesia and the Solomons) want is a Papua New Guinea descending into violence.

But the wild, enthusiastic reception given to O'Neill on his first return to Mendi after his election as prime minister was not an indicator of a gentle acceptance of change. O'Neill and his fellow ministers were honoured with a combined police and correctional services guard and greeted with a massed audience on Mendi oval. The enthusiasm for O'Neill and his 70–24 vote in the parliament may make the courts reluctant to stand up to the two other dominant formal and informal political forces in the country, the parliament and the crowd.

The potency of sentiment (but not the violence of crowds) has already been demonstrated when O'Neill went to his home electorate and the crowd claimed that he should be elected unopposed in 2012, at the University of Papua New Guinea where he was strewn with flowers, and at the National and Supreme courts where two sides gathered in support of either O'Neill–Namah or Abal–Somare. With the unexpected twists in the story so far and the speed with which unpredictable crowds can gather, it is uncertain that Papua New Guinea will have the luxury of time to establish a government that has a chance to be stable and efficient.

Sir Michael Somare failed to gain a National Court injunction to keep his seat in the PNG parliament on 20 September. AAP reports that 'Sir Michael had been seeking an injunction against his dumping from his East Sepik seat earlier this month by Speaker Jeffery Nape, who said the former prime minister had missed three consecutive sittings of parliament – grounds for dismissal under PNG law'. His lawyer, Kerenga Kua, said Sir Michael would appeal against the ruling in the Supreme Court.

Part III

Bibliography

1965

'The Missionaries and the Aborigines in the Port Phillip District'. *Historical Studies: Australia and New Zealand* 12:45, pp. 57–67.

1966

'African Analogy and the Development of Higher Education in New Guinea'. *Journal of the Papua and New Guinea Society* 1:1.

'The University's First Year'. *New Guinea and Australia, the Pacific and South-east Asia* 1:8, pp. 19–24.

1967

'Tertiary Education in Papua and New Guinea'. *Vestes* 10:3.

1968

'Papua is the Country! With a Woman to See You Through …'. *New Guinea and Australia, the Pacific and South-east Asia* 3:3, pp. 39–56. (This article also appeared in *The History of Melanesia*. Canberra: Research School of Pacific Studies, 1969.)

'*The Papuan Villager*: A National Newspaper'. *Journal of the Papua and New Guinea Society* 2:1.

A Short History of New Guinea. Sydney: Angus and Robertson. (With P. Biskup and B. Jinks).

1969

'Opportunities for Research in Papua-New Guinea and Irian Barat: History'. *New Guinea Research Bulletin* 32, pp. 207–08.

1970

'Brown Doctors: White Prejudice'. *New Guinea* 5:2, pp. 21–28.

'Contact and Administration Control'. In *An Atlas of Papua and New Guinea*, edited by R. Gerald Ward and David A.M. Lea, pp. 4–13. Port Moresby: UPNG Dept. of Geography.

'New Guinea Nationalism and the Writing of History'. *Journal of the Papua and New Guinea Society* 4:2, pp. 7–26.

A Short History of New Guinea. Sydney: Angus and Robertson. (With P. Biskup and B. Jinks; revised edition).

1971

'Hubert Murray: Private Letters and Public Reputation'. *Historical Studies* 4:56, pp. 612–21.

1972

Papua New Guinea: Black Unity or Black Chaos. Melbourne: Penguin Books.

'Presenting the Goodly Heritage: Teaching History in Papua New Guinea'. *New Guinea* 8:3. (Paper given to Section 26, ANZAAS 1972.)

1973

Readings in New Guinea History. Sydney: Angus and Robertson. (Edited with B. Jinks and P. Biskup.)

'Miners, Labourers and Officials on the Lakekamu Goldfield of Papua'. *Labour History* 25, pp. 40–52.

'Our Boys up North: The Behaviour of Australians in New Guinea'. *Meanjin Quarterly* 32:4, pp. 433–41.

1974

'Edward Stone Parker', in *Australian Dictionary of Biography*. Vol. 5, *1851–1890, K–O*, edited by Douglas Pike, pp. 396–97. Carlton: Melbourne University Press.

Papua New Guinea: Black Unity or Black Chaos. Melbourne: Penguin. (Revised edition including additional chapter.)

1975

'Living with a Blind Giant: Villagers and Foreigners'. *Meanjin Quarterly* 34:3, pp. 351–57.

'Miners and Men of the Fighting Variety: Relations between Foreigners and Villagers on the Yodda and Gira Goldfields of Papua New Guinea, 1895–1910'. *Oral History* 3:3, pp. 93–106.

1976

'History and Politics of Papua New Guinea'. In *Collier's Encyclopedia*. New York: Macmillan Educational Corporation.

'History and Politics of Papua New Guinea'. In *Merit Students Encyclopedia*. New York: Macmillan Educational Corporation.

1977

Black, White and Gold: Gold Mining in Papua New Guinea, 1878–1930. Canberra: ANU Press.

1978

'From Kanaka to Fuzzy Wuzzy Angel: Race and Labour Relations in Australian New Guinea'. In *Who Are Our Enemies? Racism and the Australian Working Class*, edited by Ann Curthoys and Andrew Markus, pp. 172–88. Sydney: Hale and Iremonger.

'Loyalties at Sword-Point: The Lutheran Missionaries in Wartime New Guinea, 1939–45'. *Australian Journal of Politics and History* 24:2, pp. 199–217.

'Papua New Guinea's Foreign Policy: Universalism, Trade, Aid and Borders'. *India Quarterly* 34:2, pp. 175–87.

'The Swinging Index: Capital Punishment and British and Australian Administrations in Papua and New Guinea, 1888–1945'. *Journal of Pacific History* 13:3, pp. 130–52.

1979

'Australians and War in the Southwest Pacific'. *Bulletin (Australia 1938–1988 Bicentennial History Project)* 3, pp. 76–87.

'Carpenter, Sir Walter Randolph'. In *Australian Dictionary of Biography*. Vol. 7, *1891–1939, A–Ch*, edited by Bede Nairn and Geoffrey Serle, pp. 567–68. Carlton South: Melbourne University Press.

'Frank Pryke: Prospector'. In *Papua New Guinea Portraits: The Expatriate Experience*, edited by James Griffin, pp. 75–100. Canberra: ANU Press.

'Inside and Outside Australia'. *Bulletin (Australia 1938–1988 Bicentennial History Project)* 3, pp. 11–15.

'New Guinea Divided: The Papua New Guinea–Indonesia Border'. *Kabar Seberang: Sulating Maphilindo* 5/6, pp. 233–42.

Papua New Guinea: A Political History. Richmond, Victoria: Heinemann Educational Australia. (With James Griffin and Stewart Firth; translated into Japanese and published in Japan in 1994.)

'War and Aborigines'. In *Handbook for Aboriginal and Islander History*, edited by Diane Barwick, Michael Mace and Tom Stannage, pp. 174–78. Canberra: Aboriginal History.

1980

'As Bilong Soldia: The Raising of the Papuan Infantry Battalion in 1940'. *Yagl-Ambu* 7:1, pp. 19–27.

'Filling Some Gaps and Building for a Nation'. In *The Hasluck Years: Some Observations: The Administration of Papua New Guinea, 1952–63*, edited by A. Ward et al., pp. 64–77. Discussion paper 1/79. Bundoora, Victoria: La Trobe University, Research Centre for Southwest Pacific Studies.

'Hold the Good Name of the Soldier: The Discipline of Papuan and New Guinean Infantry Battalions, 1940–46'. *Journal of Pacific History* 15:4, pp. 202–16.

'Miners and Islanders'. *Hemisphere* 25:2, pp. 89–93. (Reprinted in a special edition of *Hemisphere* articles for 1980.)

'Taim Bilong Pait: The Impact of the Second World War on Papua New Guinea'. In *Southeast Asia under Japanese Rule*, edited by Alfred W. McCoy, pp. 246–66. Monograph series 22. New Haven: Yale University Southeast Asia Studies.

1981

'Donaldson, John'. In *Australian Dictionary of Biography*. Vol. 8, *1891–1939, Cl–Gib*, edited by Bede Nairn and Geoffrey Serle, pp. 318–19. Carlton: Melbourne University Press.

1982

'The Australians in Papua New Guinea'. In *Melanesia: Beyond Diversity*, edited by R.J. May and Hank Nelson, pp. 143–50. Canberra: Research School of Pacific Studies, ANU.

'European Contact and Administrative Control'. In *Papua New Guinea Atlas: A Nation in Transition*, edited by David King and Stephen Ranck, pp. 10–14. Port Moresby: Robert Brown and University of Papua New Guinea.

'Looking North'. In *New History: Studying Australia Today*, edited by G. Osborne and W.F. Mandle, pp. 142–52. Sydney: Allen and Unwin.

Melanesia: Beyond Diversity. Canberra: Research School of Pacific Studies, ANU. (Edited with R.J. May.)

'Murray, John Hubert Plunkett (1861–1940)', 'Papua New Guinea', 'Papua New Guinea, Gold Mining in'. In *Historical Dictionary of Oceania*, edited by Robert D. Craig and Frank P. King, pp. 198–99, 220–24, 226–27. Westport, CT: Greenwood Press.

Taim Bilong Masta: The Australian Involvement with Papua New Guinea. Sydney: Australian Broadcasting Commission. (Reprinted in 1990.)

1983

'Presenting the Product'. *Oral History Association of Australia Journal* 5, pp. 91–98.

'Travelling in Memories: Australian Prisoners of the Japanese Forty Years after the Fall of Singapore'. *Journal of the Australian War Memorial* 3, pp. 13–24.

1985

'Banka shima no suna o chi ni somete [The Sands of Banka Island are Dyed with Blood]'. *Rekishi to Jimbutsu* 171, pp. 366–77.

'"The Nips are Going for the Parker": The Prisoners Face Freedom'. *War & Society* 3:2, pp. 127–43.

'Picking up Australia's Burden'. *Pacific Islands Monthly* 56:9, pp. 23–24 and 54. (Reprinted in *Journal de la Société des Océanistes*.)

P.O.W. Prisoners of War: Australians under Nippon. Sydney: Australian Broadcasting Corporation. (Reprinted in 1990 and 2001.)

1986

'Introduction'. In *The Australians at Rabaul: The Capture and Administration of the German Possessions in the Southern Pacific*, by S.S. Mackenzie, pp. xxiii–xxxiii. St Lucia: University of Queensland Press and the Australian War Memorial. (With Michael Piggott.)

'Murray, Sir John Hubert Plunkett' and 'Murray, George Gilbert Aime'. In *Australian Dictionary of Biography*. Vol. 10, *1891–1939, Lat–Ner*, edited by Bede Nairn and Geoffrey Serle, pp. 645–48. Carlton: Melbourne University Press.

1987

'History as Words, Noise and Pictures'. In *Finding and Keeping: Research Use of Audiovisual Materials*, edited by Marjorie Roe, pp. 9–19. Sydney: Library Association of Australia.

'Masters in the Tropics'. In *Australians 1938*, edited by Bill Gammage and Peter Spearritt, pp. 423–33. Broadway, NSW: Fairfax, Syme & Weldon Associates.

'Pictures at Tabara'. *Overland* 109, pp. 6–14.

1988

'Introduction'. In *Voices from a Vanishing Australia: Recollections of the Way Things Used to Be*, by Don Taylor, pp. 1–5. Crows Nest, NSW: Australian Broadcasting Corporation.

'Minimay: One of 6,000 Weatherboard Schools'. *Australian Cultural History* 7, pp. 5–17.

'Pryke, Frank (1872–1937)'. In *Australian Dictionary of Biography*. Vol. 11, *1891–1939, Nes–Smi*, edited by Geoffrey Serle, p. 304. Carlton: Melbourne University Press.

1989

'"A Bowl of Rice for Seven Camels": The Dynamics of Prisoner-of-War Camps'. *Journal of the Australian War Memorial* 14, pp. 33–42.

'Changing the Label'. In *Papua New Guinea: A Century of Colonial Impact, 1884–1984*, edited by Sione Latukefu, p. 19–36. Boroko: National Research Institute and University of Papua New Guinea.

'Recent POW Books: A Review Article'. *Journal of the Australian War Memorial* 14, pp. 53–56.

With Its Hat about Its Ears: Recollections of the Bush School. Sydney: Australian Broadcasting Corporation. (Reprinted in 1990.)

1990

'Ida Standley'. In *Australian Dictionary of Biography*. Vol. 11, *1891–1939, Smy–Z*, edited by John Ritchie, p. 46.

'Review Article: Turning the Talk of War into History'. *Journal of Pacific History* 25:2, pp. 260–67.

'Turning North: Australians in Southeast Asia in World War 2'. *Overland* 119, pp. 31–39.

1991

'Blood Oath: A Reel History'. *Australian Historical Studies* 24:97, pp. 429–42. (Translated and published separately in Japan.)

'The Gatekeepers: Examining the Examiners'. *Australian Historical Association Bulletin* 68, pp. 12–27.

'Recapturing the Past: The Status of Oral History'. *Australian History Teacher* 18, pp. 39–47.

1992

'The troops, the Town and the Battle: Rabaul 1942'. *Journal of Pacific History* 27:2, pp. 198–216.

'Write History: Reel History'. In *Pacific Islands History: Journeys and Transformations*, edited by Brij V. Lal, pp. 184–202. Canberra: Journal of Pacific History.

'Written and Spoken Lives and History'. In *Shaping Lives: Reflections on Biography*, edited by Ian Donaldson, Peter Read and James Walter, pp. 133–40. Canberra: Humanities Research Centre, ANU.

1993

The Burma–Thailand Railway: Memory and History. St Leonards, NSW: Allen & Unwin. Chiang Mai: Silkworm Books. (Edited with Gavan McCormack; an edition for Southeast Asia was translated and published separately in Japan.)

'Cleland, Sir Donald Mackinnon' and 'Dawes, Allan Wesley'. In *Australian Dictionary of Biography*. Vol. 13, *1940–1980, A–De*, edited by John Ritchie, pp. 440–41, 591–92.

'Gully-Rakers, Mining Companies and Parallels of War'. In *Resources, Development and Politics in the Pacific Islands*, edited by Stephen Henningham, R.J. May and Lulu Turner, pp. 11–29. Bathurst, NSW: Crawford House Press.

'Introduction' and 'Conclusion'. In *The Burma–Thailand Railway: Memory and History*, edited by Gavan McCormack and Hank Nelson, pp. 1–9, 151–59. St Leonards, NSW: Allen & Unwin.

'Measuring the Railway: From Individual Lives to National History'. In *The Burma–Thailand Railway: Memory and History*, edited by Gavan McCormack and Hank Nelson, pp. 10–26. St Leonards, NSW: Allen & Unwin.

1994

'Foreword'. In *Doctor's Diary and Memoirs: Pond's Party, F Force, Thai–Burma Railway*, by Roy Mills, pp. 9–14. New Lambton, NSW: R.M. Mills.

'Foreword'. In *Love, War & Letters: PNG 1940–45*, by Alan E. Hooper, pp. 12–14. Coorparoo, Queensland, Robert Brown & Associates.

'The Record Holders'. *Australian Historical Association Bulletin* 76, pp. 1–13.

1995

'From ANZAC Day to Remembrance Day: Remnants of Australian Rule in Papua New Guinea'. In *Lines across the Sea: Colonial Inheritance in the Post-Colonial Pacific*, edited by Brij V. Lal and Hank Nelson, pp. 25–35. Brisbane: Pacific History Association.

Lines across the Sea: Colonial Inheritance in the Post-Colonial Pacific. Brisbane: Pacific History Association. (Edited with Brij V. Lal.)

Prisoners of War: Australians under Nippon, translated into Japanese by Yoshio Sugimoto and Rick Tanaka. Tokyo: Chikuma Shobō. (Released as a Spokenword CD in 2007.)

'The Return to Rabaul 1945'. *Journal of Pacific History* 30:2, pp. 131–53.

'Sacred Trust and Self-Interest: Australia, Rabaul and Beyond'. In *The Great War: Gains and Losses – ANZAC and Empire*, edited by Craig Wilcox and Janice Aldridge, pp. 85–116. Canberra: Australian War Memorial and The Australian National University.

1996

'Grahamslaw, Thomas'. In *Australian Dictionary of Biography*. Vol. 14, *1940–1980, Di–Kel*, edited by John Ritchie, pp. 305–06.

'Kuru: The Pursuit of the Prize and the Cure'. *Journal of Pacific History* 31:2, pp. 178–201.

'Preface'. In *Voices from a Lost World: Australian Women and Children in Papua New Guinea before the Japanese Invasion*, by Jan Roberts, pp. xi–xiv. Alexandria, NSW: Millennium Books.

The War Diaries of Eddie Allan Stanton: Papua 1942–45, New Guinea 1945–46. St Leonards: Allen & Unwin. (Edited and with an introduction and postscript.)

1997

'Australia–Papua New Guinea Cultural Relations'. In *Papua New Guinea Update: Report on Proceedings of a Seminar, 11 and 12 November 1996, Canberra / Joint Standing Committee on Foreign Affairs, Defence and Trade*, pp. 93–97. Canberra: The Parliament of the Commonwealth of Australia.

'Foreword'. In *Ghosts in Khaki: The History of the 2/4th Machine Gun Battalion, 8th Australian Division A.I.F*, by Les Cody, pp. v–vii. Carlisle, WA: Hesperian Press.

'Gallipoli, Kokoda and the Making of National Identity'. *Journal of Australian Studies* 53, pp. 157–69.

'National Election: Local Decisions'. In *Challenging the State: The Sandline Affair in Papua New Guinea*, edited by Sinclair Dinnen, Ronald James May, and Anthony J. Regan, pp. 136–43. Canberra: National Centre for Development Studies and Department of Political and Social Change.

'The Talk and the Timing: Reputations and Reality and the Granting of Self-Government to Papua New Guinea'. In *Emerging from Empire? Decolonisation in the Pacific: Proceedings of a Workshop at The Australian National University, December 1996*, edited by Donald Denoon, pp. 107–17. Canberra: Division of Pacific and Asian History, ANU.

1998

'Changing Traffic across the Coral Sea: Australia–Papua New Guinea Relationships'. In *Education for Australia's International Future: The Young Diplomats Program*, edited by Rodney Sullivan, Lesley Jackman and Anne Smith, pp. 150–154. Townsville: School of History and Politics, James Cook University.

'La descolonización. De la Primera Guerra Mundial a la Actualidad. Introduccion' and 'From Frontier to Territory, Colony and Nation: Australia and New Guinea'. In *Colonizacion, descolonization y encuento cultural / Las Relaciones Internacionales en el Pacifico (Siglos XVIII–XX)*, edited by M.D. Elizalde, pp. 399–406, 671–94. Madrid: Marcial Pons.

'Doing Time: Writing of Prisoners of War'. *Locality* 8:3, pp. 12–17.

'Horses', 'Papua New Guinea–Australian Relations' and 'Prisoners of War'. In *The Oxford Companion to Australian History*, edited by Graeme Davison, John Hirst and Stuart MacIntyre, pp. 325–27, 491–93, 525–26. South Melbourne: Oxford University Press.

'Kuru: The Pursuit of the Price and the Cure'. In *Mad Cows and Modernity: Cross-Disciplinary Reflections on the Crisis of Jakob-Creutzfeldt Disease*, edited by Iain McCalman, Benjamin Penny and Misty Cook, pp. 125–66. Canberra: Humanities Research Centre, ANU, and National Academies Forum.

'Papua New Guinea'. In *Paul Hasluck in Australian History: Civic Personality and Public Life*, edited by Tom Stannage, Kay Saunders and Richard Nile, pp. 152–69. St Lucia: University of Queensland Press.

'Report on Historical Sources on Australia and Japan at War in Papua and New Guinea, 1942–45'. *Australian War Memorial, Australia–Japan Research Project*. http://ajrp.awm.gov.au/AJRP/AJRP2.nsf/2a4c0eda7a368533ca2566480011b2fe/ 2f3b86921669c57e852565b000499e78.

1999

'Crises of God and Man: Papua New Guinea Political Chronicle, 1997–99'. *Journal of Pacific History* 34:3, pp. 259–64.

'History: Lost on Paradise Road'. *Wartime* 7, pp. 66–67.

'A Map to Paradise Road: A Guide for Historians'. *Journal of the Australian War Memorial* 32.

2000

'Gallipoli, Kokoda and the Making of National Identity'. In *The Australian Legend and Its Discontents*, edited by Richard Nile, pp. 200–17. St Lucia: University of Queensland Press. (Reprint of a 1997 article.)

'Liberation: The End of Australian Rule in Papua New Guinea'. *Journal of Pacific History* 35:3, pp. 269–80.

'McCarthy, John Keith' and 'Murray, Hubert Leonard'. In *Australian Dictionary of Biography*. Vol. 15, *1940–1980, Kem–Pie*, edited by John Ritchie, pp. 170–71, 448–50. Carlton: Melbourne University Press.

'Perspectives on Crime and Blame'. In *Australia and Papua New Guinea: Crime and the Bilateral Relationship*, edited by Beno Boeha and John McFarlane, pp. 280–89. Canberra: Australian Defence Studies Centre, Australian Defence Force Academy.

'State, society and the law in Papua New Guinea's future'. *Pacific Economic Bulletin* 15:2 (supplement: 'Papua New Guinea Silver Jubilee and PNG Update'), pp. 43–49.

2001

'Introduction'. In *Taim Bilong Misis Bilong Armi: Memories of Wives of Australian Servicemen in Papua New Guinea 1951–1975*, compiled by Stephanie Lloyd, Marlena Jeffrey and Jenny Hearn, pp. 1–6. Canberra: Pandanus Books.

'Isla del Oro: Seeking New Guinea Gold'. In *Gold: Forgotten Histories and Lost Objects of Australia*, edited by Iain McCalman, Alexander Cook and Andrew Reeves, pp. 189–206. Cambridge: Cambridge University Press.

'Observing the Present: Writing the Past'. In *Pacific Lives, Pacific Places: Bursting Boundaries in Pacific History*, edited by Brij V. Lal and Peter Hempenstall, pp. 22–33. Canberra: Journal of Pacific History.

'Papua New Guinea'. In *The World Book Encyclopedia*, pp. 139–41. Chicago: World Book Publishing.

2002

Chased by the Sun: Courageous Australians in Bomber Command in WW II. Sydney: ABC Books for the Australian Broadcasting Corporation. (Published as an ebook and reprinted by Allen and Unwin, Sydney, in 2006.)

'Foreword'. In *Changi Days: The Prisoner as Poet,* edited by David Griffin, pp. 10–13. East Roseville, NSW: Kangaroo Press.

From Wagga to Waddington: Australians in Bomber Command. London: Menzies Centre for Australian Studies.

'Robinson, Alfred Lambton (1903–1948)'. In *Australian Dictionary of Biography*. Vol. 16, *1940–1980, Pik–Z*, edited by John Ritchie, pp. 113–14.

2003

'A Different War: Australians in Bomber Command'. *Australian War Memorial*. http://www.awm.gov.au/events/conference/2003/nelson.asp.

'Kokoda: The Track from History to Politics'. *Journal of Pacific History* 38:1, pp. 109–27.

'Our Great Task'. *Meanjin* 62:3, pp. 123–34.

'A Picture: From the Past and without a Past'. *Conversations* 4:1, pp. 18–29.

Taim Bilong Masta: The Australian Involvement with Papua New Guinea. Sydney: ABC Audio. (Reissued on 24 CDs and two MP3 Spokenword CDs.)

2004

'Rabaul'. In *Pacific Places, Pacific Histories: Essays in Honor of Robert C. Kiste*, edited by Brij V. Lal, pp. 153–76. Honolulu: University of Hawai'i Press.

'Study Guide: *Betelnut Bisnis – a story from Papua New Guinea*'. *Screen Education*, 36.

2005

'Bougainville in World War II'. In *Bougainville: Before the Conflict*, edited by Anthony Regan and Helga Griffin, pp. 168–98. Canberra: Pandanus Books.

'Fighting for Her Gates and Waterways: Changing Perceptions of New Guinea in Australian Defence'. State, Society and Governance in Melanesia discussion paper 2005/3, Research School of Pacific and Asian Studies, ANU.

'The View from the Sub-District'. In *The Defining Years: Pacific Islands, 1945–65*, edited by Brij V. Lal, pp. 18–38. Canberra: Division of Pacific and Asian History, Research School of Pacific and Asian Studies, ANU.

2006

'Introduction', 'The Enemy at the Door: Australia and New Guinea in World War', 'Looking Black: Australian Images of Melanesians', 'More than a Change of Uniform: Australian Military Rule in Papua New Guinea, 1942–1946', 'Payback: Australian Compensation to Wartime Papua New Guinea' and 'Zentsuji and Totsuka: Australians from Rabaul as Prisoners of War in Japan'. In *The Pacific War in Papua New Guinea: Memories and Realities*, edited by Yukio Toyoda and Hank Nelson, pp. 1–8, 124–43, 144–68, 232–51, 320–48, 423–56. Tokyo: Rikkyo University, Centre for Asian Area Studies.

'Governments, States and Labels'. State, Society and Governance in Melanesia discussion paper 2006/1, Research School of Pacific and Asian Studies, ANU.

'Have You Got a Title? Seminar Daze'. In *The Coombs: A House of Memories*, edited by Brij V. Lal and Allison Ley, pp. 235–42. Canberra: Research School of Pacific and Asian Studies, ANU.

The Pacific War in Papua New Guinea: Memories and Realities. Tokyo: Rikkyo University, Centre for Asian Area Studies. (Edited with Yukio Toyoda.)

'Papua Nyuginia to Ajia Taiheiyo senso [Papua New Guinea and the Asia Pacific War]'. In *Iwanami kōza: Ajia-taiheiyō sensō*, edited by Kurasawa Aiko et al., pp. 217–46. Tokyo: Iwanami Shoten.

'Prisoners of War and National Memory'. In *Legends and Legacies: Perspectives on Australian Soldiers' Battle and Captivity Experiences in the Far East during the Second World War*, edited by Rosalind Hearder, pp. 52–64. Canberra: Australian War Memorial.

'The State of Francis Fukuyama'. State, Society and Governance in Melanesia working paper 2006/2, Research School of Pacific and Asian Studies, ANU.

2007

Australian Prisoners of War, 1941–1945: Australians in the Pacific War. Canberra: ACT Department of Veterans' Affairs.

'The Chinese in Papua New Guinea'. State, Society and Governance in Melanesia discussion paper 2007/3, Research School of Pacific and Asian Studies, ANU.

'Foreword'. In *Surviving Sandakan and Kuching; Defying the Odds*, edited by Michele Cunningham, pp. vii–ix. South Melbourne: Lothian Books.

'Gunther, Sir John Thomson', 'Hampshire, Keith MacDermott' and 'Karava, Gabriel Ehava'. In *Australian Dictionary of Biography*. Vol. 17, *1981–1990, A–K*, edited by Di Langmore, pp. 467–69, 480–81, 603–04. Carlton: Melbourne University Press.

'Kokoda: And Two National Histories'. *Journal of Pacific History* 42:1, pp. 73–88.

'The Moti Affair in Papua New Guinea'. State, Society and Governance in Melanesia working paper 2007/1, Research School of Pacific and Asian Studies, ANU.

'The New Guinea Comfort Women, Japan and the Australian Connection: out of the shadows'. *Japan Focus*. http://www.japanfocus.org/-Hank-Nelson/2426.

'Reflections on the Experiences of Australian Prisoners of War of the Japanese' and 'Jack Dando'. In *Ōsutoraria seminā hōkokushū / POW Kenkyūkai Henshū Iinkai hen= The Australia Seminar Report / POW Research Network* Japan, pp. 16–31, 161–74. Japan: POW Kenkyūkai.

'The Rise of China in the Pacific'. State, Society and Governance in Melanesia briefing note, 2007/2, Research School of Pacific and Asian Studies, ANU. (With Paul Darcy.)

2008

'Beyond Slogans: Assessing the Experiences and the History of the Australian Prisoners of War of the Japanese'. In *Forgotten Captives in Japanese-Occupied Asia*, edited by Karl Hack and Kevin Blackburn, pp. 23–40. Abingdon: Routledge.

'*The Bottom Billion: Why the Poorest Countries are Failing and What Can be Done about It*, Paul Collier (Oxford University Press, 2007) – A Discussion'. State Society and Governance in Melanesia briefing note 2008/2, Research School of Pacific and Asian Studies, ANU.

'Collier in Melanesia: A Discussion of Paul Collier's "The Bottom Billion: Why the Poorest Countries are Failing and What Can be Done about It" (Oxford University Press, Oxford, 2007)'. State Society and Governance in Melanesia working paper 2008/1, Research School of Pacific and Asian Studies, ANU.

'The Consolation Unit: Comfort Women at Rabaul'. *Journal of Pacific History* 43:1, pp. 1–21.

'Lives Told: Australians in Papua and New Guinea'. In *Telling Pacific Lives: Prisms of Process*, edited by Brij V. Lal and Vicki Luker, pp. 243–76. Canberra: ANU E Press.

'Mystery of the Montevideo Maru Persists'. *Channel Nine Website*, 14 April.

2009

'Kokoda, Then and Now'. *Wartime* 48, pp. 12–18.

Kokoda Track–Brown River Catchment Region: Preliminary Social Mapping Study. Canberra: ANU Enterprise and Resource Management in Asia-Pacific Program for Department of Environment, Water, Heritage and Arts. (With John E. Burton, Chris Ballard, Nicole Haley and Deveni Temu.)

'Mobs and Masses: Defining the Dynamic Groups in Papua New Guinea'. State, Society and Governance in Melanesia discussion paper 2009/4, Research School of Pacific and Asian Studies, ANU.

'The Montevideo Maru: Lost at Sea, Lost from Australian History'. *Paradise* (Air Niugini), Oct., pp. 32–35.

'Tracking Kokoda'. *Inside Story: Current Affairs and Culture from Australia and Beyond.* http://inside.org.au/tracking-kokoda/.

2010

'Chinese in Papua New Guinea'. In *China in Oceania: Reshaping the Pacific?*, edited by Terence Wesley-Smith and Edgar Porter, pp. 104–17. New York: Berghahn Books.

'Foreword'. In *Footprints across the Loddon Plains: A Shared History*, by Paul Haw and Margaret Munro, pp. v–vi. Boort, Victoria: Boort Development Inc.

'The Incomplete State and the Alternate State in Papua New Guinea'. In *Nation Building, State Building, and Economic Development: Case Studies and Comparisons*, edited by S.C.M. Paine, pp. 263–76. New York: M.E. Sharpe.

'Kokoda: Pushing the Popular Image'. *Journal of Pacific History* 45:1, pp. 89–104.

2011

'Cranks Emerging'. *Inside Story: Current Affairs and Culture from Australia and Beyond.* http://inside.org.au/cranks-emerging/. (Also appeared in the *Canberra Times*, 12 Feb., pp. 8–9.)

'"Em inap nau ..." ("That's enough now ...")'. *Inside Story: Current Affairs and Culture from Australia and Beyond.* http://inside.org.au/thats-enough-now/.

'Vale James Thomas Griffin'. *South Pacific Journal of Philosophy and Culture* 10, pp. 141–42. (With Gerald Griffin and August Kituai.)

Other Work

Some journalism, including about 20 articles for the *Nation*; reviews and articles for learned journals; and reviews and articles for the *Age*, the *Australian*, the *Sydney Morning Herald*, the *Canberra Times*, the *National Times*, and ABC-TV's *24 Hours*.

Radio

Historical adviser and writer of the commentary on the 24-part radio series, *Taim Bilong Masta: The Australian Involvement with Papua New Guinea*, broadcast by the ABC from 12 April 1981 and released on cassette. Rebroadcast on Radio National several times, including in December 2003 and January 2004.

Historical adviser, writer of the commentary and an interviewer on the 16-part radio series, *P.O.W.: Australians under Nippon*, produced by Tim Bowden, first broadcast by the ABC from 3 June 1984, and released on cassette.

'Dear General: My Dear Prime Minister. Douglas MacArthur and John Curtin'. A radio feature broadcast by the ABC in 1984.

'Bush Schools'. A radio documentary series broadcast in five parts by the ABC. Released on cassette.

Edited (with Kevin Fewster) the diary of C.E.W. Bean, then read on ABC radio. Published as a double cassette, 'Frontline Gallipoli', ABC, 1990.

Writer, adviser and interviewer for six-part radio series, 'Breaking the Barriers on the Colombo Plan and Australian Volunteers Abroad', produced by Tim Bowden and broadcast on the ABC in 1993.

Adviser on structure and historical content on major radio documentaries.

General adviser and writer of questionnaires (and also did some interviewing) for the creation of the Keith Murdoch Sound Archive of Australia in the War of 1939–1945 at the Australian War Memorial.

Regular commentator on news for radio and television.

Film

With Andrew Pike and Gavan Daws, *Angels of War*, a 55-minute 16mm documentary film on World War II and the people of Papua New Guinea, released in 1982.

Associate producer and adviser for *Man Without Pigs*, a 60-minute 16mm documentary film on Tabara village, Papua New Guinea, released in 1990.

Consultant to the ABC Education 11-part television series 'Shadow Play' on Australian–Asian relations in 1988.

Historical adviser to and interviewed in *The Tragedy of the Montevideo Maru*, History Channel, November 2009, released on DVD.

Journals

Editor of the *Journal of the Papua and New Guinea Society* 1:2–3:1; on the editorial board from 1967 to 1972. On the editorial board of the *Journal of Labour History* for many years. On the board of the *Journal of Aboriginal History* for its first ten years. Editor of, and on the editorial board for, the *Journal of Pacific History*.

www.ingramcontent.com/pod-product-compliance
Lightning Source LLC
Chambersburg PA
CBHW060929170426
43192CB00031B/2882